DET ONE

U.S. MARINE CORPS U.S. SPECIAL OPERATIONS COMMAND DETACHMENT, 2003-2006

U.S. Marines in the Global War on Terrorism

by
Lieutenant Colonel John P. Piedmont
U.S. Marine Corps Reserve

History Division
United States Marine Corps
Washington, D.C.
2010

Cover: Det One prior to deploying to Iraq, during the Capstone Exercise at Indian Springs Auxiliary Airfield, Nevada, in December 2003. Here members are being briefed before the simulated and live-fire raid mission. Detachment uniforms, weapons, and equipment are shown to good advantage.

Photo courtesy of Patrick J. Rogers

Foreword

The story of the Marine Corps U.S. Special Operations Command Detachment, which became known as Det One, is an extraordinary tale. On its face, the story would not rate a minute's glance. One small group of Marines, about a hundred in number, formed, trained, and went to war. This all happened as the nation was 18 months into the Global War on Terrorism and as the Marine Corps was deploying I Marine Expeditionary Force in Operation Iraqi Freedom. Yet the story behind the basic facts is not only far more intricate and fascinating, with dramatic episodes and intrepid characters from the Pentagon to Camp Pendleton, it portended great significance for the Marine Corps.

What makes the Det One story extraordinary is the shift in Marine Corps policy that brought it about, the maturation of the special operations capabilities of forward-deployed Marine expeditionary units that made it possible, and the patriotism, valor, fidelity, and abilities of the Marines and Navy Corpsmen who manned it. Although Det One has passed now into the history books, its legacy survives in the formation of Marine Corps Special Operations Command and in the lessons learned and experiences of its members, who now continue to serve in dozens of units.

Lieutenant Colonel John P. Piedmont Marine Field Historian in Iraq in April 2004, saw the historical significance of Det One and decided to pursue its history as a project. Under the director of the History and Museums Division at the time, Colonel John W. Ripley, he was given permission to proceed with his collections with a view toward turning them into a monograph. What follows here is the culmination of his efforts, the product of two years' work, more than 60 interviews done in Iraq, Washington, D.C., Virginia, and California, and the collection of hundreds of documents.

Dr. Charles P. Neimeyer
Director of Marine Corps History

Preface

The story begins in the chow hall at Camp Fallujah on 30 April 2004. "Look, there's Colonel Coates," said the Marine I was with, pointing to a colonel seated a few tables away from us. "Do you know who he is?" "No, I don't," I replied. "Never heard of him." "He's the Det One commanding officer. If they're here, things will get interesting." In fact, things already were as interesting as one might want. The first battle of Fallujah had reached the now-famous cessation imposed from above. The insurgency soon boiled over, and I Marine Expeditionary Force (I MEF) had its hands full from Abu Ghraib prison in the east to the Syrian border in the west.

After I got a quick lecture on Det One, and guessing that Colonel Coates was someone I needed to talk to, I got up and walked over to him. I introduced myself and told him what I was doing in Iraq and that I'd like to talk to him if he had the chance. He looked up, paused, and said "send me an email."

Well, there you have it, I thought to myself. "Send me an email" translated to "forget it, I've got other things to do." But on second thought, it sounded more like an order than a suggestion, so I did send him an email, explaining in more detail what I wanted. Much to my surprise, I received an instant reply: "I will enthusiastically support the Marine Corps Historical Program." And so he has, from that minute on.

Colonel Robert J. Coates, the Marine Corps Special Operations Command Detachment's first and only commanding officer, was the first Marine I interviewed on the unit. He gave me a good hour in his office at the I MEF G-3 and provided a detailed view of the unit as it stood then. (As we spoke, it was operating in Baghdad.) He also pointed me to two other Marines who were instrumental in the formation of the detachment, one of whom, by a fortunate coincidence, was also at Camp Fallujah.

Lieutenant Colonel J. Giles Kyser IV was then commanding officer of 2d Battalion, 2d Marines. As an action officer at Headquarters Marine Corps, he had overseen the proposal and creation of what became Det One, a move that reversed nearly 20 years of Marine Corps policy. I spent an enormously informative and entertaining 90 minutes at his office near the south gate of Camp Fallujah. In his interview, he was remarkably candid, and our conversation helped me not only trace the unit's development but understand some of the deeper historical roots behind the relationship between the Marine Corps and Special Operations Command. Kyser told me that if I wanted to understand the nuts and bolts of how and why the unit was established, I needed to speak with Master Gunnery Sergeant Joseph G. Settelen and Master Sergeant Troy G. Mitchell.

Operational realities then put a stop to my Det One collections until I returned to the United States in July 2004. There, I contacted Settelen and Mitchell and arranged for interviews. Over the course of the next two years, I interviewed several dozen members of the unit as well as other Marines who had some involvement in the formation of the unit. The research and the writing together constituted, for me, a priceless professional military education. I came away with a greater understanding and appreciation for the leaders and thinkers who formed the modern expeditionary Marine Corps with its singular capabilities and ethos.

Likewise, the Marines of Det One stand out even among their peers. The most significant thing they told me was that, yes, they were a special operations force, but from first to last they were Marines. From the Corps they came and to the Corps they did return.

There are several people I must thank for their assistance in the preparation of this history. First and foremost are the Marines of Det One, with special emphasis on Colonel Coates, Lieutenant Colonel Craig S. Kozeniesky, Major Jerry Carter, and Major M. Wade Priddy. All of them—and others who will be mentioned later in the text—gave me time and attention, fielded repeated follow-on questions, and reviewed drafts of the manuscript. They gave me "warts and all" access to the Marines of the detachment and to their records and files.

Without Kyser, Settelen, and Mitchell, none of this would have been possible, both figuratively and literally. It is probably not possible for me to describe Settelen and Mitchell adequately because the details of their

v

careers will not be known for many years, if at all. Colonel Paul A. Hand told the tale from the point of view of a Marine inside SOCom and helped me understand the inner workings of that command.

Commander William W. Wilson, USN, needs to be singled out for special thanks, not only because he gave me a candid and open interview and answered multiple follow-on questions, but because he is central to the narrative. The story of Det One probably would have been considerably different were he not involved. Using his philosophy as a daily guide—"It's good for SOCom, it's good for the Corps, and it's good for the nation"—he significantly contributed to the success of the first Marine force unit to serve with SOCom.

At the Marine Corps Center for Lessons Learned—the organization formerly known as the EFCAT—several Marines willingly lent me a hand, both at Quantico and in Iraq: Colonel Monte E. Dunard, Lieutenant Colonel Jonathan T. Elliott, Lieutenant Colonel Scott Hawkins, Major Mike Dukes, and Colonel Peter A. Dotto. Lieutenant Colonel Mark A. Hashimoto of Marine Forces Pacific also stepped up and sent me volumes of material and answered questions.

At the History Division, I must thank the late Colonel John W. Ripley, USMC (Ret) and Colonel Nicholas E. Reynolds who sent me to Iraq and gave me the freedom to operate. Lieutenant Colonel David Kelly (who came out of retirement and a comfortable life in Philadelphia to go to Iraq), Colonel Nathan S. Lowrey, Lieutenant Colonel David A. Benhoff, Lieutenant Colonel Craig H. Covert, Lieutenant Colonel Kurtis P. Wheeler, Lieutenant Colonel Jeffrey A. Riley, Major Stephen J. Winslow, and Chief Warrant Officer-3 William E. Hutson all provided exceptional support in this and so many other matters. Finally, the Chief Historian of the Marine Corps, Charles D. Melson, a man of boundless knowledge and many facets, helped turn a good idea into a good product, with admirable assistance from editors Kenneth H. Williams, Gregory A. Macheak, and Wanda J. Renfrow and designers W. Stephen Hill and Vincent J. Martinez.

John P. Piedmont
Lieutenant Colonel, U.S. Marine Corps Reserve
Quantico, Virginia

Table of Contents

Foreword iii
Preface v
Table of Contents vii
Chapter 1   Concept 1
Chapter 2   Formation 17
Chapter 3   Training 31
Chapter 4   Deployment 47
Chapter 5   "Ops Normal" 55
Chapter 6   Direct Action 65
Chapter 7   An-Najaf, "Z," and Home 79
Chapter 8   A Proven Concept 91
Epilogue 99
Notes 101
Appendix A   Command and Staff List 107
Appendix B   Chronology of Significant Events 109
Appendix C   Lineage and Honors 113
Appendix D   Individual Awards 115
Appendix E   Navy Unit Commendation Citation 117
Appendix F   Meritorious Unit Commendation 119
Index 121

Chapter 1

Concept

The Rise of U.S. Special Operations Command

United States Special Operations Command—USSOCom, or simply SOCom—was formally established in 1987 by the Nunn-Cohen Act, which amended the 1984 Goldwater-Nichols Defense Reorganization Act. In the early 1980s, the nation not only faced the Soviet-dominated Warsaw Pact and other major conventional threats, but also a rising tide of terrorism emanating from radical movements in Europe, as well as a multitude of religious, ethnic, and political movements in the Middle East. The new command arose from the need to maintain capable special operations forces in constant readiness for unconventional warfare and counterterrorism, and to direct and coordinate their employment. That need had been bluntly articulated in a 1983 memorandum from Secretary of Defense Caspar W. Weinberger, which stated that the revitalization of special operations forces "must be pursued as a matter of national urgency."[1]

The legislation that established Special Operations Command did not merely create a new unified combatant command; it also created a position in the Department of Defense to oversee the policy aspects of special operations: assistant secretary of defense for special operations and low intensity conflict. Further, SOCom was imbued with certain armed service-like aspects; alone among unified commands, SOCom was directed to manage its own budgetary stream, which enabled it not only to acquire special operations-specific equipment, but also to develop and test that equipment.[2] In the years since 1986, this singular authority has provided Special Operations Command the means to equip its forces rapidly with mission-critical gear, making it the envy of the other armed services working under the more conventional acquisition rules.

Once established, the individual armed services contributed existing special operations units to SOCom: the Army assigned the Special Forces, the Rangers, and other units; the Navy assigned the Sea, Air, and Land (SEAL) teams; while the Air Force contributed its Special Operations Wings, including units such as the combat search and rescue squadrons and AC-130 gunships. Among the services, only the Marine Corps did not contribute forces.

There were several reasons that the Marine Corps made this decision, but the essential point was that the Marine leadership saw the Corps as a general-purpose force with inherent special operations capabilities that had to remain flexible in structure and maritime in nature. To place Marine units under Special Operations Command, or even to place SOCom itself under the Marines (as one member of Congress advocated), would have prevented the Corps from carrying out its primary mission for the national defense—providing maritime expeditionary forces in readiness. Behind this point was a general unease that an independent special operations command might not be a successful venture. The 1980 debacle at Desert One in Iran was a recent memory, and it left lingering mistrust among the armed services.* Finally, Marines viewed themselves as "special" in their own right and did not see a need to attach themselves to any command in order to gain in name what they held in fact.[3]

The Commandant Looks Inward

The decision not to commit forces to Special Operations Command did not mean that the Marine Corps did not adhere to the larger special operations strategy. The October 1983 memorandum from Secretary of Defense Weinberger ordered a comprehensive improvement in the organization and direction of special operations forces. The memorandum directed each armed service to "assign special operations forces and related activities sufficient resource allocation priority."[4] In accordance with these instructions, the Marine Corps leadership examined the

---
* Desert One was the code name for the site inside Iran where in April 1980 U.S. Air Force transport planes bearing the force for the rescue of the hostages in Tehran were to transfer them to Navy helicopters flown by Marines. The helicopters then were to refuel for the next phase of the operation, dubbed Eagle Claw. Mechanical problems with some of the helicopters and a collision between a C-130 Hercules and an RH-53D Sea Stallion that killed eight airmen and Marines caused the mission commander to abort. The failure of the mission and the ensuing congressional investigation highlighted joint operability issues within the special operations community and was a primary factor in the creation of Special Operations Command. The debacle at Desert One spawned bitter and long-lasting recriminations among Army and Air Force personnel on the mission and the Marines in the helicopter detachment.

issue thoroughly and formed a plan to leverage the Corps' existing structure in pursuit of enhanced special operations capabilities. What resulted was the "special operations capable" or "SOC" program.

On 14 September 1984, the Commandant of the Marine Corps, General Paul X. Kelley, ordered the commander of Fleet Marine Force Atlantic (FMFLant), Lieutenant General Alfred M. Gray, to study Marine Corps special operations capabilities and recommend ways to enhance them. A group of officers under Gray's direction met at II Marine Amphibious Force headquarters at Camp Lejeune, North Carolina, from 19 November to 17 December 1984 and produced "Examination of Marine Corps Special Operations Enhancements." This document reviewed the historical aspects of Marines and special operations, discussed current Marine Corps capabilities, and recommended options for enhancing those capabilities. The study group examination is remarkable in several aspects as it concisely articulated Marine Corps views on special operations and the Marines' capabilities to conduct them.

The common theme of this study was that Marine involvement in special operations was a historical fact, be it by units or by individuals. In the report, there was some discussion of dedicated Marine special operations units, the Marine Parachutists and Raiders from World War II, noting that their experiences were not unqualified successes. Indeed, those units rarely (in the case of the Raiders) or never (in the case of the Para-Marines) were employed in the roles for which they were formed. Both were disbanded long before the war's end, and their Marines were absorbed into conventional units. Individual Marines distinguished themselves in the Office of Strategic Services (OSS) during World War II, then in Korea, and later in the Studies and Observations Group in Vietnam. On the other hand, the report noted that conventionally organized Marine airground task forces routinely conducted certain special operations, most notably noncombatant evacuation operations (NEOs) and amphibious raids, "by virtue of organizational flexibility and forward-deployed posture."[5]

In framing its discussions, the study group stated the Joint Chiefs of Staff's definition of special operations, which, they noted, had recently changed from "secondary or supporting operations"—what the examination study called "nebulous guidance"—to the more decisive definition of "military operations conducted by specially trained, equipped, and organized Department of Defense forces."[6] The examining group compiled a list of special missions related to naval operations and constructed three broad categories of special operations capabilities:

Type A. The capability to conduct special operations tasks such as special purpose raids. This capability required unique skills, highly specialized equipment, and training far beyond that normally provided conventional forces. The forces involved were small, and were to be used in operations of short duration.

Type B. The capability to conduct amphibious raids and support other special operations missions with conventionally organized forces (normally a unit of company-size) which have been designated, intensively trained, and equipped for special operations.

Type C. The capability to conduct amphibious raids, NEO operations, and support of other special operations missions with a large, conventionally organized and equipped combined arms force.[7]

Following the general theme of the background discussion, the examination study observed that although "certain Marine Corps units have a Type C, or even B, capability, the study group found no evidence that such capabilities are other than piecemeal. Some Marine amphibious units can conduct raids; certain units perform the reconnaissance/surveillance tasks of special operations; to an extent helicopter squadrons receive the kind of training required. But, there is no cohesive approach to special operations."[8] Significantly, the study also considered whether the Marine Corps would be better served by retooling existing units or by creating something new.

The study group directed the discussion through the issues of personnel, intelligence, training, logistics, communications and electronics, aviation, command relationships, U.S. Navy perspectives (one member of the group was a naval officer from the staff of Second Fleet's Amphibious Group Two), operations and training, and the nature of hasty versus preplanned response to a crisis. Given all aforementioned points of reference and discussion, the study group examined the Marine Corps' existing special operations capabilities and came up with seven enhancement options. The underlying conclusions mandated an improvement in the overall training of Fleet Marine Force units and an immediate, specific improvement in amphibious raid capability.

The study group recommended four of the seven options for further review and action. The first was to maintain the current Marine amphibious unit structure and achieve Type C capability with one raid company. The group viewed this option as "the quick fix," a way to show action, yet something that "cannot be realized overnight." The second recommended option was to improve the existing Marine amphibious unit to a uniform Type C capability and achieve Type B capability with one raid company. This option would have required a "quantum jump in capability and cost." However, the study noted that "FMF-wide benefits are manifest: ground and aviation skills would be distributed as Marines rotated to other units. At the same time, MAUs would be better prepared to support Type A special operations."

Option three included the second option with the addition of the ground element of a small dedicated Marine special operations unit of roughly 275 men, at Type A capability, based in the continental United States rather than forward-deployed.* "When fully capable, which conservatively would take two years," the study group explained, "the FMF could provide Fleet commanders with the complete range of special operations capabilities." The study group observed that "this alternative is appealing because it is all-Marine."

Option four recommended adopting the second option and adding to it not a small Type A special operations unit, but a larger one, in this case roughly 1,000 men, with an aviation squadron containing Sikorsky CH-53E Super Stallion helicopters and Lockheed C-130 Hercules transport planes. This option, the study group noted, would probably take three years to achieve and would be "the most radical approach and extremely costly." It would contain the advantages of a smaller force but "would meet the full spectrum of special operations contingencies."[9]

Of the four, the study group favored the last option, "the most radical" as their examination study called it.[10] In doing so, the members of the group stretched the limits of their guidance since the force they advocated was a unit potentially capable of duplicating other armed services' special operations forces.[11] The fourth option was no half measure; it was an all-or-nothing proposition. It had marked advantages ("provides a highly skilled, substantial air-ground force that can concentrate solely on special ops missions") as well as stark disadvantages ("requires major additional force structure with significant impact on existing USMC structure" and "has potential for detracting from the FMF's traditional amphibious role").[12] It also contained the second option, with its significant implications for the Marine amphibious units.

The special operations capable (SOC) program is worth examining in detail as it illustrates the growth of a complementary set of capabilities grounded in historical Marine roles and missions. Background discussions on the relationship between the Marines and the special operations community seldom delve into the intellectual analysis behind the Marines' decisions to remain outside the SOCom command structure. As a result, misconceptions on the special operations capabilities of the Marine Corps persist to the present and certainly colored the issues surrounding the subject of this narrative. The importance of the special operations capable program is not only that it significantly enhanced existing Marine Corps forces and their capabilities, but also that it provided the Marines a base of individual and organizational skills that would enable the Corps to rapidly field a unit for Special Operations Command when the time came to do so.

Lieutenant General Gray Reports His Findings

Lieutenant General Gray received the results of the study group's examination and on 26 March 1985 submitted his findings on it to Commandant Kelley. Gray's findings expanded on points made in the examination study, which were necessarily somewhat discursive in nature, and placed on them the weight and imprimatur of the operating forces. In its own analysis, the report affirmed the examination's conclusions, among them that the existing Marine air-ground task force structure provided for a special operations capability found in no other armed service, by virtue of the "Marine air-ground task force concept and the well established naval command and control structure."[13]

The methodology in Gray's Fleet Marine Force Atlantic report was similar to the study group's examination: the issue in question was stated, delineated, defined, and discussed through several filters. The report drew seven conclusions and made a three-fold recommendation: that the Marine Corps held a unique capability for maritime special operations; that further developing the capability would have a pos-

---

* This notional unit bears an interesting resemblance to what would, 20 years later, become Det One, although it is larger than Det One. The notes on its conceptual task organization include some prescient language: "The S-2 support section of this company would be significantly larger than normal staff intelligence cells and for good reason . . . the unit must be capable of receipt of near real time intelligence and information, a high degree of analysis and some fusion capability. ADP [automated data processing] intelligence support will also be necessary to link the unit to national databases."

itive effect for the Corps as a whole; and that the Corps could develop a full-spectrum capability in consonance with current joint definitions. The report concluded that the Marine Corps should develop a specialized maritime strike capability based on existing doctrine; that this capability had to be in line with the needs of amphibious command relationships; that any Marine special operations force had to be complementary to existing naval special operations organizations; and finally, that the development of this capability was a crucial matter, given the world's prevalent threats.[14]

The recommendation of the Fleet Marine Force Atlantic report was that the Marine Corps develop a "viable special operations capability in order to provide fleet commanders a 'total response' capability." The three steps needed to achieve this goal were to develop an "updated maritime special operations doctrine;" to provide "additional, standardized training" for the air-ground task forces; and to create a "dedicated special operations force within FMFLant and FMFPac to conduct specialized missions requiring highly skilled forces." The study group's preferred option for an enhanced Marine amphibious unit and a large, dedicated special operations force of Type-A capability survived in a somewhat altered form; a different version of it was later offered as one course of action to the Commandant. The updated doctrine in the FMFLant report and additional standardized training were fully in line with the study group's second option.*

The final paragraph of the report's cover letter portended a significant change in Marine Corps training, organization, and capabilities: "The conclusions, recommendations, and implementation proposals, if approved, require an extensive effort to develop a unique and viable potential that exists within our current MAGTF structure. FMFLant is prepared to immediately initiate and develop this potential."[15]

The Commandant Decides

On 27 April 1985, Lieutenant General Gray met with General Kelley to review the special operations study group's findings and Gray's Fleet Marine Force Atlantic report. They discussed three options for proceeding with Marine Corps special operations enhancements. The first was to make no change, clearly not an acceptable alternative given Secretary of Defense Weinberger's guidance. The second was to "develop a *dedicated* special operations force," while the third was to "make the fleet Marine forces capable of conducting a wide spectrum of special operations with their conventional forces."[16]

Given that Lieutenant General Gray had stated that his command was prepared to take action "immediately" on the issue, it is not surprising that he came with detailed proposals. Gray's preferred course of action for a dedicated special operations force was to create a 1,000-man Marine air-ground task force complete with ground and aviation combat elements. He included a timeline for its training cycle, a list of its overall capabilities, and a scheme for a test bed unit to validate the concept. The plan for the test unit was a smaller version of the larger force, a unit of 289 men, with the ground combat element being a reinforced Marine rifle company and the aviation element made up of four CH-53D or E helicopters. The pros and cons of the plan echoed what the II Marine Amphibious Force study group and the Fleet Marine Force Atlantic report had stated: the dedicated special operations unit would provide a substantial capability, but it would have significant costs in time, money, and negative impacts on the Marine Corps' missions and structure.[17]

Lieutenant General Gray also had an alternative plan: take what the Marine Corps had and improve it. This plan had two goals. The first was to "standardize/improve a Marine amphibious unit's capability to conduct doctrinal special operations." The second was to "avoid conflict with missions of other services' special operations forces." To address the first goal, a third Marine amphibious unit would be established within II Marine Amphibious Force. Training cycles were to be expanded and standardized and the three units would be set into a sustained rotation, ensuring that one was overseas as Landing Force Sixth Fleet, one was training to take over that mission, and one was reorganizing for its training cycle, having just returned from deployment. A notional chart showed this plan at work, with continuous deployments graphed out into late 1989 and specific units earmarked for service. "The Solution," as the brief called it, continued with specifics for training improvements, including but not limited to "command and staff planning and execution skills required for special operations;" "development of infantry company/platoon skills necessary to provide a raiding force assault element, covering element, or reserve element;" and "development of aviation skills necessary for penetration/covert approach, urban operations, and withdrawal." The plan provided for a broad and valuable capability, enhanced training

---

* If it appears that both documents took pains to state and restate conclusions in a ponderous manner, consider that the language was not used loosely. "Complementary," "specialized," "unique," and "maritime" were all employed in a manner calculated to state accurately what the Marine Corps should and should not do.

across the board, and could be accomplished within the existing structure of the Marine Corps.[18]

On 7 June 1985 in a memorandum for the record, General Kelley adopted the plan to enhance Marine Corps special operations capabilities by improving the existing structure. He directed Fleet Marine Force Atlantic to begin the program, using a Marine amphibious unit as the test bed, stating that "this Marine Amphibious Unit will be tentatively designated as '—Marine Amphibious Unit (Special Operations Capable).'" He included specific guidance on what the new unit, the "MAU (SOC)," was to accomplish in terms of optimal organization; a training program focused on the all-important traditional Marine roles; any force augmentations for special missions beyond the unit's normal capabilities; special equipment; and a concept for operations with "Joint Special Operations Command (JSOC) and/or the other services" on "occasions when mission requirements dictate."[19]

Two weeks later, General Kelley communicated this initiative in writing to the Joint Chiefs of Staff and, in a separate message containing the identical text, to the regional combatant commanders and others, including the forerunner of SOCom, U.S. Commander in Chief Special Operations. Both documents clearly stated what the Marine Corps was undertaking and why—a comprehensive program to enhance existing capabilities in order to field a complementary maritime capability—and what it was specifically not doing: encroaching on the roles and missions of "special purpose organizations such as JSOC, Special Forces, SEALs or Special Operations Wings."[20]

A formal implementation plan followed in November 1986 embodying the experiences of the first special operations capable Marine amphibious unit. Continuous refinements and improvements took place, with the experiences and skills of individual Marines cross-pollinating the rest of the Fleet Marine Force as units rotated in and out of the Marine amphibious units' deployment schedule. The formal schools of the Marine Corps responded to the requirements of the program, and the rise of special operations capable units coincided with renewed interest in rigorous professional military education.

There were early instances of close, if unheralded, cooperation between the Marine Corps and elements of the new Special Operations Command, validating the particular role of the special operations capable Marine amphibious unit in operating with dedicated special operations forces.* At Camp Lejeune, North Carolina, the Special Operations Training Group and 2d Force Reconnaissance Company fielded a direct action force for the commander, U.S. Atlantic Command, known commonly as the "CINC's In-Extremis Force." As the name implied, it existed as a complementary capability for the combatant commander, available if certain special operations forces from SOCom could not respond to a crisis. This standing task force leveraged the particular maritime direct action capability that the Marines developed through the MAU (SOC) program and was linked directly to SOCom through its training and evaluation.[21]

On 5 February 1988, General Gray, who had succeeded General Kelley as Commandant of the Marine Corps, changed the designations of air-ground task forces. "Amphibious" became "expeditionary," heralding both a return to the Marine Corps' roots and an emerging philosophical change. General Gray noted that "the forces which we forward deploy around the world are not limited to amphibious operations alone."[22] Overnight, the MAU (SOC)s became MEU (SOC)s.

The decade of the 1990s cataloged a long list of operations by special operations capable Marine expeditionary units, some of which were undertaken by MEU (SOC) alone, and some of which were undertaken as part of joint operations. Marines conducted noncombatant evacuations in the Balkans and Africa, some with the involvement of SOCom units. The 24th MEU (SOC) rescued downed U.S. Air Force pilot Captain Scott O'Grady in Bosnia in 1994.[23] The 18-month U.S. involvement in Somalia provided a venue in which virtually every MEU (SOC) capability was employed, beginning with an amphibious assault by 15th MEU (SOC) and ending with an amphibious withdrawal by 24th MEU (SOC). In Somalia during one deployment in 1993 that totaled just 48 days on station, 24th MEU (SOC) conducted most of the SOC mission essential tasks, including multiple amphibious raids by small boats and helicopters; coalition

---

* One officer who will figure prominently later in this narrative, Col Paul A. Hand, was a company commander in the 26th MAU (SOC) in 1987 and remembers the unit working with "a lot of different organizations . . . including guys from Fort Bragg," an oblique reference to upper-tier elements of Special Operations Command. "At the time," he continued, "the relationship between JSOC and the Marine Corps couldn't have been any better . . . The warfighters had figured out how to make it work." Hand intvw, 26Aug05 (Marine Corps Historical Center [MCHC], Quantico, VA).

In the same vein were the highly successful maritime operations mounted by U.S. Central Command under Gen George B. Crist in the late 1980s employing elements of a MAU (SOC) with elements of SOCom forces. Gen Crist described the force: "we had really formed a new thing. It was a raid force that was totally integrated with the army at night, with the SEALs, with the navy, and hooked into air force reconnaissance, this little thing. It was a very sleek, mean little outfit." Crist intvw, 10Jan89, Gray Research Center, Quantico, VA.

support operations; tactical recovery of aircraft and personnel; numerous humanitarian relief missions; and one direct action raid by the maritime special purpose force.[24]

Operation Eastern Exit, the January 1991 evacuation of the U.S. embassy in Mogadishu, Somalia, illustrated how MEU (SOC) training standards had, at an even relatively early date, permeated the entire Fleet Marine Force. In the operation, the 4th Marine Expeditionary Brigade, afloat in the Arabian Sea for Operation Desert Shield, rapidly task-organized a small force to begin the evacuation of the embassy while the ships of the amphibious ready group closed the 450-mile distance. Every element of the operation was rooted in MEU (SOC) doctrine and experience: rapid and effective command and staff actions; a helicopter detachment that flew a task-organized force (including nine Navy SEALs) over open water at night, refueling in air more than once; and well-executed actions on the ground that accomplished a highly sensitive mission.[25]

The decade of the 1990s, however, also marked a decline in relations between the Marine Corps and Special Operations Command. A chasm developed between the Marine Corps and the special operations community that widened year by year. Although many Marines served in individual billets in SOCom and performed well, there was little or no interoperability between the theater special operations commands and the deployed MEU (SOC)s. "Love the Marines, hate the Marine Corps" attitudes persisted, often reciprocated from within the Corps. A service-level link, the SOCom/USMC board, which could and should have identified and fostered several points of common interest, lapsed into dormancy around 1996, severing all cooperation on acquisitions, training, and operations. Early unit-level initiatives such as joint operations between elements of SOCom and the deploying MAU (SOC)s and the Camp Lejeune-based CINC's In-Extremis Force also ended. By the onset of the 21st century, the U.S. Marine Corps and U.S. Special Operations Command were no longer institutionally engaged.

11 September 2001: The Landscape Changes

In the summer of 2001, Lieutenant Colonel J. Giles Kyser IV assumed the duties of head of the Marine Air Ground Task Force (MAGTF) special operations section in Plans, Policies and Operations at Headquarters Marine Corps. His position encompassed all things related to the MEU (SOC) program as well as all things related explicitly and implicitly to special operations. He was well suited for the task. In addition to a standard infantry career, he had served as

Photo by Maj John P. Piedmont

LtCol J. Giles Kyser, shown here in May 2004 as commanding officer, 2d Battalion, 2d Marines, in Camp Fallujah, Iraq. As MAGTF Special Operations action officer at HQMC from 2001 to 2003, he oversaw the creation of the first Marine force contribution to SOCom, the unit that would become MCSOCOM Det One.

operations officer of 2d Air Naval Gunfire Liaison Company and executive officer of 2d Force Reconnaissance Company. While a student at the U.S. Army's Advanced Infantry Officer Course, Kyser had met several Army Special Forces and Ranger officers. He found that he, as a Marine officer, was much more at home with them than he was with his more conventional army counterparts. Among other things, Kyser recognized that their thoughts on approaching, analyzing, and conducting missions were closely aligned with Marine Corps thinking.

Lieutenant Colonel Kyser's subsequent staff tour at Special Operations Command Europe (SOCEur) exposed him to a special operational environment and confirmed the opinions he had formed at the Army's advanced course. One of the first things he learned was that for Marines working in special operations, personal relationships were essential. The people on the other side needed to get the measure of an individual Marine and trust him; once that acceptance was in place, the possibilities for joint operations grew dramatically. Kyser observed special operations forces in Europe operating in task-organized units not unlike Marine air-ground task forces but yet lacking the synergistic integrity of the Marine organizations. This experience implanted in his mind the idea that the Marine Corps had something concrete to offer Special Operations Command, namely a self-contained, task-organized air-ground force capable of a wide range of missions and imbued with an expeditionary, combined arms ethos.

By the late summer of 2001 while assigned to Plans, Policies and Operations at Headquarters Marine Corps, Lieutenant Colonel Kyser worked on the reinvigoration of the dormant training relationship between the MEU (SOC)s and SOCom, which had lain fallow for several years. At that time no one contemplated, much less advocated, a step as radical as contributing Marine forces to SOCom.* The task at hand was simply to reengage the special operations community for the mutual benefit of the Marine Corps and Special Operations Command. But, as Kyser later pointed out, "the complexion of that landscape changed dramatically on September 11th."[26]

Lieutenant Colonel Kyser Goes to Tampa

Shortly after the attacks on 11 September 2001, Lieutenant General Emil R. Bedard, deputy commandant for plans, policies, and operations (PP&O), directed Lieutenant Colonel Kyser to go to Special Operations Command headquarters in Tampa, Florida, and begin repairing the long-broken relationship. His mission was to reestablish the moribund SOCom-USMC Board. Kyser's first act was to check in with the senior Marine in SOCom, Colonel Paul A. Hand, who only a few months before had written an "it's-a-good-idea-but" answer in *Marine Corps Gazette* against establishing a Marine Corps force within SOCom. Hand was an infantry officer with a conventional background—company command in a MAU (SOC), Amphibious Warfare School, Command and Staff College, battalion command—but no Marine reconnaissance or Special Operations Command experience. Hand regarded his background as an asset rather than a limitation. Although he reported to SOCom, Hand had received instructions from Bedard similar to Kyser's: improve the relationship; get the SOCom-USMC board going again; find ways to work together. These efforts were underway before the attacks of 11 September, but those momentous events hastened the progress.

Lieutenant Colonel Kyser next went to see SOCom's director of operations, plans, and policies, U.S. Army Major General Eldon A. Bargewell, for whom he had worked during his SOCEur days and with whom he had excellent personal rapport. Kyser discussed with Bargewell the probability that as the war on terrorism progressed over what promised to be a long time, there would be opportunities for more cooperation between Marine units and special operations forces, based primarily on the Marine Expeditionary Units' forward presence and unique capabilities. He knew what the Marines could offer special operations forces in the prosecution of the war on terrorism and was determined to make the case.

During the fall of 2001 and early winter of 2002, Lieutenant Colonel Kyser became a shuttle diplomat, with one week in Washington and the next week in Tampa. He found willing allies inside Special Operations Command and ran into ironclad opposition there, too. The same was true at Headquarters, U.S. Marine Corps. Colonel Hand was busy shepherding the placement of two Marine officers in the SOCom operations center. Shortly after 9/11, Lieutenant General Bedard had asked his counterpart at SOCom what immediate assistance the Marine Corps could provide. The answer was intelligence officers. The Marine Corps offered two, and SOCom accepted. Entrenched anti-Marine attitudes in SOCom resurfaced, however, and the two Marine officers waited with bags packed until the highest levels of the SOCom command structure cleared the way for them to be assigned.[27] Ultimately, the two were so successful that they proved what might be called Hand's corollary to Kyser's law of Marine and special operations relations: get good Marines in, let them go to work, and everything else will work out.

Lieutenant Colonel Kyser found that the prevailing argument inside Special Operations Command against any Marine Corps force contribution ran along old familiar lines: "You [Marines] have your box, we have our box, stay the hell out. . . . You decided back in 1986 you didn't want to play."[28] But the facts were that the SOCom and Marine Corps "boxes" had no significant points of connection, no places where the one's capabilities could be set to cover the other's limitations.

Anti-SOCom attitudes within the Marine Corps were just as entrenched, and in light of the events of 9/11, every bit as outdated. As recently as the spring of 2001, an unsolicited offer by Joint Special Operations Command to work more closely again with the deployed Marine expeditionary units foundered.[29] The Marine refrain that Lieutenant Colonel Kyser often heard was that "we don't need special operations forces, we can do it ourselves, there's nothing they can do that we can't do." From Kyser's own knowledge of SOCEur units in action, he knew this argument simply was not true. SOCom's training processes and resources provided for capabilities that the Marine Corps did not possess. Kyser recalled in 2004 that "all of the bravado and all of the talk in the world didn't change the facts: enthusiasm does not equal capability."[30] He also had to face age-old Marine arguments against contributing forces: if the Ma-

---

* The *Marine Corps Gazette* printed a brief exchange on a Marine force contribution to Special Operations Command in the April and July 2001 issues. The proposal for a force contribution was written by a student at Amphibious Warfare School; the riposte, detailing why a force contribution was not in the interests of the Marine Corps, was written by Col Hand, the chief of the training division at SOCom's center for operations, plans, and policies.

rine Corps gives a unit to SOCom, they will have lost control of it and will never get it back, and such a commitment will bleed the Corps of high-value Marines.*

In time, Lieutenant Colonel Kyser would turn all these arguments upside down, but the task at hand was to seize a beachhead, to gain a foothold with his audience. The objective was the SOCom/USMC board; the Marine Corps needed to engage SOCom institutionally, on a broad front, on everything from MEU (SOC)/theater special operations interoperability to equipment acquisitions to intelligence support. In the days before 11 September, interoperability between deployed MEU (SOC)s and theater special operations forces was never put to a true test, although an event like Operation Noble Obelisk, the 1997 noncombatant evacuation in Sierra Leone conducted jointly with special operations forces, proved that working together was not only possible but operationally enhancing. This operation, however, was the exception to the rule. That state of affairs may have been lamentable, but too few decision makers saw it as a potentially fatal weakness. Following 9/11, an entirely different light shone on the issue. The emerging fact was that in a war in which special operators had a leading role, the dysfunctional relationship between Special Operations Command and the Marine Corps threatened not only to keep the Marines' role in the shadows but also to deprive the nation of the well-refined capabilities of Marine expeditionary forces.

The Commandant Changes Course

By the end of 2001, Lieutenant Colonel Kyser's shuttle diplomacy and Colonel Hand's internal pressure were showing signs of success. Applying the lessons learned from their careers, they leveraged previous personal relationships to build new ones. Kyser in particular had a small network of allies and supporters wearing several uniforms who kept him abreast of developments and attitudes across the armed services and Special Operations Command. More importantly, they soon had in hand a memorandum of agreement, signed on 9 November 2001 by the Commandant, General James L. Jones Jr., and the commander of SOCom, General Charles R. Holland. This memorandum resurrected the SOCom-USMC Board and paved the way for a greater level of cooperation.

In the first week of January 2002, Lieutenant Colonel Kyser briefed General Jones and selected senior officers as a preparation for the first SOCom-USMC board scheduled to begin shortly thereafter. He wanted the Commandant's approval before he proceeded. Kyser discussed the plan for engaging Special Operations Command across a range of issues, including logistics, aviation, and others. As he recalled, when the brief concluded, the Commandant expressed approval of what he had heard and seen, then sat back and said, "If we really want to show that we are committed to this, we need to think about committing some forces to SOCom."[31] The remark was a complete reversal of the long-held Marine Corps position.

In fact, General Jones had made an early offer of a Marine force to Special Operations Command in the immediate aftermath of 9/11. He called General Holland at SOCom and offered him a force reconnaissance platoon. Holland instructed the Naval Special Warfare flag officer in charge of SOCom's resources and requirements directorate to talk with Colonel Hand and figure out exactly what Jones's offer meant. Hand received a phone call from Lieutenant General Bedard confirming the offer and then began answering the multitude of questions from SOCom.[32] How this initial offer was examined and handled foreshadowed the later discussions of a larger force contribution and revealed how things might have turned out differently in one major respect.

Shortly after the first SOCom-USMC board meeting in January 2002, Colonel Hand briefed Special Operations Command general officers on General Jones's offer of a force reconnaissance platoon. Army Special Operations Command and Naval Special Warfare Command debated where the unit would best fit. Both groups made good cases. Hand remembered that the commander of Naval Special Warfare immediately voiced the opinion that the Marine unit should align with the Navy, due to its maritime roots. The commander of Army Special Operations disagreed. Hand made no move in either direction but in retrospect said this was the first and best opportunity for the Marine Corps to have jumped ship and cast its lot with the U.S. Army Special Operations Command.[33]

Lieutenant Colonel Kyser took General Jones's instructions not just as an order to devise a Marine force contribution to Special Operations Command, but to have it ready for the first SOCom-USMC board. Fortunately for Kyser, he was a step ahead, having come to the conclusion that autumn that SOCom's tasks in the emerging war on terrorism eventually would outstrip its capabilities. He had a clear idea

---

* These two objections had been raised before, even long before the founding of Special Operations Command. For an interesting discussion of the deeper historical roots of the issue, see Maj Robert E. Mattingly, USMC, *Herringbone Cloak—GI Dagger: Marines of the OSS* (Washington, D.C.: U.S. Marine Corps History and Museums Division, 1989).

that the Marine Corps could fairly quickly field a unit—more than a force reconnaissance platoon—that would alleviate the troop-to-task burden and cover some of the missions in which SOCom units were engaged. Better still, Kyser had two Marines working for him who also knew SOCom from the inside and who could sit down and turn out a well-crafted and well-reasoned proposal.

The Marines Come Up With a Plan

Master Gunnery Sergeant Joseph G. Settelen III was the MAGTF special operations chief, working for Lieutenant Colonel Kyser. Before the attacks on 11 September, he was involved in the Reconnaissance Operational Advisory Group, commonly termed the "fix recon initiative," which General Jones had established to restore Marine reconnaissance units to a position where their particular skills and training could best be used in support of the Marine operating forces.[34]

Settelen enlisted in the early 1980s as an infantry Marine. He moved into the reconnaissance field in 1987 and served with 2d Force Reconnaissance Company. In 1997 he left the Corps for a classified billet, returning in 2000 as a master sergeant and was assigned to the special operations section at Headquarters Marine Corps. He was as uniquely qualified and fortuitously placed as Lieutenant Colonel Kyser to deal with these issues. Settelen understood the operational aspects of Special Operations Command

MGySgt Joseph G. Settelen III, the MAGTF and Special Operations Chief at HQMC. Working under LtCol Kyser's direction and using his extensive knowledge of both the Marine reconnaissance field and the special operations community, he and MSgt Troy G. Mitchell designed the structure and manning of Det One.

Photo by Maj John P. Piedmont

Photo by Maj John P. Piedmont

MSgt Troy G. Mitchell, the reconnaissance field monitor at Manpower Division, HQMC. He found the "structure," the actual manpower billets, that could be drawn from existing units to stand up Det One. Not only did he find the structure, he helped craft the requirements for each reconnaissance Marine.

from personal experience, knew Marine operations, and was fully cognizant of the current state of the Marine reconnaissance community.

Master Sergeant Troy G. Mitchell was also an original member of the fix recon initiative. He had served in several reconnaissance units and, like Settelen, had done a "dark side" tour with SOCom. He had been selected in February 2000 specifically for the Reconnaissance Operational Advisory Group and was fully engaged with that program when Kyser called on Settelen and him to draw up a plan for the first Marine unit to be assigned to SOCom.[35]

The two questions governing the size and shape of the still-unformed unit were what would it look like, and how quickly could it be formed? Lieutenant Colonel Kyser knew that Special Operations Command would not want any more of what they already had. What SOCom needed was something different—a Marine air-ground task force, a flexible, powerful unit that would be so much more than the sum of its parts. But a full-scale task force needed too much support across the Marine Corps. Kyser, Settelen, and Mitchell determined that a task force without the aviation combat element was an answer to the requirement and was doable. As Kyser put it, "What I wanted was a uniquely Marine unit that was self-sufficient and could be employed on its own . . . that was focused on special operations mission areas that we had capability in *today, right now*."[36] Looking back on his time in SOCEur, he identified four mission areas where this unit could make an immediate contribution: direct action, special reconnaissance, foreign internal defense, and coalition support.

According the Department of Defense dictionary, direct action is defined as "short-duration strikes and other small-scale offensive actions conducted as a special operation in hostile, denied, or politically sensitive environments and which employ specialized military capabilities to seize, destroy, capture, exploit, recover, or damage designated targets. Direct action differs from conventional offensive actions in the level of physical and political risk, operational techniques, and the degree of discriminate and precise use of force to achieve specific objectives." Special reconnaissance comprises "reconnaissance and surveillance actions conducted as a special operation in hostile, denied, or politically sensitive environments to collect or verify information of strategic or operational significance, employing military capabilities not normally found in conventional forces. These actions provide an additive capability for commanders and supplement other conventional reconnaissance and surveillance actions." Foreign internal defense is defined as "participation by civilian and military agencies of a government in any of the action programs taken by another government or other designated organization to free and protect its society from subversion, lawlessness, and insurgency." Coalition support involved the provision of personnel and equipment to allied forces to assist them with integrating their operations into the U.S. command and control system, and gaining access to supporting arms.[37] The Marine Corps had an excellent record of coalition support capabilities due in large part to units like its air and naval gunfire liaison companies (ANGLICOs).

The prospective Marine unit for Special Operations Command needed to be able to operate alone, with conventional forces, with other special operations units, with foreign units, or with any combination thereof. It needed to have particular intelligence capabilities. Task organization would be its strength; combined arms would be its operating principle. Lieutenant Colonel Kyser called in Master Gunnery Sergeant Settelen and Master Sergeant Mitchell and told them to design a unit that fit these criteria. Settelen remembers Kyser giving Mitchell and him the task at about 1100 one day, to be due at 1600: five hours to construct a unit completely from scratch, one that would need to be drawn "out of hide," taken from the existing Marine Corps structure, be able to deploy and operate on its own, and that would offer SOCom something it did not have. The finished proposal would go straight to Lieutenant General Bedard. Settelen and Mitchell put about 40 years of combined knowledge to work in the cafeteria of the Navy Annex with butcher-block paper, pencils, and a pot of coffee.[38] Three hours later they emerged with a plan and handed it to Kyser.

In some respects, the unit Settelen and Mitchell conceptualized was a special-purpose Marine airground task force without the aviation. It had a reconnaissance platoon and a robust support structure, including a large intelligence element. In other ways, the unit was like MEU (SOC)'s maritime special-purpose force, although much more capable. It had organic fires, radio reconnaissance, and counterintelligence sections, areas in which the Marine Corps possessed special skills, as well as the necessary staff sections that would enable it to conduct stand-alone operations. Settelen and Mitchell not only wrote down rough numbers and organization, they filled in the ranks and military occupational specialties for each billet. They designed the unit to be manned by senior Marines with many years of service and several deployments, not enthusiastic first-termers. They also intended for its members to rotate in and out of the unit and back to the regular Marine Corps, thereby addressing the old concern that the Corps would lose high-value Marines forever. In Settelen's words, the unit would be a "900-pound gorilla that could do surgery."[39]

The original Settelen-Mitchell plan showed a unit of around 110 Marines and sailors. Word came back quickly that 110 was too many, so the two Marines pared the number to 86 but advised that they were cutting into the support functions that would gird the unit's core capabilities.* As Settelen pointed out, "When you get into logistics and planning, you have to have specialists, and they don't all do the same job, so we knew support-wise we were going to need some tail to [go with] the teeth."[40]

Although the unit was conceptually a Marine airground task force, aviation was conspicuous by its absence. Kyser, Settelen, and Mitchell knew that aviation personnel and equipment pipelines, especially for a special operations unit, were so tightly scripted,

---

* Settelen and Mitchell knew what they were talking about. Det One, when it deployed in April 2004, mounted out at 99 strong. Augmentations came during the training phase when it became apparent that the modified structure of 86 was too slim.

and due to the "naval" nature of the aviation force—not completely under Marine control— that trying to include an aviation combat element in the unit would cripple its chances to form up quickly, train, and deploy. Kyser forwarded the recommended unit structure to General Jones, who gave his assent immediately. From idea to concept to rough plan in remarkably short order, Kyser had in hand an organization he could present to SOCom.

Special Operations Command Reacts

Rough plan in hand, Lieutenant Colonel Kyser traveled to Special Operations Command headquarters in Tampa in late January 2002 for the first SOCom-USMC board. In front of the future concepts working group of the board, he laid out a presentation of SOCom missions and other activities and showed how, if under a reasonable assumption that its task load increased, its tasks would soon surpass its capabilities. In his words, "SOCom would run out of Schlitz."[41] Without a pause, Kyser continued with one small step for a Marine but one giant leap for the Corps: "In the Marine Corps, we have some forces that can do some of these specific things." "Immediately," he said, "red star clusters went up— *'No! You're not SOF! You can't do these things!'*" Kyser patiently answered, "Well, look, I think we can." And he proceeded to show how.

Lieutenant Colonel Kyser, Master Gunnery Sergeant Settelen, and Master Sergeant Mitchell knew the special operations world as well as the SOCom people did. They had anticipated the objections and were ready to counter each one. Kyser fired back with a counter barrage of logical arguments. His offer to provide a ready-built force that would take on four mission areas—direct action, special reconnaissance, coalition support, and foreign internal defense—and relieve other SOCom units to focus on more pressing missions proved persuasive. Arguments old and new against a Marine unit in SOCom would continue to arise during the following months, but Kyser had made his point. He had his beachhead.

Both Colonel Hand at SOCom and Lieutenant Colonel Kyser at Headquarters Marine Corps drafted summaries of the minutes of the board meeting. Drafting was one thing; releasing was another. According to both officers, they wrote and rewrote their summaries several times, only to have them sat upon at SOCom. It took four months until SOCom released the executive summary in May 2002.* On a positive note, the summary specified leveraging the "unique capabilities of each organization" and pushing forward with interoperability between forward-deployed MEU (SOC)s and special operations forces based in the U.S. and overseas. On the less positive side from the Kyser/Hand point of view, the executive summary referred to the Marine force contribution as "possible," "notional," and "a pilot program."

In discussions that followed between Colonel Hand and Lieutenant Colonel Kyser about the nature of the Marine unit, Hand, remembering General Jones's earlier offer of a single force reconnaissance platoon, wanted to keep the unit simple and small. He wanted to send it right out to whatever component of SOCom was going to sponsor it and get it operating, believing that the operator-level relations would be a runaway success and that a small force would be more workable. Instead, Kyser's plan won the day; the Marine force contribution to SOCom was to be more than one platoon of reconnaissance Marines.[42]

Once again, Lieutenant Colonel Kyser shuttled between Headquarters Marine Corps and Special Operations Command much as he had done the previous fall. He and Colonel Hand were busy not only with selling the force contribution, but also with shepherding all the initiatives between the Marines and SOCom. As they worked trying to sell the individual service components on the potential of the Marine force contribution, Kyser still had his network of sources telling him who was saying what about the Marine unit and taking bets on when it was going to be killed off and on who would deliver the blow.

The SEALs Volunteer to Help

It was plain to Colonel Hand and Lieutenant Colonel Kyser that the center of gravity of opposition to any Marine force contribution was Naval Special Warfare. Some individual SEALs were receptive, but their command appeared to be institutionally opposed.[43] A portion of the opposition was rooted in fierce protection of roles and missions, and therefore funding, a reaction common to every service. The SEALs had built a substantial special operations capability on their own over the course of decades and were justifiably proud of it. But protectionism was not the only factor in SEAL opposition; there also was a persistent institutional memory of the 1987 decision. According to the SEALs, the Marines did not want a part of SOCom then, and they should not be

---
* Col Hand achieved the release through another direct personal appeal to Special Operations Command leadership. As the weeks went by and the minutes of the meeting went unsigned, he received phone calls from LtGen Bedard asking pointed questions about the document. Hand eventually went to see MajGen Eldon Bargewell and told him bluntly that not releasing the minutes was "destroying my reputation." Hand intvw, 26Aug05 (MCHC).

given a part of it now. That viewpoint suggested an equally persistent and widespread misunderstanding of what the Marines had to offer—a unique, complementary capability instead of a tardy knock-off—an issue that dated back at least to 1987, if not earlier.*

Determined to press ahead and not let anyone kill the issue with delaying tactics, Lieutenant Colonel Kyser wanted the future concepts working group to meet again as soon as possible to discuss the force contribution. But, as he recalled, Naval Special Warfare unexpectedly proposed that it act as executive agent within Special Operations Command to handle the issue—the Marines are a naval force, the SEALs are a naval force; there is a natural marriage.[44] (Colonel Hand had experienced the same line of reasoning when he had discussed General Jones's offer of a force reconnaissance platoon.) To Kyser, the Navy position was not the welcome development it first appeared to be. He remembered Machiavelli's dictum to keep your friends close but your enemies closer. Kyser and Hand reckoned that Naval Special Warfare wanted to gather the Marine unit under its wing not to grow it, but to kill it, or at the very least force it to serve its purposes. Both counseled against accepting the proposal.

Lieutenant Colonel Kyser and Colonel Hand, however, also knew that in Special Operations Command, the commander and the chiefs of the individual components (including Joint Special Operations Command) made the key decisions in council and that the votes might not be in the Marines' favor. Kyser and his team calculated that the commander of SOCom was on their side, and by extension the head of Air Force Special Operations Command. Army Special Operations Command was a maybe. The Joint Special Operations Command and Naval Special Warfare were thought to be opponents. "So we figured we got two definite yes's and two that could possibly be no's," Kyser recalled, "and in order to get Naval Special Warfare to allow this thing to go forward, we said OK, we'll go ahead and acquiesce to this."[45] Kyser thought they could have swayed Army Special Operations Command or Joint Special Operations Command and thus gotten what they wanted without the Naval Special Warfare's approval, but they decided to cast their lot with the SEALs. So Naval Special Warfare was designated as SOCom's executive agent regarding the issue of a force contribution from the Marine Corps.

In March 2002, Colonel Hand and Lieutenant Colonel Kyser were invited to a meeting at Coronado, California, home of Naval Special Warfare, for further discussions on the nature of the force contribution. Hand called the meeting "The Coronado Accords." For both officers, it was soon clear what the agenda was going to be. "One of the first things they wanted to do was take us in and give us the training film on BUDS," Kyser remembered. "The message was clear: *'You're not special operations forces.'*. . . Then we got a briefing from one of their teams that had been in Afghanistan on individual initiative, creativity, and small-unit leadership. Those were the strengths of special operations forces. The unspoken message was, *'they're certainly not your strengths.'*"[46]

Nevertheless, Hand and Kyser pressed ahead, briefing Lieutenant Colonel Kyser's plan and maintaining the Marine Corps' position on what the force would look like, what it would do, and what it would not do. It was evident that the SEALs liked the support and staff functions but not the platoon of reconnaissance Marines. The urge to treat the unit's support and staff capabilities as a toolbox for higher headquarters would become a critical matter up to and through its deployment in 2004.

Finding the Money in the Marine Corps

With Colonel Hand and Lieutenant Colonel Kyser fighting the deep battle, they handed the close fight to Master Gunnery Sergeant Settelen and Master Sergeant Mitchell. Settelen and Mitchell had put together a well-reasoned and detailed proposal, but the time had come to turn it into an executable plan. There were plenty of questions to answer at Headquarters Marine Corps. What was the table of organization? What was the table of equipment? Who was going to pay for it? Where were these Marines coming from, and how would they be selected? The Marine Corps had not formed a new unit in years. Settelen and Mitchell had their work cut out for them, as every man and every penny was going to have to come out of the existing Marine Corps structure.

The two Marines took what they had done and quickly filled in the detail to get an idea of what the Marines in the new unit would require to accomplish their missions. What would each Marine need to carry? What would the reconnaissance teams need? What would the radio reconnaissance teams need? What sort of equipment would the intelligence element require? As the answers emerged, Settelen and Mitchell realized that some of the gear the unit would

---

* Paradoxically, when Col Melvin G. Spiese was assigned to Special Operations Command in 1995 to serve in approximately the same billet Col Hand would fill later, he had found that Naval Special Warfare personnel were among those most receptive to greater cooperation with the Marine Corps—and some of those most opposed to it were Marines. Spiese intvw, 16May05 (MCHC).

need to work in the special operations realm, primarily weapons and communications equipment, was not anything that could be found within the Marine Corps. Special Operations Command was not going to give it to them; part of the bargain struck by the Marine Corps and SOCom was that the Marines would fund the unit's start-up costs. The price tag was going to be substantial, and many of the acquisitions would have to be made outside the normal supply channels.

Master Gunnery Sergeant Settelen tackled the table of equipment and the budget.[47] Although he had experience at Marine Corps Systems Command, the Corps' acquisitions branch, he did not know the first thing about creating a table of equipment, or a budget on this scale. He cast around for help. When he called Installations and Logistics, "I didn't get a lot of love over there," Settelen recalled, noting that Installations and Logistics had to worry about supporting and sustaining the whole Marine Corps instead of just one strange new unit. So Settelen looked elsewhere. At Marine Corps Combat Development Command he found Mr. Robert Merle, the expert on tables of equipment. Settelen's previous experience in Marine Corps Systems Command began to weigh in on the acquisitions end. At Programs and Resources at Headquarters Marine Corps he found Mary Cooney, who taught him how to do an entire budget submission package and then served as his sanity check. She looked for fat and redundancy and made sure that the numbers made sense. As Settelen compiled the budget, he estimated that it would cost $17 million to put the unit together. Including the deployment phase, down to airlift in and out of theater, he put the final price tag at $27 million.[48]

Master Sergeant Mitchell handled the table of organization. Working within the limits of the original 86-man structure, he had to balance the needs of teeth and tail, to build enough structure to support the operating elements—enough, but no extra. It was his job to find the billets and take them out of someone else's unit; as he put it, "It hurt other units to stand up this Det."[49] Billets and structure eventually meant real people, in this case high-value senior Marines who were going to be taken out of units that needed them.

Lieutenant Colonel Kyser Keeps the Pressure On

Meanwhile, Lieutenant Colonel Kyser and Colonel Hand were advancing on multiple lines. Since they had been the subjects of widespread opposition to any Marine involvement in Special Operations Command, they believed that they could mount a broad counteroffensive to get their points across. Kyser called it "an assault from all different quarters." He began lobbying the office of assistant secretary of defense for special operations and low intensity conflict, Michael A. Westphal, a former Marine, not only to garner Department of Defense-level support for the prospective Marine unit, but also to show broad progress in increasing the Marine Corps' ties with SOCom beyond a force contribution.

Lieutenant Colonel Kyser wrote the Marine Corps' response to a Department of Defense study on the future of special operations forces, demonstrating that the Marines were supporting several SOCom initiatives and programs and contributing to the effort."[50] As of July 2002, Kyser was able to detail several areas in which the Marine Corps was directly providing help to SOCom. "Some of the support," he noted, "has historical precedence and some is a direct reflection of actions taken since September 11th [2001]." Among the contributions were approximately 100 Marines filling billets directly supporting the Special Operations Command; liaison officers to SOCom and SOCCent for operational and planning assistance; operations by Task Force 58 (the 15th and 26th MEU [SOC]s) in Afghanistan, including tactical recovery of aircraft and personnel, close air support, and providing quick reaction forces; and Marine KC-130 support to Task Force-160, the Army's special operations aviation unit. SOCom apparently deemed continued KC-130 support so important that it had been mentioned in the executive summary of the first SOCom-USMC board.[51]

Lieutenant Colonel Kyser also honed his approach to Naval Special Warfare. He used a senior SEAL officer assigned to the Pentagon with whom he had served before as his sounding board to craft the arguments the Marine Corps would offer in discussions concerning the unit's prospective deployment and employment overseas.

Colonel Hand was working to get the first Marine general officer, Brigadier General Dennis J. Hejlik, assigned to Special Operations Command. Although not directly related to the establishment of the Marine force for SOCom, the assignment of a Marine general to the command would signify that the Marines had not only landed but were not going

---
* When speaking of this period later in 2004, LtCol Kyser used an example from the commanding general, 1st MarDiv: "Gen Mattis likes to talk about how it's difficult for a man to hate you when you've just handed him a cold bottle of water and it's 150 degrees outside. Well, it's difficult to make an argument against the Marine Corps being part of SOCom when at the same time we're providing assistance." Kyser intvw, 25May04 (MCHC).

Photo by Maj John P. Piedmont
Col Robert J. Coates, commanding officer, MCSOCOM Det One, shown here at Camp Fallujah, Iraq, in May 2004, almost a year after the formation of the unit. When the discussions were underway at HQMC on who would be named to command this unit, LtCol Kyser said that "We discussed several names, but every time we came back to Coates."

away. This assignment, like the placement of the two intelligence officers after 9/11, was delayed until Hand received a phone call from Lieutenant General Bedard asking whether SOCom really wanted a general officer. Tired of the delays, Hand went right up the chain-of-command at Tampa and got a final, affirmative answer.[52]

History Offers a Lesson

During the fall of 2002, Lieutenant Colonel Kyser and his team traveled to Camp Pendleton, California, and met with senior representatives from the intelligence, fire support, and reconnaissance communities. They went through several hundred record books and selected the people they wanted for the new unit.[53] For the commanding officer they recommended Lieutenant Colonel Robert J. Coates, recent commander of 1st Force Reconnaissance Company and at the time head of I Marine Expeditionary Force's Special Operations Training Group (SOTG). Coates had a strong, positive reputation in the Marine Corps as well as in the special operations community. He had served in El Salvador in the 1980s as an advisor and later with other government agencies. As Lieutenant Colonel Kyser noted, "We discussed five or six different names, but every time, we came back to Lieutenant Colonel Coates. . . . Nobody could question this man's credentials. Nobody. He was exactly the right guy at exactly the right time to put in charge of this."[54]

To ensure the longevity of the unit, it needed a lineage, according to Lieutenant Colonel Kyser. With the permission of the Marine Raider Association, he decided to put the raider patch at the bottom of the detachment's logo. Kyser saw that there was an "undeniable parallel" between the Marine Raiders of World War II and the new unit.[55] By tying his unit historically to the Marine Raiders, he sought to evoke their role as a selectively trained and equipped strike force, a unit that could hit the enemy where it lived in a way conventionally organized units could not. In order to combat the inevitable "elite within elite" argument, Kyser intended for the Marines in the unit to come from and return to the Marine operating forces in a regular rotation. The Marine Raiders had been disbanded and absorbed into conventional units, a detail that was not lost on Kyser.

The Commandant Puts it in Writing

By the end of 2002, the Marine Corps' first force contribution to Special Operations Command was about to become a reality. The unit's proponents had countered all arguments, surmounted difficulties, created a structure, identified funding, named a commander, and tied its lineage to one of the most famous units in Marine Corps history. In late October, the Commandant, General Jones, issued an executive personal communication, known as a "personal for" or "P4" message, to the leadership of Marine Corps' operating forces and supporting establishment describing the unit being sent to SOCom, his intent for its creation and employment, and what he expected of those to whom the message was addressed. He laid out how the logistical and personnel burdens would be borne and how he wanted the unit to be set up for success in material resources and training. He linked the unit and its success to the whole range of SOCom-USMC initiatives and to the continued "primacy of the Marine Corps as the nation's expeditionary strike force." Jones emphasized that "the success of this unit is a priority for me," as well as for the secretary of defense, the secretary of the Navy, and Jones's designated successor as Commandant, Lieutenant General Michael W. Hagee.[56]

Two months after General Jones's P4 message, Marine Corps Bulletin 5400, dated 4 December 2002, formally established the Marine Corps Special Operations Command Detachment as a two-year proof-of-concept test, in furtherance of the goals set forth by the USMC/SOCom memorandum of agreement signed on 9 November 2001. The Commandant's October message had provided the overview of how the unit was to be created. The bulletin detailed the who, what, where, and when of activating the unit. In accordance with the Commandant's guidance, the bulletin listed 42 units from which existing structure would be "temporarily realigned" to make the detachment a reality. As might be expected, reconnaissance and intelligence units numbered about a third of those affected, but the list covered a wide swath of the Marine Corps; among other units, all three active-duty force service support groups were listed. The bulletin stated that "the purpose of this proof-of-concept test is to determine the optimal structure and equipment required to provide appropriate Marine Corps operational support to USSOCOM."[57] Thus was born Det One.*

More than a year's worth of hard work by several dedicated Marines at Headquarters Marine Corps, Special Operations Command, and elsewhere had become reality. The year 2003 would see the new unit form up, receive millions of dollars' worth of new equipment, and begin to train for its historic deployment overseas.

---

* The "One" in "Det One" does not appear in the "P4" message or the 5400 bulletin; it does, however, appear on the unit's first command chronology, covering the period 1 January–30 June 2003, and in its subsequent reports. Command chronologies and reports at Gray Research Center, Quantico, VA.

Chapter 2

Formation

To Prove the Concept

On 14 January 2003, General Michael W. Hagee assumed the duties of Commandant of the Marine Corps. Among the many pressing matters and ongoing initiatives he inherited was the emerging détente with the U.S. Special Operations Command (SOCom). Relations between SOCom and the Marine Corps had deteriorated since the mid-1990s, but the demands of the Global War on Terrorism had forced the two organizations to resume closer ties, a development seen by certain Marines as a welcome return to the original intent of the Marine Corps policy that founded the "special operations capable" program in 1985, wherein the Marine Corps would not contribute forces to Special Operations Command but would maintain several points of contact with the command to enhance operations and training.

Yet there was more afoot than a resumption of official ties. Operations in Afghanistan and other places brought the two organizations into closer cooperation than had been the case since the late 1980s at least. The most important of all the developments was a force contribution to SOCom: the Marine Corps Special Operations Command Detachment. As January and February 2003 progressed, Det One started taking shape. "We were buying equipment," recalled Lieutenant Colonel J. Giles Kyser IV, "orders were being issued to Marines, and the detachment was beginning to form."[1]

Although the administrative works in Headquarters Marine Corps were churning out the orders and the funding to make the detachment a reality, not everything was on autopilot. One looming obstacle was the decision that had been made in 2002 to approve Naval Special Warfare as SOCom's executive agent for the Marine force contribution. This authority, however, was not a blank check for SOCom or the SEALs. On 20 February 2003, the Marine Corps and SOCom signed a memorandum of agreement codifying the nature of the force contribution—the unit "shall be employed in such a manner as to fully evaluate the MCSOCOM Det and its potential value to SOCOM"—and clearly delineating who could do what with the detachment, and when. The document reads like a business contract between two reluctant parties, full of tentative phrases and providing even for unilateral termination of the agreement before its expiration.

The memorandum provided no carte blanche for Naval Special Warfare, nor did it give the Marine Corps a free ride. It assigned definite authority to the commander of the Naval Special Warfare squadron to which the detachment would be attached to task-organize the force. The detachment's commanding officer, a colonel, would upon deployment step aside in order to invest the Naval Special Warfare squadron commander with full command and control authority. On the other hand, the memorandum sought to preserve the detachment as a unit in order to maximize its potential. The letter and the spirit of the document clearly were intended to protect the integrity of the detachment while acknowledging operational realities. Each side would hold the other to the agreement throughout the two-year period.

As early as December 2002, the press began to report Det One's formation. *Marine Corps Times* and the *San Diego Union-Tribune* picked up the story early. In the next few months, publications such as *Stars and Stripes* and *National Defense Magazine* also reported on the unit. Special interest journals such as *SWAT Magazine* and *The American Rifleman* eagerly detailed the weapons and training of Det One.

The Command Element Forms

Personnel for the Det One command element (and all officers) were directed by the 5400 Bulletin to report to Camp Pendleton, California, no later than 1 March 2003; all other Marines and sailors had until 1 June 2003 to join. It was just as well that three extra months were allotted for the bulk of the detachment to muster as the Marine Corps was gearing up for what would be Operation Iraqi Freedom. Many of the Marines earmarked for the unit would be fighting in Iraq while the command element was working to put the detachment together and would be hurried home at the end of combat. Several, in fact, ended up joining later than 1 June.

Lieutenant Colonel Robert J. Coates reported for duty on 1 March 2003. He did not have far to go to report since I Marine Expeditionary Force Special Operations Training Group (SOTG), of which he was of-

Col Robert J. Coates (far right) with Colonel John A. Toolan, commanding Regimental Combat Team 1, (second right) all shown outside Camp Fallujah in August 2004. With the Fallujah Brigade in the last days of its existence, Col Coates had a leading role in the establishment of the Shahwani Special Forces that replaced it.

Photo courtesy of Col Robert J. Coates

ficer in charge, was providing the temporary facilities for the new unit.* Other principal staff members and support section Marines soon began to check in.

Among the early arrivals, Sergeant Victor M. Guerra, the network administrator, was one of the most significant. The table of organization crafted by Master Gunnery Sergeant Joseph G. Settelen III and Master Sergeant Troy G. Mitchell anticipated the need for a dedicated information technology Marine, specifically a Marine fully qualified in his military occupational specialty who could be cross-trained in other tasks. Guerra did not have a reconnaissance background. He had spent his career in base operations at Okinawa, Quantico, and San Diego. But what experience he might have lacked in combat arms units he amply made up in network knowledge and an exceptional work ethic. This last quality would serve him well.[2]

Sergeant Guerra initially was put to work not on building or running a network, but on building and running the detachment. The detachment's communications officer would later call him "the center pole" around which the detachment grew."[3] Guerra helped lay out the utility lines for the unit's new compound near the boat basin in Camp Del Mar. He arranged for telephone service. He ordered radios and then had to learn how to employ them. When Lieutenant Colonel Coates told him to go learn the AN/PRC-148 handheld, frequency-hopping radio, the basic tactical communications gear every Marine in the detachment would be using, Guerra recalled asking himself, "OK, what's a PRC-148?"[4] Borrowing a set from Special Operations Training Group, he pored over it for two days and learned it, inside and out, on his own.

As the weeks passed, Sergeant Guerra began to work more in information technology, his area of expertise, although not less in the other areas of general support. He simply worked more at everything. As a one-man show, he had to do many things himself or they would not get done. Lieutenant Colonel Coates empowered Guerra to "wear his rank" and solve the problems. Guerra found himself in meetings—and sometimes arguments—with I Marine Expeditionary Force staff officers and base support sections, having

---

* SOTG, and then 15th MEU (SOC), would house the detachment's command element for the first three months of its existence; SOTG would even provide key personnel on loan to cover positions the slim table of organization did not provide.

to stand his ground and make sure the detachment got what it needed. As he (and others) would find out, it was not easy to get full support while virtually all hands at Camp Pendleton were concentrating on the war in Iraq.[5]

On 17 March, Major Craig S. Kozeniesky reported as executive officer. He came directly from his post as operations officer at the Mountain Warfare Training Center in Bridgeport, California, having previously served as the operations officer at 1st Force Reconnaissance Company from 1998 to 2000, when Lieutenant Colonel Coates was commanding officer. In addition to a strong U.S. Marine infantry and reconnaissance résumé, he had served an exchange tour with the British Royal Marines. By the particular arrangements spelled out in the memorandum of agreement with Special Operations Command, Kozeniesky was designated to command the detachment when it joined SEAL Team 1 for deployment to Iraq. He was also assigned under the original table of organization as the detachment's operations officer.

The original structure also did not provide for a logistics officer, so Lieutenant Colonel Coates "temp loaned" Captain Matthew H. Kress from Special Op-

Photo by Maj John P. Piedmont

MSgt James R. Rutan, Det One's de facto sergeant major. As the reconnaissance monitor he cut the orders for the Marines from that community to report to the detachment with the last set of orders for himself. Together with Capt Stephen V. Fiscus, he ran the detachment's training cell, which focused on designing, running, and evaluating exercises so that the Marines could concentrate on training.

erations Training Group. In keeping with an emerging pattern, the tall Captain Kress had been the logistics officer at 1st Force Reconnaissance Company when Coates was commanding officer. Of the same provenance was Gunnery Sergeant Monty K. Genegabus, the logistics chief. Along with Major Ronald J. Rux, on temporary duty from 11th MEU (SOC) as the acting supply officer, Kress and Genegabus shouldered much of the initial burden of ordering and accepting mountains of equipment, all of it new, and much of it non-Marine.

The senior enlisted Marine, the sergeant major in fact if not in name, was Master Sergeant James R. Rutan. The Ohio native had enlisted in 1983 as an infantryman and transferred to the reconnaissance field in 1988, where he stayed for the bulk of his career. He was involved with Det One from the beginning. As the reconnaissance field's first personnel monitor at Manpower and Reserve Affairs, Rutan had been part of the working group that sifted through the stack of record jackets to find the best Marines for the unit. Master Sergeant Mitchell had identified the billets in reconnaissance units to source the detachment while Rutan, the reconnaissance monitor, issued the orders for individual Marines, with the last set of orders being for him. (Mitchell succeeded him as reconnaissance monitor.) In Det One, Rutan's primary task would be to serve in the unit's training cell.[6] The operations chief, Master Sergeant Thomas P. Muratori, came to the detachment fresh from 1st Reconnaissance Battalion and Operation Iraqi Freedom.

The communications officer, Gunnery Sergeant James E. Wagner, joined the detachment in late May,

LtCol Craig S. Kozeniesky, Det One's executive officer, and initially its operations officer as well, is shown here outside the detachment's headquarters in October 2004. He came to the unit from the Marine Corps Mountain Warfare Training Center and had been in 1st Force Reconnaissance under Col Coates. He had also done a tour with the Royal Marines.

Photo by Maj John P. Piedmont

having been held up by the war in Iraq. A veteran reconnaissance communicator, he had served in 1st Force Reconnaissance Company for a considerable length of time, "nine years, one month, one day," including the period when Lieutenant Colonel Coates was commanding officer. He immediately took on the tactical communications matters from a much-relieved Sergeant Guerra and began to get the detachment's communications shop ready to support the training phase. When Wagner got there, the proverbial cupboard was bare: "Empty, zero . . . well, there were a couple of radios." There were actually more than a couple of radios, as much of the detachment's tactical man-pack communications gear was on hand, but the quip was essentially correct. There was a pile of gear they did not need, and some of what they did need. Wagner soon identified table of equipment shortfalls and set about correcting the problems. As time went on and they waited for deliveries of equipment, he made do with what he had, borrowing from 1st Force Reconnaissance and other commands when the situation demanded. Although he had worn the uniform for almost 20 years, Det One was a new experience. "Never have I been anywhere else in the Marine Corps where you walked into something and started it from scratch," he said. "We just pieced it all together."[7]

The Reconnaissance Element

The initial Det One structure called for four reconnaissance teams, each with six Marines and one corpsman. With the platoon commander and platoon sergeant, the reconnaissance element totaled 30. Late winter saw the first reconnaissance Marines report for duty. On 28 February 2003, Captain Eric N. Thompson reported in as platoon commander. The San Diego native had served in 1st Force Reconnaissance under Lieutenant Colonel Coates and Major Kozeniesky; from there he had gone overseas with 13th MEU (SOC), a deployment he called "very frustrating," as he watched the versatile Marine expeditionary units operate on what he saw as the periphery of the campaign in Afghanistan rather than wade into the fight and employ the full spectrum of their capabilities. Now with Det One, he would have ample opportunity to redress that frustration. He was assigned to the basic reconnaissance course at Expeditionary Warfare Training Group Pacific when he received a call inviting him to join the detachment. Captain Thompson would be the first of several former members of 1st Force Reconnaissance Company and Special Operations Training Group to fill out the ranks of the Det One reconnaissance element.[8]

Photo by Maj John P. Piedmont
Capt Eric N. Thompson, shown here in October 2004 at the detachment's compound at Camp Pendleton, was Det One's first reconnaissance platoon commander.

Gunnery Sergeant Terry M. Wyrick was assigned as leader of Recon Team 1. In addition to serving in reconnaissance units on both coasts, the Missouri native had completed an exchange tour with the Royal Netherlands Marines. He had also served with 2d Force Reconnaissance Company in the 1980s when that unit fielded the "CINC's In-Extremis Force" for the commander of U.S. Atlantic Command, and so he was familiar with the requirements of operations at the SOCom level.[9]

Like Wyrick, Gunnery Sergeant Joseph L. Morrison, the leader of Recon Team 2 had also served in 2d Force Reconnaissance. Following a tour at the embassies in Burma and the Netherlands as a Marine security guard, the slim Alabaman went west to California and served in 1st Reconnaissance Battalion, 1st Force Reconnaissance, and then the special operations training group. In late 2003, he was getting ready to retire but put off those plans when offered the Det One opportunity.[10]

The third team leader was a Californian, Gunnery Sergeant Charles H. Padilla. He had served in 1st Reconnaissance Battalion and 5th Force Reconnaissance Company. The official detachment photo showed rank on rank of stern-faced Marines, except on the left flank where Padilla, bearing the colors, appears to be not just smiling but actually laughing. Major Kozeniesky recruited him for the detachment while Padilla was in the United Kingdom on exchange with the Royal Marines.[11]

Gunnery Sergeant John A. Dailey headed Recon Team 4, reporting directly from the staff of Special

Operations Training Group. The Virginia-born Dailey—from a corner of the Old Dominion called "Mosby's Confederacy" after the hard-fighting guerrilla leader who operated there—had done a Marine expeditionary unit deployment to Afghanistan and had seen considerable action there despite the Marines' overall limited role.[12] Dailey had served with another Det One reconnaissance scout, Gunnery Sergeant Sidney J. Voss, since they were riflemen in 3d Battalion, 7th Marines. All four team leaders were long-serving reconnaissance Marines, at or near 20 years' service, and three had been in 1st Force Reconnaissance Company under Lieutenant Colonel Coates.

The reconnaissance element's platoon sergeant, Master Sergeant Keith E. Oakes, came directly from his post with the U.S. Army Ranger Training Brigade at Fort Benning, Georgia. He had served there for four years, and in 2001 had won the prestigious "Best Ranger" competition. He was also something of a rarity in the Det One reconnaissance platoon—an East Coast Marine. In terms of personality, Oakes was the quiet match to the much more outwardly aggressive and demonstrative Captain Thompson.[13]

The Det One medical corpsmen were as well qualified in combat skills as any of the Marines. Chief Hospital Corpsman Eric D. Sine headed the medical section. One reconnaissance corpsman was assigned to each reconnaissance team: Hospital Corpsman First Class Robert T. Bryan went to Team One, Hospital Corpsman First Class Michael D. Tyrell to Team Two, Hospital Corpsman First Class Matthew S. Pranka to Team Three, and Hospital Corpsman First Class Michael I. Arnold to Team Four. Pranka, assigned to Padilla's team, came to Det One by way of 1st Force Reconnaissance, straight from duty in Iraq. He was emblematic of his fellow corpsmen; his entire career in the Navy had been with the Marines. Pranka had served first with an infantry battalion and then with several reconnaissance units and had done two Marine expeditionary unit deployments and Operation Iraqi Freedom. He had been through the renowned U.S. Army Special Forces medical course and had done a clinical rotation at a hospital emergency room in Saint Petersburg, Florida.[14]

No reconnaissance Marine was a shrinking violet, and Det One gathered 30 of the most aggressive and proficient from that community under one roof. Several had been platoon sergeants in force reconnaissance companies and two had served exchange tours with foreign militaries. More than one had left the Marine Corps and came back on active duty specifically to serve with the detachment. All were well grounded in conventional infantry service before they set foot in any reconnaissance units; some had unusual life experiences as well. With a group like that—30 chiefs and no braves—one might think there might have been unseemly jockeying for position in the war party. The Marines themselves say otherwise, and the by-name selection process was designed partly to net the right sorts of personalities, men who were only focused on getting the job done. Gunnery Sergeant Dailey, for one, decided early on that his team would do whatever it needed to do to move the unit forward. "From day one I told my guys, we'll do every mission we can in training, every varied task," he recalled. Staff Sergeant Chad Baker, a reconnaissance scout on Padilla's Team 3, echoed that attitude: "I came here to be part of a team. I'll sweep floors, I'll work on vehicles, I'll be a point man, it

The reconnaissance element stands in formation during the activation ceremony on 20 June 2003. Not all the Marines had reported for duty; some were still in transit from previous commands, and a few were en route from combat in Iraq.

Photo courtesy of Maj Matthew H. Kress

Photo by Maj John P. Piedmont

Maj M. Wade Priddy, Det One fires liaison element leader and later its operations officer. An artilleryman with conventional and ANGLICO experience, he helped to shape and train the fires liaison capability that would prove its worth in Iraq.

doesn't matter—whatever they need."[15]

The organic capabilities of the reconnaissance element were substantial. The average age was over 30. Each man had several deployments under his belt. More than half were school-trained snipers; several had been instructors at the Mountain Warfare School or one of the Special Operations Training Groups. Every team leader and assistant team leader had been to Ranger School. The medical corpsmen were skilled veteran fighting men in their own right. The overall level of physical fitness was extraordinary. As a unit, they were well prepared for what lay ahead.

The Fires Liaison Element

One of the hallmarks of the Marine Corps' force contribution to Special Operations Command was the capability to integrate all aspects of fire support—planning, coordination, execution—into joint, combined, and special operations. The Marine Corps has a long history of fielding such a capability, notably its air and naval gunfire liaison companies (ANGLICOs). Composed of Marines from the artillery, communications, and aviation fields, ANGLICO supporting arms liaison teams and firepower control teams provide U.S. Army and foreign forces access to Marine and Navy supporting arms. These collective experiences proved critical for the Det One fires liaison element.

On 21 March 2003, Major M. Wade Priddy reported as the Det One fires liaison element leader. An artillery officer with both a conventional and ANGLICO background, he had been alerted to Det One's formation through an interest in the resurgence of the active duty ANGLICOs. Priddy came to the detachment from Naval Reserve Officer Training Corps duty at Texas A&M University. Later he would move more into the role of detachment operations officer and serve as Naval Special Warfare task group operations officer in Iraq.[16]

Joining Major Priddy as air officer in the fires liaison element was Major Thomas P. "Hobbit" Dolan, a Bell AH-1W Super Cobra pilot and a serious triathlete. The pugnacious former enlisted Marine was not an ANGLICO veteran, but he had been a forward air controller for 1st Light Armored Reconnaissance Battalion. He was working for Lieutenant Colonel Coates at Special Operations Training Group when Det One was formed, and he became the air officer.[17] What Dolan brought to the fight was not just the ability to call in air support, but also the ability to think as an aviator, to grasp the aviation issues of a mission, then advise, plan, and execute accordingly. Those were skills not learned in any single certification course, but over the course of a career in the air and on the ground.

The fires liaison chief did not report until after the conclusion of Operation Iraqi Freedom I. Gunnery Sergeant Fidencio Villalobos Jr. came to Det One from his post as the liaison chief of 1st Battalion, 11th Marines, 1st Marine Division, fresh from the march up to Baghdad. His career spanned 1st ANGLICO, fleet antiterrorist security teams, and conventional artillery units. Villalobos also had been, in his words, a "stealth member" of 1st Force Reconnaissance Company. After the 1991 Gulf War, he took the reconnaissance induction test, passed it, and was assigned to 1st Surveillance, Reconnaissance, and Intelligence Group. From that unit he "walked over" to 1st Force Reconnaissance Company, where, although there were no billets for an enlisted artillery observer, he lived the life of a reconnaissance Marine for four years, even going to Ranger School. Later during Det One's deployment to Iraq, Villalobos—an enormous man, with the call-sign "Big Daddy"—would take over the fire support coordination duties for a U.S. Army cavalry battalion, bridging the divide between special and conventional operations and highlighting the singular capabilities of the Det One fires element.[18]

Rounding out the leadership of the fires element was the communications chief, Gunnery Sergeant Ryan P. Keeler. A communicator whose time in Marine operating forces was exclusively served in AN-

GLICO, Keeler was as well versed in calling for fire and controlling air strikes as he was at making sure communications nets were set up and functioning. He had served in a joint communications element and in the headquarters of U.S. Central Command.[19]

The Intelligence Element

When Lieutenant Colonel Kyser, Master Gunnery Sergeant Settelen, and Master Sergeant Mitchell put Det One together on paper, they intended for it to have a "robust" intelligence capability, manned with the complete range of intelligence capabilities the detachment would need to operate independently or jointly. They wanted a substantial presence from the human intelligence (HumInt) and signals intelligence (SigInt) disciplines, as the Marine Corps has unique capabilities in both functions. Kyser, Settelen, and Mitchell wanted a complete in-house analytical and production capability. In terms of individuals, they also had in mind a specific sort of Marine, not necessarily a "snake-eater" but someone who was simply very good at his job, and who could also then move quickly into the special operations realm. The Marines who joined Det One fit all of those criteria. Lieutenant Colonel Francis L. Donovan, the unit's second executive officer, would call the intelligence element "the real strength of the detachment."[20]

Major M. Gerald "Jerry" Carter reported in as the intelligence officer and intelligence element leader on 24 March 2003. He came with an extensive résumé. Carter had been part of the initial radio reconnaissance effort during his enlisted years, and he had

Det One's radio reconnaissance chief, MSgt Hays B. Harrington, executes a magazine change during Weapons and Tactics Package I at Range 130, under the watchful eye of Patrick J. Rogers.

Photo courtesy of Det One

MEU (SOC) experience, including a recent tour in Afghanistan. He also came with the one crucial item for any Marine dealing with special operations forces—by-name credibility. Carter had done a tour—an operational tour—in SOCom. He knew the special operations realm, and he was known in the special operations realm. Both qualities would pay immense dividends. Indeed, a SEAL officer he knew and served with would later have a major role in the detachment's story.[21]

The intelligence chief was a Texan, Master Sergeant Bret A. Hayes. Hayes had no SOCom experience, but he did have a wealth of time in Marine Corps ground and air intelligence. He knew how to run an intelligence section, with its several disciplines and myriad detailed requirements. He was, in effect, Major Carter's assistant intelligence officer. The all-source fusion chief was Gunnery Sergeant Kenneth C. Pinckard, an Alabama native and a Marine tactical air traffic controller before he became an intelligence analyst. He reported to Det One in May 2003 following a tour at Dam Neck, Virginia, supporting Naval Special Warfare. As opposed to the duties of the intelligence chief, who made sure that tasks got done, the all-source fusion chief oversaw the analysts and made sure that everything got put together.[22]

A three-man signals intelligence support team and a nine-man radio reconnaissance team provided the Det One signals intelligence capability, each subdiscipline bringing its own particular capabilities. Major Carter selected Gunnery Sergeant Adam C. Toothaker as the signals intelligence support team chief. Carter knew him from the 13th MEU (SOC) and gladly tapped him for Det One. Although Carter did not know Master Sergeant Hays B. Harrington, he learned that Harrington had also done a tour in Special Operations Command, and Carter knew that he was the right man to head the detachment's radio reconnaissance section. When Harrington reported for duty, he discovered that life in Det One moved in double time. The Mississippi native and 17-year veteran of the Corps employed the time-honored stratagem of checking in on a Friday afternoon, which usually secured the Marine a weekend lull before he started his new duties. But Harrington miscalculated, as he later recounted, and the joke was on him: "I saw Colonel Coates, and the first thing he told me was get my uniform on and go draw my gear, because I'm going to the field."[23] Harrington led a section of eight highly-trained Marines, organized into two teams of four men each.

The core of radio reconnaissance is electronic warfare, but radio reconnaissance Marines bring their surveillance capabilities to and beyond the front lines as fully qualified reconnaissance scouts, going through the basic reconnaissance course, airborne and dive schools in addition to their own extensive training, which could also include language instruction. A fully trained "radio recon" Marine is a fighting man unique in the Department of Defense; Det One's radio reconnaissance team formed a substantial part of the unit's potent intelligence gathering and analysis capabilities, and it would have a profound effect on operations in Iraq.

Captain Christopher B. Batts, a prior enlisted reservist and a career counterintelligence officer, led Det One's counterintelligence section. One day in early 2003 while he was assigned to the National Counterintelligence Center in Washington, D.C., Batts called the Navy/Marine Corps Intelligence Training Center at Dam Neck, Virginia, on a routine matter. The Marine with whom he was talking asked him casually how he would like his new position—as the Det One counterintelligence officer. Surprised, he called and confirmed this assignment with Headquarters Marine Corps. Batts then got started on this new position by calling Major Carter, whom he did not know. He began to put together his part of the intelligence element, a six-man team, in much the same way as Lieutenant Colonel Coates had put the key leadership together—by seeking out known quantities, Marines he had served with before. He looked for seasoned counterintelligence Marines and kept a good balance between East and West Coast backgrounds. One detail that assured Batts of a wide base of experience was the Marine Corps' requirement that counterintelligence Marines come to the field only after serving in other military occupational specialties; one of his Marines had been a heavy equipment operator, another a mortarman. For counterintelligence chief, he chose Gunnery Sergeant Matthew A. Ulmer, a West Coast Marine with whom he had not served before.[24]

Counterintelligence Marines gather intelligence from human beings. What they do is more properly termed counterintelligence force protection source operations. Although the title suggests only a force protection task—and in fact that is part of their mission—counterintelligence Marines have evolved a particular skill set in the intelligence world. This development is due in part to the merging in the 1990s of two military occupational specialties—counterintelligence and interrogator/translator—into one, counterintelligence. The move ensured that all "CI" Marines would have a strong background in both interrogations and source operations. Where their methods differ slightly with their counterparts in the other armed services (and especially in the special operations community) is that their operations are rolled into the larger intelligence picture, no matter what the mission or target. A good bit of what they would do in Iraq resembled nothing more than old-fashioned police detective work—the relentless pursuit of wanted men. Like their radio reconnaissance brethren, most of the counterintelligence Marines would be detached from Det One to other units in Iraq, where all would make their marks.[25]

Another Marine whom Major Carter was able to secure for the detachment was Warrant Officer Kevin E. Vicinus, a meteorologist serving in 3d Marine Aircraft Wing. Vicinus provided a capability that was well known and appreciated in the aviation community, but less well valued by ground combat units—tactically relevant forecasts. Instead of just providing simple weather observation and passing on general forecasts, he could accurately determine conditions such as wind speed and direction at various altitudes, visibility, and natural illumination, and then meld the predictions with topographic and imagery analysis. The resulting products allowed the staff to plan routes and holding patterns for aircraft and vehicles. Vicinus proved his skills to the detachment by predicting, almost to the minute, the arrival of a windstorm during the Capstone Exercise in Nevada, enabling the team to avoid damage to communications operations center and loss of connectivity.[26]

Equipping the Detachment

The decision to field the detachment involved providing new equipment at a cost of roughly $17 million. The 5400 Bulletin, which had established Det One, had made clear that "unlike personnel sourcing, this equipment will not be sourced from existing units."[27] The 5400 Bulletin also declared that the money would not come from SOCom. Because of these restrictions, procurement had to come from weapons and equipment in use nowhere else in the Marine Corps, including one weapon built specifically for the detachment.

Early in the detachment's formation, it became apparent that the original table of organization was not as generous as the table of equipment. The staff sections, and in particular the logistics section, were thinly manned. Lieutenant Colonel Coates eventually levied the Marine Corps to bring some men on board to give the logistics section more depth and capability. In addition to Captain Kress, Captain Olufemi A. Harrison and Staff Sergeant Frederick L. Riano III were brought on as supply officer and supply chief as the formation of the detachment progressed. Another specialist and key member of the logistics section, Staff Sergeant Stuart C. Earl, joined as plans chief in June 2003. His job was twofold: to ensure that the embarkation and deployment plans were accurate, up-to-date, and ready for execution by strategic lift assets; and to serve as the duty "ops Marine," organizing and running the combat operations center. When he reported for duty, Staff Sergeant Earl was greeted by his former drill instructor from Parris Island, 1995—Master Sergeant Rutan, the detachment's senior enlisted Marine.

Beyond personnel needs, Det One logistical difficulties ran from the general to the specific, or more accurately, to the multitude of specifics. What set Det One's logistical challenges apart from any other unit's were, in the words of Captain Kress, "the timeline and what we had to acquire. We didn't have a piece of gear to our name."[28] Obtaining the needed equipment was compounded by the demands of operations in Afghanistan and Iraq, and in many cases, by specific shortages of special operations gear. Mundane issues bedeviled Det One's logistics section. The allocation of ammunition to Marine Corps units is governed by Marine Corps Bulletin 8011, which for budgetary reasons is planned many months in advance. When the 8011 Bulletin for 2003 was being planned, there was no MCSOCom Detachment One. Therefore, no ammunition was allocated for its use. Laying legitimate claim to ammunition in the large quantities it would need for training would be a major hurdle for the logistics section.

Another persistent problem in equipping the detachment was the process of open-purchase, which is the method by which a unit can legally buy a particular item rather than wait for its procurement and issue through normal channels. Due to its mission, the unit needed specific items, and substitution of similar items was not acceptable. Kress was asked the same question repeatedly: "Why can't you accept this thing instead of that thing?" The answer was that the table of equipment specified the one instead of the other, and the table of equipment was built around the demands of the mission. That answer did not always satisfy the questioner, who might have had a hundred M4 carbines available for issue and could not understand that it was M4 SOPMOD (for "special operations modified") carbines that Det One needed. The detachment's ultimate weapon in any dispute about resources and priorities was the Commandant's P4 message of December 2002. Kress used it when the situation warranted, yet he preferred other, "less kinetic" solutions. Like any good logistics officer, he liked to turn to the people he knew and work the system. As he put it, to say that he strained previous personal relationships in his quest to ensure support for the detachment "would be an understatement, to say the least."[29]

In another example of how much effort and forethought went into building Det One, Master Gunnery Sergeant Settelen had obtained a research, development, test and evaluation charter for the unit. In a related move, Headquarters Marine Corps also secured the services of an official at Soldier Systems Command, Natick, Massachusetts, to help identify the best equipment available, push through its critical acquisitions, and then evaluate the gear's performance. Jonathan Laplume, a former Army Ranger, worked closely with the detachment's logistics section and was responsible for getting most of the first-rate gear the unit received. He later accompanied the detachment on its major exercises and even deployed with it to Baghdad. In order to assist Laplume in the early stages of the unit's formation, Lieutenant Colonel Coates sent out Gunnery Sergeant John Dailey from the reconnaissance element. Dailey had been involved in the development and acquisition of individual equipment for the reconnaissance community in the 1990s, and he knew how the system worked.[*]

One of the key pieces of equipment that the original table of equipment did not allow for was a command and control system that could provide the detachment with its own link to national intelligence assets and communications pipelines. Major Carter, sitting one day in a planning conference on detachment communications, listened to extensive conversation about man-pack radios, but precious little on serious command and control systems. As he put it, "no one talked about how we were going to move electrons across the battlefield."[30] When he suggested that they needed to get a system called Trojan Spirit, he was greeted by polite silence.[**] Carter was con-

---

[*] Equipment for Det One sometimes arrived long after it was ordered, in some cases well into the unit training phase. Sgt Guerra, the network administrator, would receive a shipment from some long-forgotten open purchase, and think, "Did I even order this? What is this?" In one memorable instance, the detachment's laptop computers arrived months after he placed the order for them. At that time still a one-man information technology department, Sgt Guerra set up a hallway assembly line of 32 laptops and went down the row, loading software onto each one, step-by-step, mouse-click by mouse-click, into the small hours of the morning. Guerra intvw, 16Nov04 (Marine Corps Historical Center, Quantico, VA).

[**] AN/TSQ-22 Trojan Spirit lightweight integrated telecommunications equipment is a super-high frequency dual band multichannel satellite communications terminal fielded for use in intelligence communications.

vinced that the intelligence element was going to need a system that provided a stand-alone link with enough dedicated bandwidth to pass imagery and other large files directly to and from national agencies. Drawing on his education at the command and control systems course and his recent experience at the Marine expeditionary force intelligence section, he made the case for it. Having been an intelligence plans officer, Carter knew how many Trojan Spirit sets there were in the Marine Corps, where they were, and what they required for support and maintenance. Trojan Spirit—or more properly, an improved version called Trojan Spirit Lite—gave the detachment an independent expeditionary data link to the national intelligence assets and communications systems. With it, Det One could deploy anywhere in either a supporting or supported role without having to levy other units to provide it with bandwidth.

Major Carter also knew that he needed to get Marines assigned to operate and support Trojan Spirit Lite and other intelligence-related systems. Staff Sergeant Jason M. Bagstad soon joined as the electronics maintenance technician, and Gunnery Sergeant Victor M. Church came on board as the intelligence element's signals intelligence communicator. In the hands of Gunnery Sergeant Church, Det One's Trojan Lite grew in capabilities to include extra connectivity with national agencies and separate links with unclassified email and voice systems. Master Sergeant Harrington, with his detailed knowledge of special operations signals intelligence issues, would help shape that added capability. As a result, the Det One Trojan Spirit Lite became the only one of its kind in the Marine Corps, and possibly in the Department of Defense.

As the detachment increased its intelligence systems capabilities, so too did it begin to grow wheels. Gunnery Sergeant Jaime Maldonado was in charge of the motor transport effort, while Staff Sergeant Jaime J. Sierra became the motor transport operations chief. Since both were veterans of 1st Force Reconnaissance Company under Lieutenant Colonel Coates, they knew that "Motor-T" would be just one small part of their duties. As the training phase picked up in intensity, both Marines would do what the other Marines of the detachment did, in addition to their own work. During mountain training in Bridgeport, California, they would even switch for a time from four-wheeled to four-legged transport.

The table of organization authorized 18 interim fast attack vehicles (IFAVs), small, light four-wheel-drive vehicles manufactured by Mercedes-Benz that could be internally loaded on Sikorsky CH-53E Super Stallion helicopters. Based on the recent experience of 1st Force Reconnaissance Company and 1st Reconnaissance Battalion in Operation Iraqi Freedom, where the units were used in mobile operations reminiscent of the actions in North Africa during World War II, those involved in putting together the table of organization thought that the fast attack vehicles would make good platforms for Det One operations. The IFAVs offered transportability and nimble, speedy mobility. What they did not offer was the size and protection of the new armored hunekers that could fight their way in and out of a target area. Gunnery Sergeant Maldonado and Staff Sergeant Sierra remained unsure that the fast attack vehicles were the solution to the detachment's mobility needs. Events were to prove them right.

Arming the Detachment

One of the main logistics concerns was arming the detachment with the array of specialized weapons that its mission would require. The Det One armorer was Gunnery Sergeant Mark S. Kitashima, a Colorado native who enlisted in 1988. Most notable among the assignments of his career was a tour at Quantico, Virginia, as a match armorer, working on the "MEU (SOC) .45," the finely tuned .45-caliber M1911 pistol used by the direct action platoons of the maritime special purpose forces. His knowledge of weapons and weapons procurement would be invaluable in arming the detachment. When he arrived at Det One, his armory consisted only of "a lock and a chain and an open cage." He immediately set to work dealing with Marine Corps support agencies to acquire all the ordnance the detachment would need, from specialized arms to basic crew-served weapons and standard armory equipment.[31]

Although humans are indeed more important than hardware, as a SOCom saying goes, the capability to execute precision close quarter combat still required specialized equipment. Heckler & Koch MP5 9mm sub-machine guns—weapons so identifiable with special operations units as to become emblematic of them—had given way in the U.S. military in the 1990s to the M4 carbine variant of the M16 series 5.56mm rifle. The Det One table of equipment authorized 86 M4 SOPMOD carbines, one for every man in the original table of organization. Each carbine came with a suite of optics and designators to satisfy the needs of close quarter battle in full light or complete darkness.

For an individual back-up weapon, the detachment wanted the best .45-caliber pistol available.

(The Marine Corps had first suggested that it use the standard sidearm, the M9 9mm pistol, but that weapon was immediately rejected as being unreliable and underpowered.) The first answer was the MEU (SOC) .45—powerful, accurate, available in the Marine Corps supply chain, and intimately familiar to the force reconnaissance veterans in the detachment. Gunnery Sergeant Kitashima, however, knew by virtue of his Quantico tour that the MEU (SOC) pistol was not the answer to the detachment's needs.

The MEU (SOC) .45s all came from ordnance stocks in storage sites across the country, containing millions of pistols produced during and after World War II. The best of these were selected by the Marine Corps and sent to Weapons Training Battalion at Quantico, where the match armorers at the precision weapons section then rebuilt them by hand with premium parts, mating the power of the .45 cartridge with the reliability and accuracy of match-grade arms. However, the section could only turn out 60 pistols a year. The problem with the MEU (SOC) .45 was its sustainability, not its accuracy. Each one needed to be repaired by a match armorer if it broke down. (Kitashima was a match armorer, but if Det One sub-elements were operating away from the support sections, this could be a problem.) Also, each MEU (SOC) .45 had a life span of only 10,000 rounds, which in practice worked out to two complete cycles of MEU (SOC) training and deployment. After that, it had to go back to Quantico for overhaul. Det One Marines would fire more than 10,000 rounds in training alone. Given those realities, Kitashima judged the MEU (SOC) pistol to be inadequate for the detachment's needs.[32]

The solution to the Det One pistol question stretched the limits of the unit's broad open-purchase authority: a contract for the manufacture and delivery of 100 .45-caliber M1911 pistols, built to Lieutenant Colonel Coates's specifications. These guns were made by Kimber of America and dubbed the interim close quarters battle pistols, incorporating features such as an integral rail for mounting a light under the frame and an expected life span of 30,000 rounds. They were delivered in a remarkably short span of six months from date of order, in time for the detachment's groundbreaking weapons and tactics package in October 2003.[33] Until then, Det One used 50 Springfield Armory .45-caliber pistols, bought for them as a temporary measure by Marine Corps Systems Command.[34] The Det One .45-caliber was a remarkable weapon, a unique piece of ordnance, and one of the very few firearms in Marine Corps history to be stamped "USMC." Coates was issued the pistol with serial number 001.*

The detachment also was issued more standard Marine Corps weapons, such as the M249 squad automatic weapon (in a folding-stock modification), the M240G medium machine gun, the venerable Browning .50-caliber heavy machine gun, and its modern companion the MK19 40mm heavy machine gun. To ensure that the many snipers in the detachment would not lack the equipment to employ their skills, the table of equipment provided several weapons. In caliber 7.62mm, there were M14 Designated Marksman Rifles, semi-automatic SR-25 rifles, and M40A1 bolt-action rifles. In heavier weapons there were .50-caliber M82A3 Barrett special application scoped rifles, and an innovative .408-caliber sniper rifle made by Cheyenne Tactical of Wyoming—a piece used by no other Marine unit. The .408 rifles promised to deliver a solid bronze bullet beyond the effective range of the 7.62mm cartridge, thereby closing the gap between the M40A1 and the M82A3.**

Finally, in an echo of its Marine Raider heritage, the detachment was also issued with its own knife, a decision being made that Det One Marines needed a rugged utility cutting tool rather than just a sharp blade. Strider Knives of San Marcos, California, modified one of its existing designs and turned out 100 copies, each one marked with "MC SOCOM DET 1" and a unique serial number.

"Tough, Rugged, and Smart Gunfighters"

With both Marines and material arriving from March to June 2003, significant unit-level training was out of the question. Yet opportunities for individual schools abounded, and Lieutenant Colonel Coates seized opportunities to get all available people into the schools and courses they would need. The intelligence Marines, for the most part, did not require further schooling, but the reconnaissance Marines needed to send a few of their number to Survival, Evasion, Resistance, and Escape School, and some from the other elements needed to go to basic airborne school. While those selected individuals were hurriedly assigned to key school quotas, the daily

---
* The story of the Kimber .45 ICQB pistols has been told in several periodicals, most notably by Patrick J. Rogers, who assisted the author of this monograph, in the December 2003 issue of *SWAT Magazine*, and by Gary Paul Johnston in the August 2004 issue of *The American Rifleman*.

** Regarding the .408 rifles, Det One was authorized to seek out new weapons and test them for their utility in military operations. Likewise, the .45 pistol was designated the interim close quarters battle pistol, with the intention being not only to provide a serviceable weapon but to test its features for future production models.

tasks of building and housing the detachment continued.

The detachment's initial command post was in the offices of I Marine Expeditionary Force Special Operations Training Group. Having outgrown that space with even a limited number of Marines on deck, they moved into the headquarters of the 15th MEU (SOC), which was deployed at the time. While this was an acceptable interim solution, there was no way the unit could effectively execute command and control from such arrangements. Det One needed a place of its own where it could house its members and their equipment and plan and execute its training schedule. But the Marine Corps 5400 Bulletin that established the unit specifically foreswore permanent new facilities. Instead, the unit found a site in the Del Mar boat basin at Camp Pendleton, California. It was not large, but it was big enough for basic facilities, and it had the advantages of being close to the water (for training purposes) and relatively close to the I MEF command element, where the detachment's intelligence section continued to work because the nature of their daily operations required existing buildings and special communications.

The detachment compound evolved on a single lot, surfaced with asphalt and surrounded by a chain link fence. The unit erected three buildings, tent-like devices, durable yet temporary, made by a corporation with an appropriately descriptive name, Sprung Instant Structures. The three buildings were big enough for the staff, the reconnaissance element, a classroom, and a conference room and could provide some supply storage as well. The motor transport section had plenty of lot space for its growing fleet of vehicles.

Having a compound solved the problem of a home base, but it brought on several new tasks. Telephone and data services, both unclassified and classified, had to be connected for the staff to have true command and control capabilities. The detachment's man for all seasons, Sergeant Guerra, handled these tasks, venturing into territories where sergeants rarely tread. He found low-cost, readily available solutions to a host of problems and composed the detailed letters and orders that would enable to the detachment to keep and maintain the sensitive classified network equipment they needed.

The nascent unit also faced challenges beyond personnel and equipment issues. The nuts and bolts of integration with Naval Special Warfare Squadron One, built around SEAL Team One, had yet to be addressed. The 20 February 2003 memorandum of agreement with Special Operations Command spelled out the command relationships between the units but left the detailed coordination to be done by the Marines and SEALs involved. In late March 2003, the Det One staff held its first planning conferences with SEAL Team One and the unit's parent command, Naval Special Warfare Group One. The Marines presented their training plans and their views on integration. The SEALs reciprocated. It was clear to Det One's leadership that the SEALs' interpretation of the clause in the memorandum that gave them the authority to task-organize based on "operational requirements" differed from the Marines' reading, as they consistently sought to maintain the integrity of their force, in keeping with the Marine Corps' warfighting philosophy.[35] The group left other questions unresolved, such as when actual integration would take place and the extent to which training events before that date would be jointly run and evaluated.

In addition, there was still no firm word on the unit's operational destination, which presumably would have informed the training plan. Would it be the mountains of Afghanistan or the urban sprawl of Iraq? Or would the detachment land somewhere else, such as the Horn of Africa or the Philippines? In the spring of 2003, Afghanistan seemed to be a likely option. For much of the training phase, Naval Special Warfare had a split deployment in mind for the detachment, with the unit divided between U.S. Pacific Command and U.S. Central Command. In the absence of knowing the destination, the best answer was to develop a mission training plan to address the four core competencies—direct action, special reconnaissance, limited foreign internal defense, and coalition support—and then make adjustments when circumstances dictated.

The mission training plan the detachment staff put together for Lieutenant Colonel Coates's signature was all encompassing, firmly directive, and remarkably blunt. From ensuring that all Marines were prepared for promotion boards by completing their required professional military education, to dire warnings on cutting corners on safety, to a plain language assessment of what he desired from of his Marines, the commanding officer set the stage for a truly grueling training schedule. One line under the paragraph "General Guidance" spoke volumes: "Remember most of all: I want tough, rugged and smart gunfighters. In our profession and in a gunfight, second place is last place!"[36]

Activation

On 20 June 2003, the Marine Corps U.S. Special Operations Command Detachment was officially activated in a ceremony at the Camp Del Mar compound. In a compact formation, arrayed by elements, stood 89 Marines. Family, friends, fellow Marines, and guests packed bleachers and the seats. Among the dignitaries were figures that had prominent roles in the detachment's formation, directly or indirectly, such as the former Commandant, General Paul X. Kelley, and the assistant secretary of defense for special operations and low intensity conflict, Michael A. Westphal. Brigadier General Dennis J. Hejlik and Colonel Paul Hand from Special Operations Command were there, as were representatives from each armed service at the command. Naval Special Warfare was represented by its commander, Vice Admiral Albert M. Calland III. Charles Meacham, a veteran of World War II and the president of the Marine Raider Association, looked on as the commanding general of Marine Forces Pacific, Lieutenant General Earl B. Hailston, presented Lieutenant Colonel Coates with the detachment's colors, and Det One officially came into being.

Chapter 3

Training

"Brilliance at the Fundamentals of Our Craft"

Det One's unit training phase began officially on 1 July 2003. Although selected Marines would attend various schools during the second half of the year, the individual training phase was over. The time had come to train the detachment as a whole. From this point on, every Det One exercise would end with an internal or external evaluation.

Looming ever larger was the single fact that colored so much of the detachment's formation and training, and what Colonel Robert J. Coates (promoted 1 July) labeled their "critical vulnerability": the short period of time before deployment.[1] The ability of Det One to operate at the Special Operations Command level rode on its own ability to train itself to the highest standards with no time to spare for remedial events. The singular (and not always well-received) by-name selection of the Marines for the detachment would prove its worth by forming a solid foundation on which it could build and train. The command chronology for this period understated the full-speed-ahead nature of the schedule by noting the absence of what it called "white space" on the calendar. Master Sergeant Charles H. Padilla, the leader of reconnaissance Team 3, put it less elegantly but more descriptively: "It was one big kick in the nuts."[2]

Even after activation, there were still Marines joining the detachment. One was Captain Stephen V. Fiscus, another 1st Force Reconnaissance Company alumnus and recent Iraq veteran, who reported for duty as the assistant operations officer. His job was twofold. First, as the assistant operations officer, he supervised the execution of the training schedule and day-to-day operational issues. Second, and of greater significance, he formed the training cell with Master Sergeant James R. Rutan. The importance of this small organization would become apparent as the training phase gathered momentum.[3]

The requirements of the mission drove the training schedule—despite the lack of a clear deployment assignment—and the training schedule governed the detachment's collective life. Far from being a sort of pilotless drone, the Det One training schedule was an ambitious and complex undertaking, full of moving parts and rife with potential pitfalls. It was a certainty that adjustments to the schedule would have to be made, given the demands of the Marine Corps and ongoing operations. That proved to be the case, as Major Thomas P. Dolan observed that "every event changed or moved in some way."[4] Proving Clausewitz's timeless observation that the simple becomes difficult and the difficult becomes impossible, routine training matters, such as scheduling the use of firing ranges, took on maddening complexity. The range scheduling systems at Camp Pendleton, Yuma, and other bases did not recognize MCSOCom Det One as a unit, thus MCSOCom Det One could schedule no ranges. No ranges, no training. Time and time again, Marines from the operations section had to patiently explain who they were and what they were trying to do.

This is not to suggest that the whole West Coast Marine Corps stood against them. On the contrary, almost everyone the detachment staff members encountered was willing and eager to help once they had explained the matter, but they certainly lost some time in telling the same story again and again. They dealt with the few real obstructionists they encountered as needed, usually by working around them, but sometimes by invoking the name of Marine Forces Pacific (the detachment's actual higher headquarters) or even by employing General James L. Jones's "P4" message. Captain Matthew H. Kress certainly had to use the "P4" as his ultimate argument. Major Dolan admitted having to "pull the MarForPac punk card" once. Colonel Coates, however, made the decision early on not to leverage the "special" part of their title, knowing that it would be the fast track to alienating people from whom they needed support—and to reinforcing the perception of the special operations unit being an elite within an elite.

Immediately following the activation ceremony, Colonel Coates and Major Craig S. Kozeniesky attended a conference of Marine Corps and Special Operations Command flag officers. Even at this late date, despite the 20 February memorandum with Special Operations Command, there continued to be ominous noises from outside the Marine Corps concerning how the detachment would be employed. Coates briefed the detachment's status and "received wide-

Photo courtesy of Det One

Members of the intelligence element at Bridgeport, California, during the "Man-Ex" of October 2003. Col Coates wanted all hands to have "hard feet and strong backs" and be able to operate in any clime or place. Maj M. Gerald Carter wanted all of his Marines to remember the experience so that when they analyzed the topography and planned a route for the reconnaissance element to follow, they knew that there was more to the terrain than lines on a map.

spread support from the assembled Marine generals that they would strongly resist efforts to split the detachment for deployment as proposed by Naval Special Warfare."[5] Widely divergent views concerning the basic employment of the Marine unit did not bode well for coordinated training and integration.

Execution of the mission training plan proceeded even as the ultimate nature of the deployment was unclear. There was no lack of clarity to the intent of Colonel Coates's mission training plan: to make sure that his Marines were "brilliant at the fundamentals of our craft—being able to shoot, move and communicate," as well as equipped to excel at their individual tasks.[6] For Det One, shooting would include not only small arms but also close air support. In Det One, moving would mean proficiency at mounted operations as well as "strong backs and hard feet," as Coates said. For all Det One Marines, communicating would mean using handheld radios as well as complex tactical data links.

The entire detachment went through a combat trauma course in the last week of June 2003, the goal being "to provide each detachment member with medical training required to immediately identify, effectively treat, and evacuate a battle casualty."[7] The reconnaissance element took this training to the logical conclusion by conducting two days of simulated casualty evacuations by helicopter.

Throughout the first three weeks of August, all members of the detachment trained on the full range of communications equipment and procedures. The communications section drilled the Marines in every aspect of the long-range radio equipment the detachment would be using, including high frequency, satellite, and imagery transmissions, with an emphasis on the tools used in special reconnaissance. Subject matter experts from the radio manufacturers, Harris RF Communications and the Thales Group, as well as personnel from Marine Corps Systems Command, attended those sessions to provide the Marines with firsthand answers and technical reach-back. Det One then reinforced classroom instruction with a practical application exercise: the reconnaissance element, augmented by the radio reconnaissance teams, took up positions in the urban combat training facility at Marine Corps Air Station, Yuma, Arizona. Over the course of the next four hot August days, they transmitted reports and imagery to the detachment operations center back in California at the Del Mar boat basin.

Also in August, the Det One fires liaison element, augmented by selected Marines from the reconnaissance element and the counterintelligence and radio reconnaissance teams, went to Hurlburt Field at Eglin Air Force Base, Florida, for a week of joint special operations close air support. The Marines learned to call for fire from AC-130 Spectre gunships and coordinate that aircraft's considerable surveillance and communications capabilities with their operations. These exercises certified the fires liaison Marines as joint terminal attack controllers, an important addition to their capabilities, as they would find out later in Iraq.

The other major event of central importance for the entire unit was range work with the M4 carbines and the .45-caliber pistols. Weapons and Tactics Package I began with the reconnaissance element on 7 July 2003 at Camp Pendleton's Range 130, the Special Operations Training Complex. This range contained the sort of specialized facilities the detachment needed, and since the majority of the reconnaissance Marines had been in Pendleton-based units, it was familiar ground for them.

When the reconnaissance Marines moved off Range 130 after a week's firing—and an enormous amount of ammunition expended—Marines from the other elements took their place. Every Marine is a rifleman, and Colonel Coates had decreed that every Det One Marine would be proficient at the basic tools of the gunfighting trade.* This training package began with the fundamentals—grip, stance, sight alignment, sight picture, trigger control—and progressed through tactical reloading procedures and immediate action drills, all under a time limit and under pressure. Each man was able to put his weapons through their paces, get accustomed to the combinations of optics and other devices, then test his magazines, discard the unreliable ones, and modify his gear layout. The Marines shot so much that some came away astounded at how many rounds they sent downrange. As Major Jerry Carter recalled, "I never thought that in the Marine Corps I would shoot so many rounds through a weapon that I would be tired of shooting and my trigger finger would be numb."[8] All came away with considerable, substantive confidence in their gunfighting skills.

After their first week at Range 130, the reconnaissance Marines continued weapons and tactics fundamentals at one of the training areas at Camp Pendleton. They went into two more weeks of patrolling, team tactics, contact drills, marksmanship, and then moved on to infiltrations and live-fire attacks. Joined by the radio reconnaissance Marines, they capped off the event with a 10-mile infiltration march and a live-fire raid on a target. In this case, weapons and tactics "fundamentals" is a relative term; Captain Eric N. Thompson observed that the quality of the Marines in the platoon—"independent thinkers and independent operators"—enabled them to start off at a fairly high level and progress quickly, so that he did not have to concern himself overly with matters of safety and individual weapons proficiency and could concentrate instead on training.[9] This theme recurred throughout the detachment's training period and provided continuing proof that the right Marines had been chosen for the unit.

Thanks to the existence of the unit's training cell, Thompson did not have to pull himself, or his platoon sergeant, or a team leader off the line to actually run the range, nor did he have to devote time to develop the scenario and the target. The training cell handled these matters and left the leaders free to attack the mission. As the calendar progressed and the exercises became more complex, the ability to keep the Marines focused on the mission rather than the exercise would become a key element in the detachment's success.

For the Marines from the other sections, the biggest challenge was balancing their own weapons training with their duties to support every ongoing evolution, as well as the need to plan for future operations. Marines "one-deep" in their functional areas, like Gunnery Sergeants Mark S. Kitashima and Monty R. Genegabus, felt it the hardest. Colonel Coates's insistence on brilliance in the basics in every area, as painful as it was during the training phase, proved its worth in Iraq, when Marines from the support sections had to serve as machine gunners and drivers on direct action missions and members of the radio reconnaissance teams found themselves fighting for their lives in Baghdad.

In addition to all these events, there was also physical conditioning. From the beginning, Captain Thompson and Master Sergeant Keith E. Oakes instituted a demanding physical training program for the reconnaissance Marines. "Through the entire workup, whether we were in the field or whether we were in garrison, we always did a hike every week," Thompson recalled. "That's something that a lot of recon units I found got away from . . . but that's one of the fundamentals of being a good reconnaissance Marine."[10] Oakes had initially decreed platoon physical

---

* The emphasis on essential combat skills for all hands presents another contrast with the prevailing attitude in other special operations units, which seem to prize the "shooter" as the zenith of operational capability. In Det One, with its deeply rooted air-ground task force philosophy, shooting was a skill not a job description and the "shooter," the Marine in the team making entry into the target building, was but one part of the larger capability.

training twice a week, but after discussions with the team leaders, he scaled back to once a week, and by default that once a week became the road march—the hike. Because he wanted his Marines to see their steady progress week by week, Oakes chose a standard route: "We would always park up at [Camp] Flores, work up into the mountains, and then down on the beach," he remembered. "We always finished here on the compound."[11] The Marines made the hikes with full gear and full loads, about 60 pounds per man, including food and water. In a platoon like the Det One reconnaissance element, it was a reasonable expectation that the Marines knew all the tricks of marching long distances and of arriving ready for operations. But even in this case, the veteran Ranger instructor in Master Sergeant Oakes had a few points to share. "The biggest thing was teaching them how to eat and drink properly, which was what the Rangers taught me," he explained. "I could not afford to have guys that would hit the wall."[12] The weekly hikes proved to be excellent preparation for the coming exercise at Bridgeport, California, as well as an all-around conditioning tool.

Bridgeport: "The Man-Ex"

The summer of 2003 ended on a sad note as one member of the reconnaissance element, Sergeant Christian W. Myler, died in a motorcycle accident on 6 September. The detachment paused its training for memorial services and then resumed the march toward deployment.

The first item on the schedule for September was two weeks in the cold waters off the Southern California coast practicing the skills of reconnaissance in support of an amphibious landing. As the detachment's destination for deployment was at that point still not known, this block of training was part of the requirement to maintain the core competencies, with these skills also being a true Corps competency. The Marines practiced long-range nautical navigation, hydrographic surveys, scout swimmer techniques, and other skills pertaining to this highly specialized art. They again demonstrated the depth and breadth of experience in the reconnaissance element as the Marines took only a day of rehearsals in the Del Mar boat basin before they mounted out on a full-mission profile, at night, in open water. Right before this event was scheduled to begin, a helicopter flying over the San Onofre beaches—where the hydrographic survey was to take place—spotted and photographed an altogether too realistic opposition force: two great white sharks.[13]

With amphibious training checked off the list, the entire detachment prepared for a fortnight at the Mountain Warfare Training Center, Bridgeport, California. Few of the Marines were strangers to Bridgeport. The detachment was packed with trained mountain leaders, and Major Kozeniesky, Master Sergeants Padilla and Muratori, among others, had been instructors and staff members there. What made this mountain training package different from any previous experience for the Det One Marines was the speed at which Colonel Coates took them from acclimatization and a basic skills refresher to a high-altitude crucible over the toughest terrain in the center.

The Bridgeport exercise began with a review in the technical skills of military mountaineering, the use of which they would require later in the event. There were perils at this stage, even for the experienced Marines in the unit. Gunnery Sergeant John A. Dailey, leader of Recon Team 4, took a fall while rappelling that nearly sidelined him for the entire exercise. Loss of a Marine due to injury was something the unit could ill afford. For some of the Marines, military mountaineering skills also included parachute jumps on the high-altitude drop zones of the center. Within a few days, the training schedule moved the detachment higher into the mountains for the next evolutions.

Marines from the support sections were as involved in the training as they were in the support of the training. Although the logistics section could have supported the entire exercise from Camp Del Mar, part of Colonel Coates's intent was to get the entire detachment out into the field and put it under a microscope. Among other events, support section Marines went through an abbreviated version of Bridgeport's mule-packing course, the only such program of instruction in the U.S. military. Mules can go where vehicles and helicopters cannot go and would have been valuable transportation assets had the detachment been sent to Afghanistan, as likely a course of action as any at the time. This was a novel experience for the motor transport section. Military vehicles, although not without their own peculiarities, do not bite or kick or throw off their loads. Gunnery Sergeant Jaime Maldonado and Staff Sergeant Jaime J. Sierra learned how to pack the mules, feed them, and then get them headed up into the mountains loaded with food, water, and ammunition. "The animals, they do their own thing," Maldonado recalled. "When we were packing them, it was okay, because they got fed as they were getting packed. But the minute we step off, they just keep going, they don't stop."[14] As Gunnery Sergeant Genegabus, the logistics chief, said: "The animals themselves are just hard-headed.

Photo courtesy of Patrick J. Rogers

GySgt Jaime Maldonado and SSgt Jaime J. Sierra prepare for a mission during the Capstone Exercise in Nevada, December 2003. Every Marine in Det One was issued with the same equipment and weapons, and every one was expected to master the basic skills such as gunfighting, communications, first aid, and driving.

We had one guy kicked off, one guy kicked, and one guy bit."[15] Despite the hardheadedness of the beasts, they could carry substantial loads. The detachment subsequently used a mule train for resupply during one phase of the tactical problem. As strange a military event as mule-packing might seem, Gunnery Sergeant Genegabus, for one, did not see it as far-fetched at all, given the U.S. Army Special Forces' recent experience in Afghanistan.

The Bridgeport exercise served as the welcome-aboard package for a new member of the fires liaison element, Captain Daniel B. "Shoe" Sheehan III, brought on board as the forward air controller after the original table of organization was augmented to give the battle staff more depth. A Bell AH-1W Super Cobra pilot just returned from Operation Iraqi Freedom, Sheehan was not only a new-join but also new to the ground operations business. He had not served in an air and naval gunfire liaison company (ANGLICO), nor in reconnaissance units, nor in a Special Operations Training Group. He had two Marine expeditionary unit deployments under his belt, the second involving both a substantial period in Djibouti working with a joint special operations task force, as well as combat flying in Iraq. He had tried but not succeeded to gain entry into another arm of Special Operations Command. That unit's loss became Det One's gain.

The final week at Bridgeport was a memorable navigation and "terrain appreciation" exercise with "visits" to the highest peaks, where units normally do not train.[16] The experience level of the detachment as a whole made training in the roughest parts of the center possible, as did Major Kozeniesky's recent service there as operations officer. Captain Thompson of the reconnaissance element described the last seven days as "half mountaineering skills and half gut check, to make sure that we had the right crop of guys that could march up and down mountains with 70-pound rucks, operate in the high altitude, and not have a total mental meltdown."[17] He saw it as a "Man-Ex," a straightforward test of each Marine's manliness. Colonel Coates described the Bridgeport exercise as the detachment's "selection," revealing something of his intent for the exercise beyond the utility of a tactical problem.[18]

The "terrain appreciation" exercise was a two-day hike by element and team. Major Kozeniesky chose the route with his intimate knowledge of the base and designed the exercise to test each man's ability not only to hike at altitude with a heavy load, but also to negotiate the terrain with tactical and technical expertise. Major Dolan, who had trained there many years earlier as an enlisted Marine, called this particular phase "very, very difficult, hard stuff."[19] Master Sergeant Padilla—former Bridgeport instructor, Royal Marines mountain instructor, and trained mountain leader—said it was "probably the hardest training" he had ever seen a unit do at the Mountain Warfare Training Center.[20] The last phase of the Bridgeport exercise also illustrated the line separating special and conventional operations: in special operations, the performance expectations increase rather than decrease, even as the conditions get tougher.

The culmination of the "Man-Ex" was a direct action mission, preceded by another route march. The Marines—two teams for reconnaissance and surveillance, and then the task-organized assault force—were inserted approximately 20 miles from the objective. The mission, according to Major Dolan, "required a two-and-a-half day movement, across two ridgelines, going over 10,000-foot passes."[21] Groups of Marines from an infantry battalion training at Bridgeport were out looking for the reconnaissance and surveillance teams, adding to the realism of the exercise. Then, as the helicopters arrived to extract the force after the successful strike, the training cell had one more "kick in the nuts," as Major Kozeniesky put it. The aircraft set down unexpectedly in separate landing zones, and the pilots handed the Det One Marines notes that read: "The helicopters have just crashed; execute your evasion and recovery plan." The evading Marines linked up according to plan, with counterintelligence teams that guided them to safe territory.[22]

Executing this surprise event meant "another 8- or 10-hour movement across some horrendous terrain," according to Major Dolan, who recalled that by that time, there were "not a lot of happy campers left." But the evasion exercise taught the Det One Marines lessons about seeing the operation through to the very end.[23] It also validated the critical requirement for detailed planning to cover contingencies, and it exercised a significant capability of the counterintelligence section, again demonstrating how the detachment could use what other special operations units might call the "non-operators" as integral parts of the whole plan.

The experience at Bridgeport had the intended effect: it raised the stress level and gave the commanding officer an opportunity to examine every man under extreme pressure. The crucible of the "Man-Ex" also brought out some unarticulated personality conflicts. At the reconnaissance platoon debrief, a gathering of some "unhappy campers" after the surprise evasion exercise, Master Sergeant Padilla spoke up to provide some constructive criticism for the platoon commander. The ensuing acerbic exchange, recounted with humor some 18 months later by participants and witnesses alike, cleared the air and cemented the personal and professional understandings between the reconnaissance element leadership.

Close Quarters Battle Training

A major qualitative leap in the reconnaissance element's tactical capabilities came in October 2003 on the heels of the Bridgeport exercise. Returning to Camp Pendleton's Range 130, the reconnaissance Marines immersed themselves in a groundbreaking close-quarters battle package unlike anything they had ever experienced. The reconnaissance element

GySgt John A. Dailey's and SSgt Jack A. Kelly's teams during the Capstone Exercise. These Marines, task-organized for reconnaissance and surveillance with the addition of radio recon and fires Marines, bore the brunt of the cold weather in the high desert of Nevada.

This photo shows both the protective clothing, procured for them by Jon Laplume at Soldier Systems Command, as well the Full Spectrum Battle Equipment, which could be tailored to each Marine's duties and personal preference.

Photo courtesy of Patrick J. Rogers

knew its business individually and collectively from several years of deployments. It was also a platoon loaded with close-quarters battle instructors: Master Sergeant Oakes and Gunnery Sergeant Morrison, to name only two, had spent time as special operations training group shooting instructors. All were experienced marksmen and tacticians, giving them the right foundation to rapidly achieve a higher level of proficiency. But they were about to be challenged to begin thinking critically about how they needed to conduct their operations.

In order to break away from the Marine Corps close quarters combat model, the detachment contracted directly for the services of a retired U.S. Army Special Forces soldier, a veteran of a tier-one Special Operations Command unit. He first observed them as they breached and cleared a structure. He did not like what he saw and told the Marines that what they were doing was not going to cut it against the opponents they would be facing. The new set of tactics and techniques he taught them was "vastly different from what we did, as Marines, up to this point," said Captain Thompson. He called the experience "very enlightening."[24] No substantial change is easy, and not all of the Marines immediately embraced the new methods.

Staff Sergeant Alex N. Conrad, one of the reconnaissance scouts, described the difficult but constructive change. The instructor "taught us what we needed to do," but then "we went into the house [the specially constructed building for live-fire close quarters battle training], and we reverted back to our old tactics." Conrad remembered that the retired Special Forces soldier yelled "'stop, stop. Stop right there.' He just told us, 'this is not going to work. Here's what we're going to do, and this is how we're going to do it. Get back out of the house and re-do this, one thing at a time.'" He told them bluntly that their old tactics were going to get them killed. When he demonstrated how their methods were slower and less effective than his—by having some Marines watch from a gallery in the house while the others went through the problem using both ways—he got his point across.[25] Conrad credits him with engineering a complete reversal in the reconnaissance element's tactical mindset. "He changed our way of thinking. I think that was the turning point."[26]

The main issue the experience highlighted, and the one that cut to the essence of the larger USMC/SOCom relationship, was the divergence of Marine Corps close quarter battle tactics with those used by the upper-tier SOCom units. "Basically," said Master Sergeant Padilla, "we were using dinosaur tac-

Photo courtesy of Patrick J. Rogers

Det One's armorer, GySgt Mark S. Kitashima, conducts instruction on the M2 .50-caliber heavy machine gun during the Capstone Exercise, at Mercury, Nevada, in December 2004.

tics."[27] The big switch was a change from their familiar "initiative-based tactics" to the more fluid and dynamic "team-based tactics." Initiative-based tactics relied on a single point of entry into a target house. Team-based tactics, on the other hand, enabled the Marines to simultaneously hit that target from more angles, then flow rapidly from room to room, maintaining the speed, shock, and violence of action they needed to gain the upper hand and prevail.

The new tactics prompted a structural change in the detachment. The reconnaissance platoon reorganized from four teams of seven Marines each to six teams of four or five Marines each. Staff Sergeant Jack A. Kelly, assistant team leader in Master Sergeant Terry M. Wyrick's Team 1, and Gunnery Sergeant Sidney J. Voss from Gunnery Sergeant Dailey's Team 4 became the leaders of Teams 5 and 6. (Although the detachment received no new corpsmen to fill out the new structure, the platoon had enough certified emergency medical technicians—Staff Sergeant Kelly being one of them—to cover the basic requirements.)

The introduction of team-based tactics to Det One's reconnaissance element was more of a significant single addition to its toolbox than a wholesale replacement. Some of the younger Marines in the platoon took to team-based tactics more readily than the older ones and saw it as a day-and-night change, but the more wily and seasoned among them adopted a comprehensive view. Master Sergeant Wyrick pointed out later that most of the detachment's direct action missions in Iraq were conducted using individual-based tactics because of the nature of many of the targets in that close-in urban setting precluded attack from multiple angles. Yet the Det One Marines were nearly unanimous in assessing the team-based tactics as a major improvement in thinking, in how they looked at a target as a whole, not just the actions on the inside. It was that change in the Marines' approach that produced the enduring improvement in their capabilities.

The Det One staff was also undergoing an important training session during the month of October, a two-week staff integration exercise with SEAL Team One, which had become Squadron One after taking on its full complement of attachment and augments. The detachment was only half the size of the squadron but brought completely different capabilities. The squadron had six platoons of operators; the detachment had one platoon of reconnaissance Marines, who averaged more than a dozen years each on active duty. The squadron had an intelligence officer and some intelligence specialists, whereas the detachment had its self-contained 30-man intelligence platoon, capable of independent communications with national assets and organic fusion from all intelligence sources. The squadron had SEALs who were certified in supporting arms; the detachment had the fires liaison element, including two combat pilots. Fully drawing out the combined capabilities with Squadron One was a prickly process, requiring a great deal of patience and flexibility on both sides. Much of the efforts centered "defining how we fight as institutions," as Major Kozeniesky put it—the differences in how the SEALs and Marines view tactical problems and solutions. The process of integration was not helped by the fact that the destination for the deployment was still being debated at the service level.

Practice on skill at arms continued into November 2003, when the fires liaison element took the reconnaissance and radio reconnaissance Marines to the Air Ground Combat Center at Twentynine Palms, California, for a week of planning and calling close air support. Like other Det One training events, this exercise deviated significantly from similar events in other units. A conventional unit would have set up an overt observation post on one of two or three prominent terrain features and called in mission after mission. Major Dolan, however, devised a more practical exercise for the Det One element tailored to situations a reconnaissance team might encounter on a mission, far away from supporting units. The Det One Marines did a half-day of refresher training on the "nine-line brief," the close air support call for fire,

and then ascended the rocky desert hills where they constructed tactical observation posts and ran live missions more in line with their operations. The missions concentrated on calling for support while breaking contact with the enemy, therefore involving synchronization of the helicopters with small-arms fire, individual movement, and the dozen other actions that a team needs to perform to get itself out of a tight spot. Dolan's work was made easier by the same qualities in the Marines that Captain Thompson and others had remarked more than once: they had been through this training before and they knew their business. Refresher training always strengthens and hones the skills that are prone to atrophy, but the Det One Marines had enough experience and prior knowledge to go from rehearsals to live runs on targets within one day.[28]

The other significant event in November was the arrival of the detachment's 18 Mercedes-Benz interim fast attack vehicles to add to their small fleet of all-terrain vehicles. The motor-transport section leaped to the task of making these machines ready for service. Gunnery Sergeant Maldonado and Staff Sergeant Sierra needed to get the vehicles inspected, set up, and modified for Det One operations and then get several dozen Marines licensed to drive them before the detachment's capstone exercise, scheduled for the following month, in which the vehicles would see heavy use.

Finally, no mention of the month of November would be complete without reference to the Marine Corps Birthday. The commemoration of this event proceeds in lesser or greater form wherever Marines are stationed throughout the world, as conditions permit; the Det One Marines, after training hard for months, chose a venue that let them play hard too. The command chronology for the period mentions "well-deserved liberty and revelry" and celebration in "grand fashion" at a Las Vegas hotel, but it is uncharacteristically silent on further details.

The Capstone Exercise

Just as Marine expeditionary units progress to "special operations capable" certification and then deployment through a series of ever more complex and challenging exercises, Det One continued to set its own bar higher as 2003 drew to a close. In December, the detachment deployed en masse to Nevada for the capstone exercise, a full test of the unit's capabilities. Although not the ruck-humping "Man-Ex" of Bridgeport, the capstone exercise tested the complete range of the unit's operational abilities in trying conditions and against exceptionally difficult targets.

It was also the last major event scheduled before actual integration with the SEALs, the final chance to nail down the procedures and hone the fighting edge. Selected observers from I Marine Expeditionary Force Special Operations Training Group and Headquarters Marine Corps (among them Master Gunnery Sergeant Joseph G. Settelen III) were on hand to evaluate and critique.

The U.S. Department of Energy's Nevada Test Site is located 65 miles from Las Vegas. It is a big chunk of high desert, larger than many small countries, and just the place Det One needed for this exercise.[29] The terrain, climate, isolation, and facilities provided the perfect venue for the detachment's second to last operational test. The Nevada Test Site was also new terrain, as none of the Marines had ever trained there before.

The detachment's first task was setting up the forward operating base at the Indian Springs Auxiliary Airfield, the basic living and working spaces where the unit could house its command and control functions, and where the Marines could prepare for missions and refit afterward. Although fixed facilities were readily available, Colonel Coates chose to make the unit's footprint as expeditionary as possible—to "do it all in the dirt," as he put it—in order to ensure that all of the detachment's elements addressed and worked through any problems that might arise from

A Det One Marine backs an Interim Fast Attack Vehicle onto a KC-130 Hercules for a long-range insertion during the Capstone Exercise in Nevada, December 2003. That exercise marked the first heavy use of the vehicles, which, as the photo shows, were almost brand-new. Unfortunately, just before the deployment the Interim Fast Attack Vehicles were found unsuitable for the assigned direct action missions the detachment in Iraq.

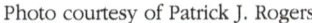

Photo courtesy of Patrick J. Rogers

being away from Camp Pendleton. Within 24 hours, Det One Marines had set up the tents and basic utilities and were preparing to execute the training schedule. Never one to mince words, Captain Thompson described the austere Indian Springs camp as a very good replication of "a Third World shit-hole."[30] The communications section set up the Trojan Spirit Lite and had connectivity within an hour; the combat operations center was functional within six hours.[31]

Marines from Company K, 3d Battalion, 5th Marines, provided the opposition force for the exercise, but the real adversary was nature itself. Although the detachment's records make no mention of the weather, Det One Marines remember it clearly. Sergeant Guerra's network equipment was the first casualty of the cold high Nevada desert. The nonexpeditionary servers, hand carried from Camp Pendleton and crucial to the detachment's command and control, did not work. Guerra had what he called "the four most stressful days of my life." He had brought out three servers, all quality pieces of gear in a garrison setting. In the field, two failed immediately. While he worked to get some information systems capability up and running, he hounded the manufacturer to send out replacements. The manufacturer delivered, but not in time to spare Guerra the unwanted attentions of the staff: "Every five minutes I get, 'Is the network up? Is the network up? Is the network up?'"

Sergeant Guerra's private nightmare continued as the one Marine he had working with him became ill, and the one server he had managed to get working crashed. Guerra had to rebuild the entire network from scratch, by himself. What was normally a few hours' work took four days.[32] Although he did not appreciate it at the time, the painful experience at the capstone exercise served him well on the deployment, when he had his networks up and running within hours of arrival at the detachment's compound in Baghdad. The weather did not single out Sergeant Guerra; it affected the intelligence section, too. The intense cold froze the ink in the plotters that printed out the maps and other intelligence products, at least temporarily disrupting a critical piece of the staff work.[33]

Marines in the assault forces and reconnaissance and surveillance teams also were lashed hard by the weather. The detachment's expensive equipment—in this case, the latest layered clothing system procured by Jon Laplume from Soldier Systems Command at Natick, Massachusetts—again proved its worth and kept the sniper teams functioning in their hide sites. Still, there were other aspects of the weather they could do nothing about. Master Sergeant Padilla vividly described the result of a very long movement in their interim fast attack vehicles during the exfiltration phase of one of the direct action missions. "We should have known better, but we had taken off all the windshields. . . . I don't know what the hell we were thinking. . . . With the wind chill it must have been -10 degrees. Guys were just freezing."[34] Hospital Corpsman First Class Matthew S. Pranka, the corpsman in Padilla's team, agreed: "It was just nasty. They picked the absolute worst time."[35]

The detachment executed two full-mission profile raids during the capstone exercise: one was a simunitions raid and the other a full live-fire raid.* The live-fire attack included both sniper shots and base-of-fire support from M240G machine guns manned by Marines taken from the support sections, which allowed the detachment to concentrate the reconnaissance element in assault force.[36] In their after-action report, the observers from I MEF Special Operations Training Group noted the use of non-reconnaissance Marines in precision fire support.

The first mission was a raid on a missile site suspected to be under terrorist control. The Det One training cell and the I MEF Special Operations Training Group had crafted a difficult target, including underground tunnels and other features that would confound all but the most careful observation and analysis and possibly draw the assault forces into a trap. The reconnaissance and surveillance teams, task-organized with the addition of fires and radio reconnaissance Marines, were quickly inserted, established their hide sites, and began reporting back to the combat operations center while the assault force was forming its plan and rehearsing its actions. The plan called for insertion of the assault force in fast attack vehicles; the final assault would be made on foot. One of the primary training objectives for the members of reconnaissance element was to shake out the fast attack vehicles, equipment still so new that the paint was clean and the tires dark black. They learned a good deal on how to employ the vehicles in raids, not just how to drive them and maintain them, but how many it would take to get the full raid force to the objective.[37] The plan was further enhanced by loading the reconnaissance and surveillance teams and their vehicles on Marine Corps KC-130 Hercules transport aircraft, flying them to a dry lakebed, and disgorging them at night in a "hot unload" while the plane's engines were still turning. Even though the close-quarter actions on the objective would be done with simunitions, the plan included live-fire close air support to isolate the objective. Providing the outer cordon for the operation were Marines from Company K, 3d Battalion, 5th Marines, some of whom were also providing the "enemy" on the target site.

The raid was a success, due as much to careful analysis, good staff planning, and rigorous rehearsals as to the skillful actions on the objective. The detachment's intelligence analysts had constructed an accurate picture of the target site and had spotted indications of underground works, so the assault force was able to plan accordingly. Master Gunnery Sergeant Settelen, posted on the roof of the target building as an observer, watched the assault unfold: "Right on their timeline, they came up out of the shadows, set up, and did a simultaneous multiside breach into the facility, and then the gunships sealed off the other side of the objective to make sure that they didn't have 'squirters' [enemy personnel escaping through gaps in the cordon]."[38] The fog of war reigned inside the building when smoke generators emplaced to create a haze malfunctioned and instead created what Settelen called "a black hole." He also noted, with some satisfaction, that even in the confusion, noise, and smoke, the assault force refused to be sucked into the underground trap the exercise designers had laid for them: "They isolated both sides of the tunnel based on excellent geospatial analysis, and then they just pinned [the enemy] in there and kept them in there while they sensitive-site-exploited the rest of the target," eliminating several enemy and seizing the high value target they were looking for, aided by photographs for positive identification."[39]

It is the job of the evaluators to take even a successful mission and pick it apart, to mention the little things that can be improved, and to highlight mistakes that can cost dearly on actual operations. Again, Master Gunnery Sergeant Settelen provided the best commentary: "SOTG dinged the snipers a little bit because they were on the forward slope and a real seasoned evaluator was able to pick up the difference in the camouflage between some of the hides. As far as an untrained eye [being able to do that]? Maybe not, but we were being real critical on

---

* Simunitions are training rounds fired from modified weapons that exhibit ballistic performance similar to live ammunition at short ranges. They are ideal training aids for close quarters combat.

* Sensitive site exploitation (SSE) is the critical process of quickly but thoroughly searching a target and removing anything of potential intelligence value. Items and people seized in SSE frequently yield intelligence for the prosecution of other targets, as Det One operations in Iraq would show.

Photo courtesy of Patrick J. Rogers

Following Col Coates' dictum that every Det One Marine would be a gunfighter, Marines from the headquarters sections were regularly integrated into the raid force regardless of specialty. Sgt Victor M. Guerra and another Marine are shown above on a M240G 7.62mm machine gun in support of the live-fire raid during the Capstone Exercise in Nevada.

ourselves. We didn't want to make any mistakes."[40]

Also observing from the roof, and with an equally critical eye, was Commander William W. Wilson, USN, commanding officer of Naval Special Warfare Squadron One and Det One's future task group commander. This proof-of-concept operation with Det One was Wilson's first experience with Marine Corps units. His previous assignments had taken him in directions away from the amphibious Navy and Marine operating forces, although he had served with individual Marines in other places and at other times. Significantly for the detachment, one of those individuals was Major Jerry Carter. If he was new to working with Marine units, Wilson was no stranger to the Marine Corps; his father was a Marine officer, and he had grown up on and around Marine bases across the country.[41] The veteran SEAL had a vested interest in closely examining how far the detachment had progressed in training to Special Operations Command standards. He liked what he saw, especially the ability of the entire unit to execute a successful hit on a complex and difficult target from the staff planning to reconnaissance and surveillance, then assault, exploitation, and extraction.[42]

Colonel Coates issued the warning order for the second raid within 24 hours after the conclusion of the first mission, once the after-action reviews were done and the troops had had a chance to recover. The target this time was a simulated terrorist training camp, and this mission would be a full live-fire hit. Again, reconnaissance and surveillance teams were inserted and began reporting and transmitting imagery. As they had with the first mission, the intelligence element used a versatile computer program to produce detailed models of the target buildings, using the imagery they pulled in from various sources. "Literally, it looks like a video game," said Gunnery Sergeant Kenneth C. Pinckard; the topographic and imagery analysts "can actually build their own models" in virtual reality and then have the assault force "walk through" the buildings or the route to the target. The detachment had had the program, called Sextant, for some time, but the capstone exercise was its first real opportunity to put it to the test.[43] Staff Sergeant Benjamin J. Cushing of Recon Team 4 figured out how to take the waypoints stored on a global positioning system receiver and download them as a file to a laptop computer, then transmit that file by radio to the combat operations center. In that way, the assault force had instant access to the results of the reconnaissance and surveillance teams' navigation and scouting, the routes, the hide sites, and the covered and concealed positions.[44]

By exploiting the imagery, the information sent back from the observation posts, and the resulting Sextant models of the target site, the staff divided the target into thirds and devised a plan to take it. Master Gunnery Sergeant Settelen also observed this mission, although not from a rooftop inside the site. He described how the supporting machine guns engaged the target: "On cue—they were using red, white, and blue as the flare signals—they were lifting and shifting fires on each third of the camp as [the assault force] went in," with the beaten zone of the machine gun fire only meters in front of the assault force and keeping pace with its advance. Marines from the fires element controlled live close air support as the assault force swept the objective, consolidated and did a quick site exploitation, then withdrew quickly in good order to the vehicles for a long, frigid, exfiltration back to Indian Springs. There was a casualty exercise thrown in at the height of the assault that was handled by the detachment's corpsmen, and a helicopter flew in for casualty evacuation while the fireworks were still underway by the fires liaison element.[45]

Elements of Squadron One, in addition to Commander Wilson, were also on hand for approximately one week. However, their training and the Marines' training were handled as separate events. Integrated operations at the platoon level were never a goal and therefore not an issue. The gap remained at the staff level. Since the staff integration exercise in October, no one had made much progress on that level. Det One leadership strongly believed that closer staff cooperation during the capstone exercise would have been highly beneficial for both groups.*

In direct action missions, the assault force tends to receive the most attention, but every element of the detachment was fully employed and tested during this exercise. The reconnaissance and surveillance teams endured the vile weather while performing every conceivable task in support of the missions. They found the routes, scouted the positions, guided the assault force, provided sniper support, and reported what they saw and heard. The fires liaison element was able to work live close air support on the targets and bring aircraft into a landing zone during an assault. The support sections did their critical but unheralded work and then manned the crew-served

Photo courtesy of Patrick J. Rogers

Team leaders and Maj Craig S. Kozeniesky (back to camera) prepare for a mission during the Capstone Exercise in Nevada. While Kozeniesky checks the settings on his AN/PRC-148 tactical hand-held radio, the other two pass last-minute information on the mission.

weapons for base-of-fire operations. The intelligence element employed the entire spectrum of its disciplines, from weather forecasting, to connectivity with national assets, to analytical work, and to distribution of photographs of the "high value targets" to every member of the assault force. The intelligence Marines also got an unexpected bonus out of the exercise: a good look at the Air Force's Predator unmanned aerial vehicles, which were home-based at Indian Springs. Seizing this opportunity, they integrated a few Predator flights into their reconnaissance and surveillance plans, learning much about the platform.[46]

The training cell was justifiably pleased with the results of the capstone exercise. Captain Fiscus summed up the experience: "We built some exercises that stretched the detachment's limits physically, mentally and emotionally." He admitted it was "a very difficult evolution to put together, supervise, and execute." "But," he continued, "it paid huge dividends, as we noticed our shortfalls, we pushed the operating limits of our equipment and our personnel and our planning procedures."[47]

The senior enlisted Marines also assessed the exercise as a significant milestone. Master Sergeant Rutan echoed Captain Fiscus's opinions, believing that the capstone exercise, even more than Bridgeport "Man-Ex," forged the detachment into a cohesive operational unit. Master Sergeant Oakes agreed: "It brought out a lot in the platoon that I liked. We did a lot of long-range missions—very long range—

---

* Cdr Wilson stated that a conscious decision was made in the Naval Special Warfare hierarchy to allow the Marines to conduct this exercise without oversight or participation by NSW elements.

60- to 100-kilometer round-trip missions, nighttime driving, long-range navigation . . . a long distance to move and a tight timeline to get there. . . . It was a 'bringing together.'"[48]

Major Kozeniesky looked beyond the immediate results of the exercise to the unit's deployment, still months away. He pointed out that before the capstone exercise, "we largely engaged in element and platoon training," but at the capstone exercise, "we formed the raid force which later became Task Unit Raider and started to figure out a concept of employment." The Marines demonstrated what they had been saying for months: that the value of the task force was greater than the sum its parts.[49]

Integration

The year 2004 began with a combat trauma training package for the fires and intelligence elements, identical to the course run six months previously for the reconnaissance element. Other events in January included more sniper training for the reconnaissance Marines, a naval gunfire refresher for the fires liaison element, and an off-road driving course for Marines from across the detachment.

The long-awaited full integration with Squadron One—the certification exercise—was scheduled for late January. However, according to the command chronology, "uncertainty about the location and organization of the deployment" suddenly put the event off.[50] For much of the training phase, Det One members thought that their destination might very well be Afghanistan. At one point, the probable destination emerged as the Horn of Africa. Another option lingering for months had the detachment divided between U.S. Pacific Command and U.S. Central Command, which the Det One leadership and the Marine Corps hierarchy resisted strongly, maintaining that a split deployment was not in keeping with the letter or spirit of the memorandum of agreement with Naval Special Warfare. By January 2004, all of those options were out; Iraq was the destination, with the detachment to be used primarily in urban direct action.* The abrupt decisions on the deployment postponed the certification exercise and caused the detachment staff to rethink several aspects of their preparedness.

Conveniently, the rescheduling of the exercise opened a gap in the detachment's calendar. The staff deftly turned this unexpected "white space" on the training schedule to the detachment's advantage. In order to maintain the edge and refine procedures, the unit moved to Camp Talega, a remote site at Camp Pendleton, for a concentration on direct action. Although not as meteorologically challenging as the exercise in Nevada, the Talega exercise provided another opportunity for the detachment to work full mission profiles out of an expeditionary setting, putting into practice the lessons the Marines learned in the capstone exercise and leaning more in the direction of urban warfare rather than special reconnaissance. To this end, they were able to leverage an ongoing event in the abandoned housing area at March Air Reserve Base, Riverside, California—Project Metropolis, an effort employing extensive use of role players in training Marines units headed for Iraq—and experience a "very realistic opposition force" on one direct action mission.[51] The realism became clear later to some of the Det One Marines. "It was right on the money for our training," recalled Master Sergeant Oakes. "We didn't know it at the time, but that March Air Force Base, with the urban environment, with Iraqi actors, was exactly what we were going to be doing in the future."[52] The Talega exercise further refined the capabilities of the raid force that was built at Mercury, but it also suffered from the same deficiency: it was a Marine-only show, on the eve of a Navy-Marine certification exercise and deployment.

In early February 2004, on the heels of the Talega exercise, a small party consisting of Major Kozeniesky, Major Carter, and Captain Kress flew to Southwest Asia with members of Squadron One's leadership for a pre-deployment site survey. Their first stop was the Naval Special Warfare support unit in Bahrain, the administrative headquarters of all SEAL forces in the region. Next they flew to Baghdad, where they visited Naval Special Warfare Squadron Seven, which they would shortly relieve.

The site survey team came back with a "much better understanding of the requirements for the deployment," according to Major Kozeniesky. During their five days in Baghdad, the Det One officers saw how their units would be laid out, based on Squadron Seven's operations: one task unit in the North, one task unit in the West, and the headquarters and two task units in Baghdad. Concurrently, they saw that their interim fast attack vehicles, newly acquired and thoroughly exercised in Nevada, were not what they needed for urban direct action. They needed hunkers, and in particular a new special op-

---

* The decision for deployment to Iraq did not occur until "December 2003, at the SOCom-USMC Warfighter Conference," wrote Col Coates. SOCom commander Gen Bryan D. Brown "made the decision for the detachment to deploy to Iraq with the possibility of a follow-on deployment to Afghanistan when I briefed him on the status of the detachment and the proposed split deployment." Col Coates email to author, 13 April 2006.

erations-specific model based on Squadron Seven's in-house modifications of armor and assaulting equipment. A resolution to that problem, as important as it was, would have to wait.[53]

Finally, Commander Wilson and Major Kozeniesky visited the headquarters of the Combined Forces Special Operations Component Command in Qatar. Det One's executive officer was dismayed to find that the special operations headquarters did not know that the detachment was coming with Squadron One, in fact barely knew of its existence, and thus had not planned for the employment of its capabilities. Combined Forces Special Operations Component Command, for its part, was quite pleased to have an extra direct action force emerge from nowhere.

Following the snap evolution at Talega, the detachment was informed that the certification exercise would now be held in late February 2004. As such, the detachment's training phase command structure also ended, and Det One came under the actual control of Naval Special Warfare Command, as spelled out in the memorandum of 20 February 2003, although on paper the detachment had come under control of Squadron One in December.

The certification exercise saw the end of Det One as a self-contained task force. The principle staff officers were absorbed into the squadron staff: Major Kozeniesky became the senior Marine and squadron operations officer; Major Carter became the squadron intelligence officer; and Major Priddy and Major Dolan respectively became the squadron fires and air officers. The individual staff sections assumed a role of direct support to the task group as a whole, not just the Marine task unit. Marines from the intelligence element—counterintelligence, radio reconnaissance, and some analysts—were detached out to support the task units, providing those capabilities and skills that these units did not otherwise possess. Few Marines, especially on the staff, were happy about the new assignments.

At the same time, Det One received a welcome addition from Squadron One, four explosive ordnance disposal (EOD) technicians, who were promptly added to the rolls. This critical military occupational specialty was not represented in the Det One table of organization—a deficiency noted by SOTG evaluators at the capstone exercise.[54] Headquarters Marine Corps had refused to draw on the EOD community to staff the detachment, anticipating that operations in Iraq would require every available Marine EOD technician. In the final event, the addition of Navy EOD technicians rather than Marines was the right course of action since, as Major Kozeniesky noted, "they multiplied our combat power more so than Marine EOD due to their consistent work with special operations forces."[55] All four men were absorbed into the reconnaissance element.

The certification exercise was designed to simulate how Squadron One expected its task units would be employed across Iraq, based on how Squadron Seven was addressing the mission and the anticipated requirement to do likewise. Edwards Air Force Base, California, served as the "Baghdad" hub, where Squadron One would have its headquarters. Two task units were sent to outlying locations that, in Iraq, would be in the West and North. Two other task units were retained at the hub. During the five days of the certification exercise, the squadron executed four full mission profiles, a taxing operational tempo by any measure, as the staff had to support three sites spread over hundreds of miles. The Marine task unit, comprised mostly of the reconnaissance element, performed up to and beyond standards and expectations.

Most Det One Marines remember the certification exercise as a good evolution but not an exceptionally tough one in the sense that Bridgeport and Nevada were. Gunnery Sergeant Dailey noticed some new aspects of integration, "tweaks" to the operating procedures and briefing points, but neither of their two direct action missions, including the one they conducted in conjunction with a SEAL task unit, elicited

A Marine from Company K, 3d Battalion, 5th Marines, serving as a "terrorist" during the Capstone Exercise in Nevada, pauses to eat his Meals Ready to Eat. The flak vest, gloves, helmet, face guard, and light colored bands on the barrel of his rifle all indicate the use of simunitions, the realistic training tool for close-quarters battle.

Photo courtesy of Patrick J. Rogers

much commentary.⁵⁶ That second mission was led by Major Kozeniesky as overall raid force commander. A few of the more senior enlisted Marines noticed some undercurrents of the old, highly competitive Marine/SEAL relationship at work but took it in stride. "It's frustrating," remarked Master Sergeant Wyrick, "but at the same time I've done this enough to know that if you just keeping doing what you do, and you do it well, eventually they're going to have to give you the ball. They're going to have to because you're going to show that the capabilities and competencies you have exceed what they have."⁵⁷ Gunnery Sergeant Pinckard, the All-Source Fusion Chief, regretted the rapid mission cycle in the certification exercise not because it was demanding but that it left no room for "any decent analytical work."⁵⁸

As is frequently the case in any military operation, the views from opposite ends of the chain-of-command differed. Since activation, the detachment had trained intensively on its own, commanding and controlling itself. The staff integration exercise with Squadron One provided a baseline for joint work, but before the certification exercise there had been no evaluated evolutions run with an integrated staff under one commander. Then the detachment command element found itself broken up, absorbed into a larger whole, no longer focused solely on its unit, and in the middle of a zero-defects evaluation in front of a tough audience. Many Marines in the command element looked back on the Nevada and Talega exercises and shook their heads ruefully at the missed opportunities to achieve the "same gain with less pain." Here at the eleventh hour, for better or for worse, was the product of the separate-but-equal training schedule and the whole host of tensions between Special Operations Command and the Marine Corps. The new arrangement worked, but it was to few Marines' liking. As Major Carter put it: "It showed us that the baby was ugly."⁵⁹ But the offspring, ugly or not, need to be loved because it was alive and kicking and headed for Iraq. The Det One staff members shouldered their packs and joined their SEAL brethren in making the exercise a success, showing that the Marine Corps warfighting ethos and basic Marine Corps staff work were completely relevant in the SOCom realm.

Commander Wilson, who had both a golden operational opportunity and an unenviable task, must get the lion's share of credit for making the arrangement work. No one, including Wilson himself, was truly happy with the shotgun wedding, and all the Marines sensed that Wilson faced enormous pressures from within his own community. It was clear that he had authority to make changes in task organization, and if he wanted the whole unit to increase its capabilities, he had to make some hard decisions. That he immediately supplanted some of his own staff with the principle Marine staff officers suggests that he recognized what they could do for the whole unit, and that he would not hesitate to do what he thought was best. Command is not, after all, a popularity contest.*

Integration issues aside, most of the Det One staff officers described the certification exercise as a good test for conditions in Iraq. Even Major Dolan, admittedly no fan of Naval Special Warfare, called it a "top-notch exercise."⁶⁰ The Marines received high marks from a host of observers and evaluators. Naval Special Warfare Group One, the squadron's higher headquarters, declared the unit mission-capable and ready for the fight.**

Last-Minute Preparations

After the certification exercise was over, the detachment turned to last-minute issues. The intelligence element provided a range of briefs on Iraq and the situation there. Others Marines busied themselves packing gear and staging it at the Camp Del Mar compound while the staff made refinements to the deployment plans. All hands looked forward to pre-deployment leave. The support elements of the detachment went back to Range 130 to revisit their individual weapons skills, while the reconnaissance element looked to broaden its tactics, techniques, and procedures for close-quarters combat.

Meanwhile, the motor transport section faced a major problem. The relatively late realization that the detachment would need a new set of vehicles threw a big wrench into the predeployment works. When Major Kozeniesky brought back the word on vehicles—"we needed hunekers and we needed them in a big way"—there was no time to get the new gear before the onset of the certification exercise, and then no time during the exercise since all hands were fully

---

* In the post-deployment study on the detachment by Joint Special Operations University, the Squadron One Command Master Chief succinctly described Cdr Wilson's dilemma and his success: "Has this been harder? Yeah, it's been harder on the boss. . . . [He] has had to try to take our side and their side and it's been a monumental struggle to do it so that nobody's pissed off. . . . Commander Wilson's probably the only guy that could've done it." Joint Special Operations University study, C-5.

** Maj Wade Priddy pointed out later that when Group One declared the unit ready to deploy, it did not include a specific certification of Det One by itself. He was told at the pre-exercise conference that Group One had no authority to decide such a matter, and it was left up to the Marine Corps. Maj Priddy email to author, 31 August 2006.

involved.⁶¹ By the time the dust had settled from certification exercise, it was clear that Det One was not going to receive the vehicles it needed before deployment. There were none to be had on such short notice, and not even SOCom's authority nor the detachment's own acquisitions prowess could pull that rabbit out of a hat. Gunnery Sergeant Maldonado and Staff Sergeant Sierra were ordered to go find whatever hunekers the Marine Corps had, grab the best ones they could, and then get to work on modifying them.

The two went immediately to Marine Corps Logistics Base at Barstow, California, to see what hunekers were available in the cast-off lot. Not surprisingly, all they found were wrecks, hulks in various states of disrepair. Many had been out in that desert lot for years. Sierra, a certified civilian mechanic who gained those credentials before he enlisted, put on his coveralls and crawled in and around the vehicles while Maldonado wrote down the discrepancies. Choosing the "best" vehicles they could find, they had about a dozen of them transported back to the detachment compound. There, giving up their own predeployment leave, the two Marines worked day after day to strip the hunekers down and get them back in basic running order. Making the special modifications—armor, assault platforms, infrared headlights, scaling ladders and machinegun mounts—would have to wait until they got to Iraq. When the time came to deploy, not all of the rebuilds were finished, but they were ready enough to get on and off the aircraft.

Ready for Deployment

By April 2004, after an unprecedented stand-up and training period and with full integration into Naval Special Warfare Squadron One just completed, the Marine Corps Special Operations Command Detachment was at the highest pitch of readiness. The Det One Marines were fully trained and thoroughly exercised in their individual fighting abilities, their particular disciplines, and now their roles in the squadron. In a remarkably short time span, the detachment had progressed by leaps and bounds into a first-rate special operations force, fully capable of executing the missions assigned to it. And it was a uniquely Marine force, even if somewhat altered by full integration into the squadron, not a copy of any existing Special Operations Command unit.

On 6 April 2004, the first of four U.S. Air Force C-5 Galaxy transport planes carrying Det One Marines and their gear lifted off from Naval Air Station North Island, San Diego. Like the storied Marine Raiders of World War II, the Marine Corps Special Operations Command Detachment was on its way to take the fight directly to the enemy.

Chapter 4

Deployment

Naval Special Warfare Task Group—Arabian Peninsula

The first planeload of Marines from Detachment One landed in Baghdad on 6 April 2004. It was the same date they had taken off from San Diego, but in reality, they touched down on a different day and in a vastly different place. The next two loads arrived without difficulty, but the last, carrying the bulk of the reconnaissance element, was vexed by delays and mechanical problems and did not arrive for two weeks.

In late March 2004, Iraq had exploded. On 31 March, four American contractors from the private security firm Blackwater USA were waylaid, murdered, and burned by a mob, their bodies hung from a bridge in the city of al-Fallujah, approximately 45 miles west of Baghdad. These acts drew the I Marine Expeditionary Force, newly in charge of the area of operations encompassing the western third of the country, into full-scale combat operations as the insurgents in the predominantly Sunni region were emboldened to rise up in growing numbers. Other towns and cities in the surrounding al-Anbar Province followed suit. The fledgling Iraqi security forces melted away, and American casualties mounted. In the cities and rural areas, rocket and mortar attacks on Coalition bases increased in volume and accuracy, and across the country, improvised explosive devices became the insurgents' weapon of choice.

From the south came Shi'a militias, on the march against the Americans and other Coalition forces. This was an unwelcome development at a distinctly inopportune moment. These forces had not taken the field in large numbers, if at all. The Shi'a uprising, instigated by a radical cleric with ties to Iran, Muqtada al-Sadr, severely restricted the lines of communications south to Kuwait and at more than one point threatened to sever them entirely. It complicated an already-dark political scene and portended nothing good for the formation of an Iraqi governing coalition.

Matters in Iraq were at an exceedingly delicate stage, with a transition of sovereignty to an interim Iraqi government in the offing even while there was all-out fighting in several cities. The initiative was in the hands of the insurgents. The U.S.-led Coalition needed to mount effective offensive operations across the country to regain the initiative.

This was the environment that greeted the Marines and SEALs of Naval Special Warfare Squadron One when they landed in Baghdad and began to organize for operations. Det One Marines on that first load, most of them from the logistics and intelligence sections, spent the first night manning the base defenses. The first week included daily indirect and small-arms fire.

Special operations forces in Iraq were grouped under Combined Joint Special Operations Task Force Arabian Peninsula. Commanded by a U.S. Army colonel, the task force had under its command not only Naval Special Warfare Squadron One, but also other units, such as the 2d Battalion, 5th Special Forces Group (Airborne), and later the 1st Battalion. The Det One Marines would form close working relationships with both units. There was also a unit from the Polish special operations force, called the GROM after its Polish name, Grupa Reagowania Operacyjno Mobilnego (Operational Mobile Response Group). Squadron One, now properly called Naval Special Warfare Task Group Arabian Peninsula, was the special operations task force's primary direct action arm.*

In accordance with the hub-and-spoke plan that was conceived during the predeployment site survey and tested at the certification exercise, Commander William W. Wilson dispatched task units to outlying cities, the "spokes" that radiated from the Baghdad hub. One task unit went to northern Iraq, augmented by one counterintelligence Marine and four radio reconnaissance Marines. Another task unit went west to al-Anbar Province; it was augmented by the Det One intelligence chief and counterintelligence chief. Wilson sent another counterintelligence Marine to the "Green Zone" in Baghdad to be the task group liaison to other government agencies.

Initially, the use of counterintelligence Marines in special operations was, despite their capabilities,

---
* From this point forward, the term "task force" will refer to Combined Joint Special Warfare Task Force—Arabian Peninsula, and the term "task group" will refer to Naval Special Warfare Task Group—Arabian Peninsula.

Photo courtesy of LtCol Craig S. Kozeniesky

Det One's compound in Baghdad was named Camp Myler in honor of Sgt Christian W. Myler of the reconnaissance element who was killed in a motorcycle accident in September 2003. The sign proudly displays the insignia of Det One's forbearers, the Marine Raiders of World War II.

problematic. The crux was legal, not operational. Human intelligence specialists in Special Operations Command (SOCom) were certified in advanced special operations techniques (ASOT), a skill set very similar to the Marine Corps' human source intelligence (HUMINT) exploitation, but counterintelligence Marines did not have the certifications that their SEAL or Army counterparts did, which were tied to specific provisions of U.S. laws governing intelligence collection. According to Commander Wilson, "A lot of folks [in the special operations forces] were very nervous about [Marine HUMINT] guys getting into activities that could be perceived as the environment of ASOT."

Wilson recognized the Marines' particular skills and capabilities, however, and he needed a dedicated tactical human source intelligence capability. With the task force commander's full support, Wilson decided to take a risk and use his counterintelligence Marines in the roles for which they were trained. The key was Wilson's personal trust in Major M. Gerald Carter, only one of many times that officer's personal stature would prove important. This arrangement allowed Wilson to make the best use of his assets; the counterintelligence Marines could do tactical human source intelligence while the SEALs, trained in advanced special operations techniques, could work with the task force intelligence section, where Wilson had specific tasks for them. There was plenty of work to go around, as Wilson noted.[1]

Task Unit Raider

Task group staff integration, begun at the certification exercise, continued in Iraq and settled into a workable structure. Major Craig S. Kozeniesky remained as commander of Task Unit Raider but dropped the collateral duties of task group operations officer, even though for a brief period he also filled in as the task group deputy commander. Major Carter was assigned as the task group intelligence officer, and Captain Christopher B. Batts was designated as the task group "special activities officer," dealing with all aspects of human source intelligence, including interrogations. Major M. Wade Priddy ascended to the post of task group future operations officer, and Captain Stephen V. Fiscus functioned as Task Unit Raider's operations officer. Major Thomas P. Dolan handled the air officer duties for the task unit but devoted part of his time to working air operations issues of the task group.

Out of the original 30-man intelligence element, only two analysts, four radio reconnaissance Marines, and one counterintelligence Marine remained in direct support of Task Unit Raider. All others were in general support of the task group or in direct support of other task units. The fires element remained intact under Task Unit Raider, as did the logistics section and the communications section.

Colonel Robert J. Coates, at the insistence of the commanding generals of Marine Forces Pacific Command and Marine Forces Central Command, went to Fallujah on 23 April and was attached to I Marine Expeditionary Force staff as Marine Forces Central liaison officer.

After the reorganization of the task group and dispatch of the outlying task units, the first order of business for Task Unit Raider was to get settled in its own compound, sort out the logistics situation, then leap into the targeting cycle and begin hitting targets. The Marines made a home near Baghdad International Airport, naming it Camp Myler after Sergeant Christian W. Myler, the reconnaissance Marine who had died in September 2003. They claimed their corner of the complex, where the Seabees constructed additional buildings, and set up their working spaces, then identified ranges and buildings they could use for assault rehearsals. The duties of camp commandant were assigned to the Det One parachute rigger,

Gunnery Sergeant Jason T. Kennedy.

Confusion reigned for a time. Det One Marines were coming and going on a variety of urgent matters and being detached to serve with the outlying task units. The logistics situation was shaky; the normal uncertainties attending a newly arrived unit were compounded by the constrained supply situation. One of the staff's previous assumptions was that once in Iraq, the detachment would be able to plug into the Marine expeditionary force for support since Baghdad and Camp Fallujah were not far apart, about the same distance as Camp Pendleton to San Diego. But attacks on the main supply routes took that course of action out of consideration. Until supply lines opened, the Marines had to get their support from the special operations task force structure and from the many Army units that dotted the Baghdad area.*

The lack of proper fighting vehicles had to be addressed quickly. The hunekers as they came off the planes were in no shape to roll out of the gates on missions. They lacked armor and many other modifications, such as infrared headlights, communications equipment and navigation aids, and additional machine-gun mounts. The first daily situation report from Iraq identified vehicle issues as the number-one impediment to Task Unit Raider's ability to mount out and hit targets. The same comments recurred repeatedly during the first few weeks in country.[2] By the time-honored method of scrounging (or "exploiting opportunities," as one report termed it) in and around Baghdad over the first two weeks, the logistics section was able to procure enough armor kits to get six hunekers battle-ready.[3] The improvement in readiness came just in time, as the first targets were being designated for execution.

Ammunition was also an immediate problem, and not just because of the general supply situation. In a maddening variation of the training phase ammunition problem, some shipping containers with specific munitions Task Unit Raider needed to operate and conduct sustainment training were lost in the ammunition dump in Kuwait. It was such a conundrum that the imperturbable Captain Matthew H. Kress was compelled to sort it out himself, noting that "it was a matter of me going down to Kuwait and physically driving the desert to find these containers."[4] A substantial load of ammunition, but by no means the whole lot, arrived on 22 April and gave the Marines enough of the supplies they needed to begin and sustain their operations.[5]

Making the most of the material at hand and what could be obtained locally, Marines from all elements soon established daily routines. The logistics section took over base defense in addition to its regular duties, augmented by others as needed. The communications section had the radio nets and data networks up and running within hours, with the all-important Trojan Spirit Lite passing a steady stream of electrons back and forth to a station in the United States. Sergeant Victor M. Guerra profited from his experience in Nevada; he had protected his gear during travel and consequently had his networks in operation right away. Staff Sergeant Chad E. Berry set up and maintained the power and environmental controls. By billet he was the detachment's small-craft mechanic, but he stepped into the rarely publicized but always critical role of keeping the utilities operational.

The reconnaissance element turned to stropping its collective razor: small arms sustainment training, "flow drills" for close-quarter battle (now on structures of indigenous construction materials methods, something they had not experienced before), and a host of other actions. All hands turned to incorporating the rebuilt hunekers into their operating procedures, working out the differences between the capabilities of the bigger, heavier armored vehicles versus the fast attack vehicles. Almost every aspect of vehicle operations needed to be reexamined and

Col Robert J. Coates (right) and an unidentified Det One Marine in Iraq. This was after the detachment had been allocated separate missions, based on skills and aptitudes as needed by the Naval Special Warfare Task Group.

Photo courtesy of Col Robert J. Coates

---
* The agreement with SOCom had specified that the Marine Corps would fund the detachment, hence the plan to plug into I MEF for support. MarForPac and MarCent helped clear the way for funding to flow to the detachment through SOCom and Army channels.

digested. How would a fully loaded humvee perform at high speed? What were the driver/gunner/commander dynamics in the comparatively spacious humvee instead of the cramped fast attack vehicle? What was the quickest way to get a humvee ready for towing if the need arose? Answering these and other questions occupied much of the Marines' days and nights in those first few weeks.

Members of the Task Unit Raider staff and the intelligence element immersed themselves in establishing relationships with adjacent commands and finding their place in the targeting process—getting a feel for the "atmospherics," identifying the main malefactors, and devising ways to track, strike, and exploit them. Commander Wilson established two priority information requirements: first, who was attacking the Iraqi security forces? And second, who was attacking Americans? The answers to these questions provided the basis for the targeting process.

Wilson then established two criteria for launching a direct action raid: first, was there a good legal case on the target, something that would keep him in custody? And second, what more would this kill or capture lead to?* The answers to these questions provided the operational basis for a raid.[6] The overall plan was to hit one target after another, using the intelligence gained from one hit to lead to the next. The key was to start with the smaller, more vulnerable targets. "You don't go after the big guy at first—you can't get to him," Wilson explained. "You work your way up through the guy who's welding the brackets for the rockets that they're firing. You get the guy that's supplying the mortar rounds; you get another guy who's a mortar trainer. . . . You work your way up and you take out an entire structure."[7]

Striking high-value targets was Task Unit Raider's reason for existence, and the targeting cycle was what the intelligence element was specifically designed to do. Through some early missteps not of their making, Majors Kozeniesky and Carter found that the targeting cycle would be a "bottom-up" search rather than a "top-down" push, meaning that the Marines would have to take the lead in developing most of their own targets.[8] On 23 April, Kozeniesky reported that the detachment was "fully deployed and preparing for operations."[9]

Early Operations

In Iraq in April 2004, there were several agencies and entities collecting intelligence. This was both a good thing and a bad thing from Task Unit Raider's point of view. On the positive side, it promised a wealth of exploitable intelligence; on the negative, there was no single point of contact in higher headquarters who was fusing the data and passing it down the chain in an actionable form. Nor was there necessarily any uniform quality control, as the Marines saw it, in the intelligence products available to them.

By later April, missions began to percolate. On the 21st, the task group received a warning order from Combined Joint Task Force 7, the highest military headquarters in Iraq, and the task unit staff began planning the first direct action mission, dubbed Objective Rhino.† The order alerted the task group to large numbers of hard-core enemy personnel concentrated at a location west of Baghdad and east of Fallujah. The planners zeroed in on the area and began a thorough examination of the terrain and the enemy. Within a few days as more information became available, the nature of the target evolved slightly and the name was changed to Objective Rat.[10]

Further study and close coordination with 2d Battalion, 5th Special Forces Group, verified that a large number of known insurgents were concentrated in the neighborhood. Intelligence sources also identified the building housing them—Abu Ghraib prison. The information from higher headquarters was technically correct—large numbers of known insurgents in a given location—but essentially worthless. The weekly situation report tartly noted that "the planned [mission] has obviously been shelved and a thorough review of targeting procedures is recommended."[11]

Were it not deadly serious business, the Rhino/Rat episode might have been amusing. It highlighted problems with the quality of the targeting intelligence being passed down the chain-of-command. Its only value lay, perhaps, in being a realistic paper drill, a command post exercise under operational conditions. Major Kozeniesky, although irritated, chose to close the episode on a positive note, writing that "Task Unit Raider, while disappointed with the poor coordination and targeting from higher headquarters on Objective Rat, established good lateral contacts with friendly conventional forces and special operations forces."[12]

As it turned out, the first mission for Task Unit

---

* A reference to making a case against an individual in the legal sense is not just an analogy. As the transition to Iraqi sovereignty progressed, the strength of the evidence against a target could mean the difference between his being released and his being detained for a long period of time.

† All Task Unit Raider missions had codenames beginning with the letter "R." Objectives had two components: an individual or cell, and a location. Thus, the same individual or cell could have more than one operation planned or mounted against them, as locations changed.

Raider was not a full-scale direct action, but rather a "close target reconnaissance." It proved to be a good test for two Marines, and it handed the intelligence element what it wanted most, a solid piece of actionable intelligence. It began with one of the detachment intelligence officer's frequent liaison visits to higher headquarters. From his ever-widening circle of contacts, Major Carter discovered that agents in the Federal Bureau of Investigation cell in Baghdad had a source that had named a female Iraqi, employed by a U.S. contractor, as an insurgent sympathizer. It appeared that the woman, code named "Rachel," had leaked information concerning several linguists employed by the contractor, resulting in their murders. She needed to be found, apprehended, and questioned. The murders limited the ability of Coalition units to work with the Iraqi population on a number of important projects. The target fit all of Commander Wilson's criteria, and Carter gladly took ownership of the mission.

The task group staff analyzed the mission and came up with a plan. They knew very little about the woman and had to get a positive identification. A small team would be sent to find her, starting with her last known location. Once they got sight of her, they could develop a plan to track her and eventually take action. The mission carried some risk, but it promised both a good payoff and a foot in the door of the targeting cycle. A small victory would also satisfy Commander Wilson's other goal: an early success.

Gunnery Sergeant John A. Dailey, leader of reconnaissance team 4, took charge of the mission. He headed what could be called a small combined joint task force, which consisted of Dailey, Gunnery Sergeant William M. Johnston from the counterintelligence section, a SEAL assigned to HUMINT duties, and an operator from the Polish special forces unit, the GROM, reportedly the best sniper in that organization. The GROM member was also a woman, an important factor since they were dealing with a female target. The task group staff coordinated with other government agencies, the Army commands involved, and the contracting company's officials and sent the four in civilian clothes and civilian vehicles to where "Rachel" was supposed to be working.

When the four arrived at the target's reported place of employment, they were told that she no longer worked there, but that she was employed at a base outside the city. Gunnery Sergeant Dailey wanted to go on to the second site and find her, so he conferred with Commander Wilson and Major Kozeniesky, who approved his request to continue the search and the capture if conditions permitted. At the second location, members of the combined joint task force received the same answer. Their contacts pointed them to a third site, to which they proceeded immediately.

The four took a low-key approach to the mission, and this helped them in their quest. Civilian clothes concealed their pistols and soft body armor, and they kept their M4 carbines and other combat gear stowed in their vehicles. The smooth-talking HUMINT specialists were adept at asking questions without raising eyebrows. According to Dailey, "This was one of those times that being able to wear civvies and having your hair at the outer limit of regulation really helped."*

Arriving at the third site, they located the target's former office, but they were told that she had quit. Rather than let the trail go cold, they discussed the matter with the U.S. Army officer for whom she had worked, without going into too much detail about why they wanted her. Together, they devised a simple trap: "Rachel's" former employer located her phone number and called her to come get her last paycheck. Much to the group's surprise, she agreed. At this point, with nothing to do but wait—the woman had promised to be there in 20 minutes, but Dailey knew that in Iraq, 20 minutes could mean "20 minutes, or four hours, or whatever"—he went to see the base commander to let him know what was going on. After Dailey explained to a skeptical colonel what was afoot—Dailey, in civilian clothes and sporting a slightly non-Marine haircut, was sure that the Army officer did not believe that he was who he said he was—the base commander gave his full support.

To this point, the mission was coming together. The small combined joint task force would be able to identify "Rachel" and probably take her into custody. But if she was indeed working for the insurgents, there was always the possibility that she would resist capture. If she had a male escort, as she surely would, would he (or they) also put up a fight? The last thing anyone wanted was a gunfight on a crowded base frequented by civilians. That would mean an early disaster, not an early success. Speed, surprise, and deft execution would be vital to a successful conclusion, and the group worked out a plan. Dailey posted Gunnery Sergeant Johnston and the GROM member behind the door of the office where "Rachel" would go to pick up her pay. He positioned the SEAL and himself outside to handle whomever she might have with her.

---

* Personnel in civilian clothes carrying weapons were not unusual sights on coalition bases in Iraq. What would seem outlandish in any other setting was commonplace.

Their patience was rewarded. As "Rachel" and a male escort came into the facility, Dailey gave the signal to stand by. When she walked into the room, Johnston shut the door, and the female GROM member quickly got her under control. Dailey and the SEAL overpowered and flex-cuffed the male. The encounter was over in an instant and not a shot was fired. The task group bundled the pair into civilian vehicles and sped back to Camp Myler so that Captain Batts's interrogators could go to work.

Questioning soon revealed that "Rachel" was not actively involved in passing information to the insurgents, but that she was probably doing so unwittingly through ill-considered chatter. The male likewise was not an insurgent, but he provided useful information and produced the key that turned this operation into a minor coup. He knew a few details about the linguist murderers, and he knew some other things about unsavory people involved with bombs and rockets. The interrogators asked whether he would be willing to accompany a raid force and identify the individuals. The man agreed, and the information he supplied became the basis for Objective Racket, Task Unit Raider's first true direct action mission.

Objective Racket

"Rachel" and her male escort were taken on 2 May. Planning began immediately afterward in order to exploit the information they had given the interrogators. "Rachel's" escort provided details about a man who lived in a certain neighborhood of Baghdad with his wife and two children. This man worked as a repairman at a shop not far away. He was involved in the linguist murders as well as in the construction of rocket launchers used to attack Coalition bases. He hated Americans. His relatives reportedly were involved in the car bomb trade, and one of them was suspected of being the suicide bomber in a recent attack on an Iraqi police station. This case was an opportunity tailor-made for the Marines of the intelligence element. They pulled in data from every corner of the command structure in Iraq and fused it into a comprehensive whole, corroborating and amplifying bits of information as they proceeded. They identified this man's house and his workplace on imagery taken from various platforms, and they mapped his daily routine.

The way the mission was planned, coordinated, and executed provides a look at Task Unit Raider's template for a direct action mission. In traditional Marine Corps fashion, the actions during planning were not strictly sequential but rather more concurrent, and collaborative rather than hierarchical. Later, other more complex missions featured different planning and coordination aspects, but this first one was emblematic of the process.

All hands contributed to the planning. The staff analyzed the mission and came up with courses of action, which were briefed to Commander Wilson. The chosen course of action was then planned out in detail. The operations section posted a tentative timeline for execution; arranged for close air support; coordinated with conventional forces in whose territory they would be working; and kept track of the countless small tasks that need to be accomplished. The intelligence element continued to draw information and to monitor its sources while it assisted the planners.

The assault force wanted to know dozens of pieces of information. What did the target look like, and what did his house look like? What was the composition of the structures, doors, and windows? Did the target have guard dogs or some other form of early warning? Would his neighbors be watching on his behalf, and would they join in a defense? What were his probable reactions to the assault? Would he fight, or would he try to run? How much starlight and moonlight would there be? The list was long, but the intensive training phase had provided detailed templates for mission planning, and there was little that had not been anticipated.

Concurrent with the planning were vehicle preparation, rehearsals, and refinements. What was the vehicle order? Who was assigned to which vehicle and what were their duties? In the event of a vehicle breaking down, what was the "bump plan" to shift the load to the other vehicles, and what was the recovery plan? What were the call-signs and frequencies for the supporting arms? Who was providing the quick reaction force? Where were the helicopter landing zones in case of a casualty evacuation? Every man was assigned specific responsibilities. Every man had a backup and was himself a backup to someone else. Before mounting out, all hands test-fired their weapons and checked their night-vision goggles, then checked and rechecked the vehicles.

At a predetermined time, every man involved in the mission gathered for a confirmation brief. The mission was restated and an intelligence update was provided. (The one major item for Objective Racket that the intelligence section did not have was a photograph of the target, which would end up causing some confusion.) The intelligence Marines had once again done their part by fusing imagery and topographic analysis to produce three-dimensional "drive-through" models of the route and the objective area, overlaid by detailed mobility diagrams to show which routes were trafficable and which were not. Warrant Officer Kevin E. Vicinus briefed the weather conditions and their possible effects on the operation. The key leaders in the mission stood up and briefed their elements' roles in the mission, from pre-assault rehearsals to post-assault actions. They answered all last-minute questions on target minutiae, ironed out any wrinkles in the plan, and rebriefed these details so that every Marine understood them. The leaders described the route to the target, in this case one of Baghdad's main thoroughfares, the infamous bomb-studded "Route Irish." Briefers indicated the various checkpoints along the route and the points in the neighborhood where the force would split up, drop off the assaulters, and finally rendezvous for extraction.

The two key elements on this and every other mission were surprise and a good breach, as the assault force needed to get into the target house before the occupants could react. "Once we're inside the target and we've got a good flow of people in it," explained Master Sergeant Terry M. Wyrick, "we're going to win that fight. . . . That's just the nature of close-quarters battle."[13] Events on this target and every other would prove him right.

The task unit had the deck stacked in its favor: the Marines had the initiative and they had chosen the time, the place, and the form of the attack. Even so, tensions ran high since on this, their first target, they would face not an instructor with simunitions or obliging role-players, but a thinking, breathing, armed adversary with a will of his own. Nine months of hard work were going to be put to the ultimate test.

The assault on Objective Racket launched at 0100 on 4 May, when the convoy of armored hunekers containing Task Unit Raider rolled out of the gate at Camp Myler. The vehicles were blacked out, and the Marines were driving fast on night-vision goggles. Devices mounted in the vehicles combined global positioning system technology and imagery and provided real-time aids in navigating the Baghdad roadways. Prior coordination with adjacent units allowed them to bypass roadblocks and other obstacles. Their speed provided a measure of protection against ambush; sophisticated electronic counter-measures protected them from radio-detonated roadside bombs. According to Master Sergeant Keith E. Oakes, the unit was "a traveling fight waiting to happen."[14] High above and in radio contact with the Marines were an AC-130 and two HH-60s, providing over-watch on the route ahead and keeping tabs on the status of the target area.

After a quick stop at Baghdad International Airport, the convoy continued on and eight minutes later reached the set point. There they split, with one section going to the target's residence and the other to his shop, five blocks away. Reconnaissance Teams 2 and 3, under Master Sergeants Joseph L. Morrison and Charles H. Padilla, advanced to the residence. Teams 1 and 6, under Master Sergeant Wyrick and Gunnery Sergeant Sidney J. Voss, moved to the workshop. Teams 4 and 5 provided drivers and the gunners for the vehicles, augmented by Marines from the support sections. Two Marines from the fires element, Captain Daniel B. Sheehan III and Sergeant David D. Marnell, got on top of a nearby structure to get a better view of the whole area and through the aircraft kept an eye on any movement that might signal the force had been compromised. Master Sergeant Hays B. Harrington and his radio reconnaissance Marines kept their ears on the target and scanned the spectrum for enemy traffic.

The Marines had brought the source with them on the operation, the man rolled up by Gunnery Sergeant Dailey's team barely two days previous. When the source positively identified the residence of the target, the breaching team went to work. Marines in Team 3 placed ladders against the wall surrounding the house and were scrambling over it when the Navy explosive ordnance disposal technician attached to them saw a figure in a first-floor window. The technician sprinted forward, seized the man through the metal grate over the opening, and pinned him to the bars to prevent him from sounding an alarm or grabbing a weapon. Working quickly, Padilla's assistant team leader, Staff Sergeant Chad D. Baker, placed his explosive charge on the door, and seconds later detonated it, blowing the door in. Five blocks away, a Marine from Team 1 used a shotgun to break the lock on the doors of the shop. The time was 0129.[15]

Once inside the house, the assaulters flooded the interior as they had practiced many times before. Master Sergeant Padilla described the sensations of time and motion: "When you get off the vehicle, you know exactly where you're going. . . . Everything is moving, sometimes you think you're making a lot of noise, but you're not. . . . You start off nice and easy, like you've been rehearsing. At the breach point, you slow down a little bit—climbing over the wall to get to the breach point, you slow down—then once the breach goes, the fastest man in the house wins."[16]

Inside the residence, the stunned occupants surrendered without a fight. The Marines took one man outside, where the source for the operation identified him as the target. However, a woman told them that the target was actually next door. The helicopter circling overhead alerted the Marines that a man had jumped from the residence's rooftop to the adjoining structure.[17] Morrison's Team 2 quickly breached and entered that house, where they seized another man, who was waiting for them with his hands in the air. He was taken out and positively identified as the target of Objective Racket; the first man was then identified as his brother-in-law and was subsequently released.[18]

Marines from the intelligence element, assisted by the assaulters, searched the house on sensitive site exploitation and took away several items, having been previously briefed on what to seek. The searches at the residence and the shop were finished by 0157. By 0206, the raid force was accounted for and headed back to base, and by 0321, Task Unit Raider was inside the wire at Camp Myler, where the Marines turned over the detainee and the intelligence materials.[19]

"Pleased to finally have a successfully completed mission under our belt," read commander's comments in the 2 May daily situation report on Objective Rachel. "Although not a dramatic operation itself, it marks a milestone for the USMC/SOCom relationship and will hopefully lead to destruction of a cell that has targeted Iraqis assisting the coalition."[20] After the follow-on hit, the daily report from 6 May continued the thread: "Successful execution of Racket was the fruition of many months of hard work by every member of the Detachment. More pointedly, it was the culmination of the intelligence cycle started with Objective Rachel, which produced the actionable intelligence for this follow-on operation."[21]

Rachel and Racket were indeed successes for Detachment One, with the second raid launched less than 48 hours after the first operation ended. The operations proved that the unit could take a scrap of information and use it to develop a high-value target, then fix it, strike it, and exploit it. Major Kozeniesky and his staff worked through formal and informal command relationships, operating as easily with other government agencies as they did with conventional units. The quiet capture of "Rachel" affirmed to their special operations peers that individual Marines had the experience and tactical savvy to operate independently and think on their feet. The subsequent direct action hit validated Task Unit Raider's training and modus operandi. If these two targets lacked the difficulty that would characterize later missions, they made up for it in scope for failure, which, had it occurred, would have set the whole task group back and jeopardized its ability to operate. The Marines of Detachment One, and Commander Wilson as well, had every reason to be pleased with the outcome.

Major Kozeniesky's comments in the 6 May report concluded the Rachel/Racket discussion: "While [Rachel] and last night's evolutions [Racket] were noteworthy events in the history of the detachment and the Marine Corps, we look forward to the time when it is all considered 'ops normal' for the Raiders."[22]

Chapter 5

"Ops Normal"

The Hunt for "X"

Within days of the Rachel/Racket operations, Task Unit Raider launched a series of actions against a significantly more serious target. "X" was an insurgent facilitator who had come to the coalition's attention after one of his associates was captured in March. He was a figure of importance in the insurgency, on a much higher level than Rachel or Racket. Originally targeted as Objective Raccoon, "X" was mentioned under that code name as early as 1 May, while the Rachel operation was still in the planning stages, and he and his organization were a constant topic in operational documents for the next several weeks.

"X" was a canny operator. From his ability to evade surveillance and elude capture, the intelligence section concluded that he had had some military or intelligence training. A previous task group had targeted him several times and each time had come up frustratingly short. Because of the pressure being put on him, "X" had assumed a low profile but had not ceased his anti-Coalition operations. The one consistent problem in the raids launched against "X" was the inability to positively identify him. This fact, plus the difficulty in establishing a trigger for his presence at a given location, meant that actually capturing or killing him in a single operation was an elusive goal. Commander William W. Wilson, Det One's task group commander, and Major Craig S. Kozeniesky, commander of Task Unit Raider, reasoned that striking at "X" and his associates in a series of raids would produce a disruption in his operational capabilities, force him on the defensive, and as the targeting cycle quickened, eventually result in his capture.

Operations against "X" began with close coordination between the task group and the various cells in other government agencies, where Major M. Gerald Carter and Captain Christopher B. Batts were frequent visitors, and where Gunnery Sergeant William M. Johnston was embedded.* Those agencies had sources close to the "X" organization, whose information was good but not complete enough to tell the whole tale. Operatives were able to track the movements of a van that drove between several sites of interest to those targeting "X" and his people. Det One intelligence analysts matched the times and locations of the van's movement with the information being fed to them by the source and were able to zero in on the residence of a subsidiary figure and associate of "X," located on the northeast edge of Baghdad. The operation was named Red Bull.

During the first two weeks of May while the Marines of Task Unit Raider prepared for the hit, the other agencies were working through their sources to lure "X" to the associate's residence on the night of 11–12 May. Late on the evening of 11 May, as the raid force waited by the vehicles staged for the convoy, the task group and task unit staffs were working to establish the trigger for the raid with the case officer assigned to them, who was in contact with a source placed to monitor the associate's house. Moments after the source gave the signal that the person suspected to be "X" was onsite, the convoy launched.

The basic template for Red Bull resembled the template for Racket, except there was one target site instead of two. In the five days since that first operation, Task Unit Raider had absorbed lessons learned and refined its procedures. The size and strength of the raid force was much the same; one particular difference was that Chief Hospital Corpsman Eric D. Sine and Major M. Wade Priddy were to be aloft in a helicopter to provide medical support in case of a casualty evacuation as well as general airborne overwatch. The U.S. Army's 1st Squadron, 5th Cavalry, provided the quick reaction force.

The movement to the target area was, in the words of the after action report, "uneventful," except for a quick maneuver to block traffic by the second vehicle, carrying Master Sergeant Charles H. Padilla's Team 3. Actions on the objective also proceeded smoothly. The Marines detained three men and took away some significant items after sensitive site exploitation: parts and batteries—all improvised bomb components. One of the men was subsequently identified as the owner of the house, the associate also targeted in the raid.

---

* Johnston, who accompanied GySgt Dailey on the Rachel operation, was the face of the task group to those agencies. An Illinois native who joined the Marines in 1990, he was the perfect choice to be the liaison as he had served with another government agency's office of military affairs during a tour at Headquarters Marine Corps. Johnston intvw, (Marine Corps Historical Center, Quantico, VA.

The one thing missing from the target site was "X" himself, as he again demonstrated his ability to evade capture. During the after action review, the Marines determined that a short gap occurred in communications with the source, coinciding with a brief time in which the source also lost visual contact with the target site. In that small window of opportunity, the wily "X"—whether or not he knew what was afoot—slipped out and disappeared into the Baghdad night.

The raid was a success on other levels. The associate of "X" turned out to be a known bomb maker who had been targeted by coalition forces several times before, and who was reportedly schooled in remote-control bomb-making by "X." The haul of intelligence materials, notably information gathered through onsite tactical interrogations by Staff Sergeant Scott J. Beretz of the counterintelligence section, gave the intelligence Marines a rich pile of raw material to feed back into the targeting cycle. But the prize was still "X," who remained at large. Over the next four weeks, Major Carter drove his Marines to use every trick and technique at their disposal to target any place or person known or suspected to be associated with him.

After the execution of Red Bull, "X" struck back. Another source close to the investigation was murdered, as was his young daughter. These acts lent a more personal, urgent motive to the hunt, and they were proof that the task group was getting closer to its most-wanted man. Major Carter's Marines worked every angle they could devise in order to track the man and pin him down. By the third week of May, they decided to hit the next target, code named Objective Raccoon, which the Marines' growing files indicated was "X's" residence. If he was not there, they expected that several of his family and associates would be there and that the action would further penetrate his comfort zone and disrupt his activities. Objective Raccoon consisted of three target sites; the Marines planned to hit the first building, break contact while a security element searched the place, then hit the next two simultaneously. The target sites were located south of Baghdad in a semi-rural area. The three buildings were a few hundred meters apart.

Just before midnight on 21 May, Task Unit Raider descended on Objective Raccoon. The assault force conducted a hard hit on the first site after being informed by the covering aircraft during the approach that there were figures moving outside the buildings. The Marines found several people onsite and detained one male. While the security element was combing the residence and grounds, the assault force remounted its vehicles and sped off to hit the next two sites, where the entry and containment teams took another six men into custody, including one who provided the only drama of the night by trying to escape on foot. The aircraft circling overhead vectored Master Sergeant Padilla's Marines on a 20-minute foot chase, which ended with the man's capture. Items of interest seized in the raid included suspected bomb-making material as well as a van observed at several locations monitored during the surveillance on "X." Without further incident, the entire raid force re-embarked and sped back to Camp Myler where, after dropping the detainees at the task force headquarters, they arrived at 0114.

Again, "X" had eluded the Marines. However, the exploitation of the site and the interrogations conducted by Staff Sergeant Beretz, Captain Batts, and the task group's interpreters uncovered information that fully justified the decision to hit the insurgent chief's suspected locations. A few of the men taken off the Raccoon sites were related to "X." All would eventually reveal much useful information, but even if they had remained silent, their faces gave away the prize: a strong family resemblance. Major Carter and his Marines now had a good idea of what their man looked like. As Major Kozeniesky later reported, "At a minimum, we believe that we have significantly disrupted his operations by pursuing him at several of his favorite spots."[1]

Major Kozeniesky's assessment proved true. One of their government agency sources fled with his family to Jordan, obviously trying to avoid the fate suffered by the first source, murdered following the Red Bull operation. Even with the loss of two sources (and a temporary interruption of direct action missions), by early June, the task group and the other agencies had collected enough solid intelligence to target "X" again, this time at another semi-rural location south of Camp Myler.

On 8 June, Task Unit Raider attacked Objective Razor, looking again for "X." During the approach, a vehicle bogged down on a road by a canal, only 400 meters from the set point, delaying the assault by 15 tense minutes. Given those conditions, Major Kozeniesky made the decision to conduct a "soft" hit, by foot instead of by vehicle. The Marines isolated and breached the first of three structures, and while a team searched that location, the rest of the force assaulted the other two buildings. Fourteen men were present at the site, but 12 were quickly released. One of the remaining two matched the description of "X." Both were taken back to Camp Myler by the raid force, which was back in the wire by 0423.

Over the next several days, the man matching the description of "X" sparred with his interrogators, steadfastly maintaining that he was not who they said he was and adamant that the Americans had wrongly detained him. Despite his well-crafted denials, Major Carter and Captain Batts were sure they had their man, and they grilled him relentlessly. Their confidence grew when relatives identified him from a photograph taken after his capture.

Finally, the man admitted that he was "X," but he maintained that he had done nothing wrong, was involved in no illegal activities, and was only a peaceful man trying to survive the war. The intelligence Marines knew otherwise, and his continued evasions and denials got nowhere with them. Their problem was that they needed him to admit to his involvement in a string of atrocities in order to make sure that they had a solid case against him. But they could only go so far in their interrogations, due to the Abu Ghraib scandal, in applying anything that even hinted at coercive methods. There was also a limit on the length of time they could hold him before they had to let him go or pass him to another facility. They suspected that "X" knew all of this and was banking on his ability to outlast his interrogators.

His smug confidence proved his undoing. Major Carter floated a bold proposal to Commander Wilson and Major Kozeniesky. If "X" would not talk to Americans, how long would his defiant act play in Kurdistan? Carter wanted to take him north and put him in front of a few Kurdish interrogators, reasoning that the shock and uncertainty of the new circumstances would crack his resistance. Wilson and Kozeniesky got approval from their superiors and gave assurances that the matter would be handled carefully. Carter and a small escort flex-cuffed him, threw a hood over his head, and bundled him onto an aircraft waiting to take them to Kirkuk. When "X" was put in a chair and the hood removed, he saw only three Kurdish security service officers staring at him across a table. (What he did not know was that Major Carter was standing behind him with other government agency representatives, just to make sure that things did not get out of hand.) Choosing discretion over valor, he started talking.

The hunt for the target known as "X" was a case study in the capabilities that Detachment One brought to SOCom, particularly the ability of the intelligence element to track and identify a previously unidentified individual through the fusion of disparate bits of information and incisive analytical skill. It was, to use a law enforcement analogy, excellent detective work.* The interrogations by Captain Batts and Staff Sergeant Beretz illustrated the central role of counterintelligence Marines in the targeting cycle. Sharp intelligence work and nimble staff action were backed up by rapid and ruthless execution on the target sites. To borrow one of the central points of Marine Corps doctrine, Det One got deep inside the target's decision cycle and acted on him faster than he could act on them.

On any given day in late May and early June 2004, Task Unit Raider was operating on several lines at once. Direct action operations were launched on 11, 18, 20, 21, and 26 May and 8 June, three of them "X" missions and three others unrelated but no less important. On 18 May, for example, the unit was involved in two operations in the planning stages, the execution of one operation "currently underway," a major planning session with 2d Battalion, 5th Special Forces Group concerning the period leading up to the 30 June 2004 transfer of sovereignty, personnel augmentation to the task group, and the recovery of other personnel from a safe house in Baghdad. The hoped-for "ops normal" was becoming a relative term.

Hunting Murderers

The insurgent "X" was the biggest single catch in May-June 2004, but he was not the only fish in the sea. In addition to that series of raids, Task Unit Raider addressed three other targets and planned for several more. All were aimed at higher-level individuals in the Baghdad terrorist networks that were trying to prevent the emergence of an interim Iraqi government. On 18 May, Task Unit Raider executed its third direct action mission, Objective Rambler. The mission was to capture or kill an individual responsible for facilitating anti-Coalition forces by coordinating the funding, training, and movement of foreign terrorists. Rambler was a short-fuse operation and was not even put into the detailed planning stages until 17 May, although it was part of a general set that had been under discussion for a few days.[2] It was based on intelligence gained from 2d Battalion, 5th Special Forces Group, and its subordinate units. The ability of the special forces teams to gather information quietly and effectively was substantial. Major Kozeniesky called them "probably the best collectors of information in the country."[3]

The target site for Objective Rambler was the individual's residence, with a possible secondary site at

---

* Not only good detective work, but good police work as well. MSgt Joe Morrison, among others, noted that Task Unit Raider's direct action missions were much like "SWAT teams serving high-risk warrants."

his farm just a mile north of his residence. The two sites were near the sharp bend in the Tigris River that defines Baghdad's southeastern side. Photographs of the man and two of his associates showed a group of portly, established, middle-aged men. Appearances belied realities, as intelligence indicated that these three were well placed in the networks that moved foreign fighters into and around Iraq.

In the early hours of 18 May, Task Unit Raider, augmented by special forces operators and their sources, assaulted the residence of the primary individual targeted in Objective Rambler. While Teams 2 and 6 isolated and contained the area, Team 3 made a foot approach to the target with the sources in tow. After scaling the wall—a standard feature of nearly every Iraqi house—they encountered a guard. Fortunately for all concerned, including the guard himself, he was "extremely compliant" and was quickly put under control. The assault force backed up a humvee and attached a chain to the metal gate blocking the driveway. The humvee ripped the gate off its hinges and the assaulters breached the door and flooded the house. The subsequent sensitive site exploitation produced a pile of damning evidence, some of it stashed in hidden compartments. The team collected hundreds of pounds of documents, including approximately 50 passports and a "large quantity of currency from a variety of countries." The Marines apprehended the high-value target, "briefcase in hand," as he attempted to escape out the back door. In addition to the tangible results, Major Kozeniesky and his staff assessed one of the most important outcomes of the operation as the close cooperation with the special forces unit and its teams.[4]

Two days after Rambler and again in conjunction with a special forces operational detachment, Task Unit Raider launched Objective Revenge, appropriately named as it targeted three Iraqis suspected of having participated in the brutal murder of American telecommunications worker Nicholas E. Berg. "This is one we were pretty amp'ed to do," said Master Sergeant Terry M. Wyrick, explaining that the brutal murder gave the mission an additional, personal importance for every Marine. On Objective Rambler, intelligence had predicted that the occupants of the target house would opt for flight when the assault began. On Objective Revenge, Task Unit Raider expected a fight.

The Special Forces soldiers provided "exceptional atmospherics and positive target building identification, to include a very clear hand-held image of the building frontage," according to the operational summary.[5] One of the specifics that the planners learned from the intelligence they gleaned through other government agencies was that these suspects had been raided by coalition forces before and had used the roof as an avenue of escape. Another was that the upper floors were occupied and likely would be defended. One vital detail that the planners also observed on the photographs supplied by the Special Forces was that a fence instead of a wall surrounded the house. With all of that taken into account, Major Kozeniesky directed that the assault force attack with the maximum possible shock and violence and ensure that the second floor and roof were secured at the same time as the ground floor was being assaulted.

This raid had had none of the stealthy finesse of Rambler. It was, in Master Sergeant Wyrick's words, "fairly dynamic." The hunekers carrying the assault teams went straight at the house. As Wyrick described it, "Picture three vehicles going over the fence at the same time, three teams unmanning the vehicles, and [two teams] moving to the breach point as one team is throwing flash-bangs and climbing up a ladder to jump up on a ledge."[6] When Wyrick's team began scaling the ladder, they found that part of the structure prevented their vehicle from getting close enough so that the top of the ladder could touch the house. Beyond the end of the ladder was four feet of pitch-black nothing. Without hesitation, Staff Sergeant Alex N. Conrad hurled himself in full gear from the top rung of the ladder to the balcony across and slightly above him while his fellow Marines tossed flash-bangs in second-floor windows to keep the occupants from shooting at him. Four men, including the primary target and both secondary targets, were detained.[7] The expected fight did not materialize because the Marines of the assault force achieved maximum shock and surprise and allowed the occupants no time to react.

On 26 May, Task Unit Raider initiated a direct action raid on Objective Ricochet, the target of which was a former Iraqi intelligence officer believed to be a significant figure in a ring of former regime officials in Baghdad. This operation was the third of the co-ordinated series of raids undertaken with 2d Battalion, 5th Special Forces Group, during the period leading up to the 30 June transfer of sovereignty and was also based on intelligence gathered by the unit. The Marines knew that the man they were after on Ricochet was a hard target and would probably put up a fight if given even the slightest chance.

On the raid against Ricochet, Master Sergeant Wyrick's Team 1 had the breach with Staff Sergeant Andrew T. Kingdon as the lead breacher. After scaling the wall around the target house, the team approached the entrance and took cover behind a wall partially masking the doorway. Kingdon crept around the corner and squared up to the door. He quickly and quietly placed his charge on the lock side of the big, heavy wooden door, then withdrew behind the wall to protect himself from the blast. While doing so, he thought he heard part of the charge come off the door, so he went back to check it, and seeing the charge still in place, drew back again. He announced over his radio, "breaching, breaching, breaching" and detonated the charge.

The subsequent blast knocked Kingdon off his feet, shattered his weapons and gear, and momentarily stunned the Marines right behind him. Something had gone wrong with the breach, and although he did not know what it was, he definitely knew he was injured. While he was down on the ground, stunned and wounded, Hospital Corpsman First Class Robert T. Bryan began to work on him, and the rest of the assault force initiated the backup breaching procedures. Master Sergeant Wyrick looked at the door and the charge and thought at first that it had only partially detonated, or "low-ordered." He called for the secondary breach, which used sledgehammers and a wrecking tool appropriately called a "hooligan." When that approach failed, Wyrick called for a third method, another explosive charge, which got the door open. The alternate breaching took only a few extra seconds, but now the all-important elements of shock and surprise were gone.[8]

Leaping over the prostrate Staff Sergeant Kingdon or dashing around him, the assaulters burst into the house and began to flood the interior. Just inside the entry was a room with an open doorway. Master Sergeant Wyrick moved down the hallway, past the doorway, and button-hooked back to clear the inside of the room, flashing the bright white light attached to his M4 as he passed to assess the situation. He saw nothing, but concealed in the shadows of the room was the target himself, awake, alert, and armed. Shots rang out from inside the room, and one of the assaulters shouted, "He's shooting through the door!" Wyrick threw in a flash-bang and entered. Right behind him was Staff Sergeant Glen S. Cederholm, who saw the armed Iraqi in the corner positioned to shoot Wyrick and killed him with precise fire from his M4 carbine.[9]

Outside the house, casualty evacuation procedures were in motion. Further examination revealed what had happened to Staff Sergeant Kingdon. The explosive leads with the blasting caps and booster charge had come loose from the main charge and were coiled up under his M4 carbine, which hung down on the right side of his chest. When he initiated the detonation, the blasting caps and booster charge exploded and also set off a sympathetic detonation of a flash-bang. The main charges still attached to the door were unprimed and therefore untouched, leading Wyrick to think that they only partially functioned. Kingdon's body armor shielded most of his torso, but his unprotected right arm took the full blast.

Lying there while the assault progressed, he heard Wyrick call for the alternate breach, then saw the assault teams flood past him into the house. "Doc" Bryan placed a tourniquet on his arm and that, according to Kingdon, hurt worse than the blast itself. He heard the gunshots from the house, then heard Master Sergeant Keith E. Oakes call for a body bag. Not knowing that the body bag was for the now-dead target of the raid, he wondered who it was for.[10] There was also another Marine casualty. Hospital Corpsman First Class Michael D. Tyrell was hit in the leg with one round from the burst fired by the target of the raid. Despite the wound, Tyrell continued with the mission of clearing the house and even went outside to assist in treating and evacuating Kingdon. When he went back into the house to help with the search, Major Kozeniesky ordered him to stop and be treated.[11]

While the house was being searched, three or four Marines took Kingdon to the designated casualty evacuation vehicle to get him to the helicopter. Master Sergeant Hays B. Harrington, the radio reconnaissance leader, jumped into the driver's seat and sped off to the primary landing zone. He found it unusable, fouled by wires, and headed for the secondary zone. The helicopter pilots, seeing another patch of clear ground that looked better than the secondary zone, vectored Harrington there instead. The helicopter flew Kingdon to the Army's 31st Corps Support Hospital in Baghdad, where he was immediately taken into surgery.*

---

* Kingdon was sent from Baghdad to Landstuhl, Germany, from there to Naval Hospital in Bethesda, Maryland, and eventually back to Camp Pendleton. On 24 March 2005 he recounted the details of the incident to the author. When the blast happened he thought he had blown his arm off. Two things immediately worried him. Displaying admirable cool headedness and a keen sense of priorities, he assessed his own condition: "I had Doc Bryan check to see that my nuts were okay"—they were—"and then I took my own pulse just to make sure that I had one." The wry humor belied what were very serious, life-threatening injuries: "a nearly severed arm, a broken artery, a four inch chest compromise, and burns to the chest and groin area." HM1 Bryan would receive an award for his speed and skill in treating him. At the time of his interview, Kingdon had been promoted to gunnery sergeant, was back on full duty with Det One, and his arm was working at "98 percent."

Photo courtesy of Det One

GySgt James A. Crawford of Det One's radio reconnaissance section puts his .45-caliber pistol through its paces at Range 130 during Weapons and Tactics Package I. The skills that Crawford and others learned there— marksmanship, mindset, and gun-handling—came into play later in Iraq.

Despite the problems during the breach and the injuries to two men, the raid achieved its objective. The target was killed and several items were taken during sensitive site exploitation. The intensive training that the detachment had gone through for a year paid off. "Prosecution of the target continued fluidly and simultaneously while the casualty was treated and evacuated," wrote Major Kozeniesky. Objective Ricochet was the only direct action operation in which a Det One Marine was wounded, and moreover, the only raid in which any shots were fired during the actual assault. Shortly after Ricochet, the entire task group received an order that stopped all direct action raids.

Supporting Task Unit North

While Task Unit Raider operated in Baghdad, the Det One Marines with the outlying task units were busy as well.

Gunnery Sergeant James A. Crawford, one of the two radio reconnaissance team leaders in the Det One intelligence element, arrived in Baghdad on the first planeload. The quiet Georgian and former infantryman spent his first week sorting out the situation on the ground, then was instructed to take his team and one counterintelligence Marine to support Task Unit North. Switching out one member of his team for another—he had two Arabic linguists and needed to leave one at Camp Myler—they departed on 15 April 2004.

Crawford's team consisted of Sergeant William S. Benedict, Sergeant Daryl J. Anderson, and Staff Sergeant William B. Parker. Parker had joined the Marine Corps later in life than most of his colleagues; when the detachment deployed to Iraq, he was in his late thirties but was still a relatively junior Marine. A man of many talents, he had formal instruction in Arabic and would use that skill to good effect.* Also part of the team was a bespectacled former mortarman from the counterintelligence section, Staff Sergeant Daniel L. Williams. Although Williams looked like a misplaced computer programmer, he was in fact a shrewd and experienced HUMINT operative who had honed his skills in the Balkans and Afghanistan. Just prior to deployment, Williams went to a six-week Arabic immersion course and came away with some basic skills, although nothing like he would need to operate without a translator. Despite being the sole Marine HUMINT collector in the city where they deployed, his work would have an immediate impact on the insurgent cells there.

The SEALs made the Marines feel welcome. "They treated us like we were somebody," said Crawford, having half-expected the opposite.[12] They allotted the Marines good living and working spaces and more importantly, allowed them the operational freedom to use both their technical skills and their gunfighting abilities. Williams was stunned at the reception: "We landed on the airstrip, and they [the SEALs] had two trucks full of guys who unloaded all of our gear for us, stacked it up, had coffee and snacks waiting, then drove us over to our trailers. They gave us everything we could have asked for or wanted."[13] The next day, Crawford and Williams gave a short capabilities brief, the gist of which was: "we're here to build targets for you to hit, and this is how we're going to do it." One SEAL expressed reservations that they could deliver. Crawford and Williams made it a point to make sure that they over-delivered.

Within a week after arrival, Task Unit North exe-

---
* He had been, among other things, a garbage man. He took that job in order to satisfy his own curiosity; it would not be incorrect to say that the same impulse led him to the Marine Corps.

cuted its first hit. Staff Sergeant Williams worked closely with the other intelligence cells in the city and with the task group in Baghdad, and based on information derived from them, he produced actionable intelligence on a target. When the task unit drove out of the gate on the first mission, the Marines were fully integrated into the raid force. Staff Sergeant Parker, with his language skills, did most of the radio reconnaissance work; Gunnery Sergeant Crawford and Sergeants Anderson and Benedict were "average Joes," but Benedict manned a machine gun as well as an electronic jammer. The radio reconnaissance Marines also handled the items taken in sensitive site exploitation, especially phones and other electronics. Williams filled his role as the one-man HUMINT element, waiting to do tactical interrogations of detainees. The SEALs brought 14 detainees off the first target, and Williams interrogated them all, assisted by a Navy (and former Marine) linguist and Staff Sergeant Parker. The subsequent intelligence enabled them to roll up most of the local terrorist network, methodically, mission by mission, over the next several weeks. One of the first 14 detainees was the leader of a cell tied to Ansar al-Sunna, an al-Qaida affiliate.[14]

The work that Williams did so well had its downside. His operational cycle was "two days on and four hours off," a good indication of his dedication to duty but a reminder of why counterintelligence Marines are usually employed in pairs. Working with other agencies, running sources, going on missions, interrogating detainees, and reporting up the chain-of-command was a tall order for one man, even for a short duration.

Williams's most important duty was interrogations. Staff Sergeant Parker helped him, using his Arabic skills at times more to keep an eye on the translator than to translate.* The linguist had to say exactly what the interrogator said, mimicking his tone and emphasis. If the translator faltered, Parker knew enough Arabic to say, "You're not translating that right. I know what he [Williams] said, and I know what you said." He then would point out the discrepancies.[15]

Staff Sergeant Williams had his own detention facility to house detainees from Task Unit North's raids, and guards to run it. His operations coincided with the revelations of the Abu Ghraib scandal, and its effects were quickly felt. But the task unit had good procedures that both protected them and looked after their detainees. Each was medically checked when he came in and when he went out, both by the SEALs and by third parties. Some of the Iraqis who were guests of the task unit howled at the treatment in an effort to make trouble for the Americans. Williams weathered more than one investigation, but nobody could fault his procedures or adherence to the rules. The Abu Ghraib incident produced substantial changes in interrogations and detainee handling, not so much in the methods used—although some methods were curtailed—but after Abu Ghraib, interrogators had more people looking over their shoulders, which acted as a psychological constraint on them. Not being wedded to questionable methods, Williams and the other Det One interrogators relied on classic techniques to get the information they needed, and invariably they succeeded.[16]

Even though they were sometimes stymied by the language barrier, Gunnery Sergeant Crawford's radio reconnaissance Marines did a variety of collections, even in their off hours. On a few occasions, they could hear people talking about them as they drove out on missions. Setting aside the somewhat off-putting nature of this discovery, they saw an opportunity in it. One night they went out for the sole purpose of intercepting the traffic that seemed to give away their movements. Staff Sergeant Parker and his fellow Marines triangulated it and identified the source location. Fortunately, it turned out that the transmitters were not enemy forces, but local levies just practicing bad communications security. They were unwittingly tipping off anyone who was listening to the operations of the task unit. Crawford passed the word up his chain of command, and through delicate liaison with higher headquarters, those responsible were persuaded to cease and desist.*

In the month and a half on station, the Marines with Task Unit North went out on approximately 18 raids. Through their efforts, the task unit was able to identify, target, and disrupt the local insurgent structure and completely eliminate three of its cells. What stopped Task Unit North from getting the rest was not enemy action, but an abrupt change in the task group's mission.

Supporting Task Unit West

Det One supported Task Unit West in al-Anbar Province as well as in northern Iraq. Major Carter se-

---

* The interpreters, or "terps," that Williams and Parker were concerned with were not SEALs, but contractors, native speakers whose loyalties were sometimes in doubt. Parker referred to dealing with the interpreters as "terp wrangling."

* MSgt Harrington and his Marines made a similar discovery in Baghdad. Some American personnel at Baghdad International Airport were heard freely discussing Task Unit Raider's movements over unsecured nets when the raid force exited the base. The practice was immediately and firmly corrected.

lected Master Sergeant Bret A. Hayes, his intelligence chief, to go out to al-Anbar Province with Gunnery Sergeant Matthew A. Ulmer, the counterintelligence chief. Because the task unit's base was not far from the base of the 1st Marine Division's Regimental Combat Team Seven, the reasoning behind sending only two Marines (albeit very senior ones) was that they could leverage the capabilities in the intelligence sections of the Marine units. Hayes knew the 7th Marines intelligence officer and intelligence chief very well; Ulmer likewise knew the counterintelligence Marines.

The two Marines received a less enthusiastic welcome than their northern counterparts but were quickly rolled into Task Unit West operations. Master Sergeant Hayes noted that the SEALs, in his experience, tended to treat support personnel as outsiders, but they accepted the Marines as "operators." In one instance, Hayes asked the task unit commander for permission to detail a Navy intelligence specialist to fly in a helicopter to take photographs of a site of interest near Haditha Dam. The answer he got was that the sailor was not a SEAL and therefore was unsuitable for the task. Hayes went to 7th Marines' intelligence section and borrowed a lance corporal, who went up and got the images that Hayes needed.[17]

In contrast to tight urban areas like Baghdad, Task Unit West had a huge operating area, all of western Anbar province, where population centers were separated by vast amounts of nothing. The differences in distances were evident as Task Unit West executed its first mission the night after the Marines arrived, an operation near Haditha Dam on the Euphrates River. To illustrate the distances involved, Task Unit Raider's first operation involved an approach lasting no more than a few minutes; the convoy for Task Unit West's first mission took an hour and 40 minutes to arrive on target. The mission was a success, and the SEALs brought the man they were seeking back to their compound. The post-operation actions were similar to those in Baghdad, except out west, they lacked certain facilities. Gunnery Sergeant Ulmer interrogated the detainees at his small detention facility, but he had to hand them off to the 7th Marines after about 24 hours. As with Task Unit Raider and Task Unit North, there were Army Special Forces teams in this area. Both teams excelled at HUMINT and cooperated closely with the SEAL task unit.

After the first few weeks on station, Task Unit West leadership traveled to Ramadi to confer with the 1st Marine Division on operations in and around Fallujah. The division was planning a major sweep around the city. The task unit leadership made contact with the Marines' tactical fusion center (which had absorbed much of I Marine Expeditionary Force's intelligence section on top of its own assets) and with the local special forces team. The members of the task unit then moved down to Camp Fallujah, where they conferred further with the commanders of 1st Marines and 7th Marines and formed a plan. Task Unit West would provide sniper support but would also maintain an on-call direct action capability to seize high-value targets of opportunity. (Staff liaison with 1st Marines was helped by the fact that the regimental executive officer had once been Master Sergeant Hayes's company commander. Hayes and Ulmer were also glad to be able to spend some time at Camp Fallujah with Colonel Robert J. Coates.) When offensive operations in Fallujah ceased indefinitely, Task Unit West was turned to running counter-mortar and counter-rocket patrols in an area near the Marine base. Following that task, the task unit was released from duty in and around Camp Fallujah.[18]

After Fallujah, Task Unit West returned to its home compound, where it resumed operations. Some were directed at insurgents, targeting a three-pronged intersection south of Haditha where roadside bombs were all too common. Members of the unit also started planning a major operation in conjunction with the 7th Marines in which the SEALs of Task Unit West would assault a site to seize two high-value targets while the Marines would roll in with vehicles to cordon off the area. The task group in Baghdad supported the planning by filling Master Sergeant Hayes's extensive "laundry list" of intelligence requirements. Task Unit West continued to run operations throughout its very large area of operations, including more joint operations with the special forces. One mission rolled up a suspect who led them to actionable intelligence on bomb makers in Husaybah and al-Qaim, important towns and constant trouble spots right on the Syrian border.[19]

On 18 May, Master Sergeant Hayes went home to the United States, where his wife was giving birth. During the brief time he was gone, the nature of task group's deployment changed, and when he returned to Iraq, Task Unit West was in Baghdad. He and Gunnery Sergeant Ulmer were rolled back into general duties supporting the task group and Task Unit Raider. Almost two months into the deployment, Hayes was finally doing his job as Det One intelligence chief, and Ulmer was serving once again as counterintelligence chief.

Colonel Coates in Fallujah

On 23 April 2004, Colonel Coates departed Baghdad for Camp Fallujah. Due to the provisions of the memorandum of agreement between the Marine

Corps and Naval Special Warfare, he stepped aside but retained his command of the detachment. Rather than have him return to Camp Pendleton, the commanding general of Marine Forces Central Command sent him to I Marine Expeditionary Force (I MEF) as his liaison officer, where his experience in unconventional warfare could be best employed.

When Colonel Coates arrived at Camp Fallujah, the situation was in a tense stalemate. Marine units occupied a quarter of Fallujah but were held in their positions by orders from commands higher than I MEF. An agreement had been reached with the elders in the city—those who could be found and persuaded to negotiate—to turn in all heavy weapons and munitions, but no true cease-fire existed. Fire fights were common; one Marine company commander joked that the insurgents apparently interpreted the agreement to hand over their weapons and munitions as "giving them to us one round at a time."[20]

Lieutenant General James T. Conway, the I MEF commander, needed to solve the problem. The most effective course of action, a rapid and violent thrust to seize the rest of the city, was no longer available to him. At this point, on or about 21 April, a former Iraqi general appeared on the scene with an interesting plan. He said that in a matter of days, he could form and field an indigenous force to address the security of Fallujah. He would take orders from General Conway, and the Marines would pay and support the force. Taken on face value, this plan held great promise: an Iraqi solution to an Iraqi problem. Moreover, it was a Sunni-based solution and was supported by the emerging interim government. Once the plan was implemented, Marines could be withdrawn from the city and redeployed to the areas from which they had come, and they could begin to redevelop the operational themes of security, stability and reconstruction.

For better or for worse, the Fallujah Brigade, as it quickly began to be called, became the best choice on a very short list of options. It offered a solution to the prevailing operational dilemma, the imperative to keep the pressure on the insurgent groups in Fallujah while not engaging in direct offensive action. It promised a way to engage and shape the city and force the Iraqis to deal with their own problems. A success would be significant and would portend good things for other trouble spots in Iraq. The risk was that the whole scheme would fail.

Lieutenant General Conway selected Colonel Coates to be the point man with the Fallujah Brigade. He would deliver Conway's intentions and instructions and would pay the Iraqis as agreed. He would also seek to keep them focused on the task at hand, hold them to their agreements, and report back to the commanding general on their performance. Coates needed every scrap of his experience in unconventional operations to keep the organization in line and working toward the right goals, harkening back to his time as an advisor in El Salvador. Accompanied by an Arabic-speaking Marine officer, Captain Rodrick H. McHaty, and a small detail of Marines, he went to meet with his new charges on 30 April. The next day, Coates confirmed that the first battalion of the brigade, numbering approximately 300 men, had reported for duty, with several hundred more expected in a few days' time.*[21]

Throughout the late spring and summer of 2004, Colonel Coates and his team were in and out of the Fallujah Brigade's lines on a regular basis. Much of his work was simple communication, telling the Iraqis what they needed to do, reminding them what they said they were going to do, ensuring that supplies were being distributed, and then either delivering or withholding payments as the occasion warranted. This was certainly a laborious process. The enemy's agile information machine had spun the Americans' withdrawal from the city as a defeat. One story attributed it in part to divine intervention in the form of a horde of "heavenly camel spiders" descending upon the invaders and forcing them out. The Fallujah Brigade soldiers or *jundi* gleefully accepted this peculiar assessment as an article of faith, even though they were ostensibly on the coalition's side. Coates's tasks included trying to disabuse them of strange notions and to get them operating on concrete lines. As he told the credulous jundi, "There are no spider bites," and he rolled up his sleeves to prove it to them.

Once the odd new unit was in place and assigned its own sector, a curious thing happened: the fighting stopped. There was much debate within the Marine headquarters over whether this development was a product of the Fallujah Brigade asserting itself over the insurgents or allying itself with them. It was an open secret that many of today's *jundi* were probably yesterday's (and possibly tomorrow's) insurgents, but given the uncertain nature of unconventional warfare, to say nothing of the importance of the mission, the Marine leadership was willing to give the initiative an opportunity to stand or fall on its own merits.

---

* The MEF G-3, Col Larry K. Brown, remarked somewhat harshly, but not without justification, in an interview with the author that when the first contingent of the Fallujah Brigade fell into formation as promised, it was the first time he had seen an Iraqi "do anything he'd promised, on time."

More importantly, perhaps, than simply ending the fighting was the intelligence the Marines gained from the Fallujah Brigade on the situation inside the city. Colonel John C. Coleman, the MEF chief of staff, noted that "we gained a window into the insurgency that we would otherwise have spent months wrestling to understand."[22] It turned out that the insurgency inside the city was no monolith; it had fault lines and fractures. At the same time that the Marines were working hard to direct the Fallujah Brigade, they were also profiting from a new vantage point, gathering intelligence and honing tactics, techniques, and procedures.

Colonel Coates took a long-term view of the Fallujah Brigade and was under no illusions about instant operational miracles. Counterinsurgency operations are measured in years, not weeks or months. If the venture succeeded, then so much the better in his opinion, but he knew from his daily contact that it was a shaky proposition. He wanted to make sure that the Marines extracted the most value they could out of the Iraqi unit, so that if the time came again when coalition forces had to mount a final operation to take the city, there would be no question that the command had fought smart as well as hard, and had exhausted all means to crack this very hard nut.[23]

Some of the attractive aspects to the brigade were also its weak points, namely that it was full of locals who identified with the old Iraqi military. After its initial successes, the Fallujah Brigade's inherent contradictions began to tell, and its effectiveness declined as the summer of 2004 progressed. Contact between insurgents, Fallujah Brigade units, and American forces increased, and indirect fire on Marine bases once again became a daily event. The hearts and minds of the brigade's leadership were in the right place, but they could not address the hard-core elements and fully assert themselves over the city. As the Iraq unit became less of an asset and more of a liability, Colonel Coates lent his expertise to unpublicized operations aimed at exploiting divisions in the insurgency and then assisted another Iraqi unit that could and did fight.

By the end of May 2004, Detachment One and its elements were deeply involved in a wide range of operations. The main body, Task Unit Raider, had found its operational niche and was operating in an increasingly efficient battle rhythm. A handful of Marines in the two outlying task units were providing critical intelligence support to their SEAL brethren. Colonel Coates was engaged in a momentous effort to direct an indigenous force to deal with the biggest problem in Iraq.

On 28 May, Commander Wilson received word that his mission was changing. He was ordered to shift focus from offensive operations to a defensive operation, protecting the four principal figures of the interim Iraqi government.

Chapter 6

Direct Action

Protecting the Iraqi Leaders

After he received the order on 28 May 2004 to cease direct action operations, Commander William W. Wilson pulled in all his forces, including Task Unit Raider, and reorganized them for the new protective mission, the personal security detail. Wilson's two priority information requirements shifted to a single overriding question: who was trying to kill the interim Iraqi government leaders? Every action that any member of the task group took from that point on was dedicated to keeping the Iraqi president, prime minister, and two vice presidents alive. The personal security detail became, in the words of Wilson and many others, "the most important mission in Iraq."[1]

Task Unit Raider's Marines were assigned to cover one of the two vice presidents, Rowsch Shaways, a Kurd. Captain Eric N. Thompson was assigned as the "agent in charge" of the detail, and as such, he was offered an interesting view of Kurdish politics as well as a look at the workings of the interim Iraqi government and the Coalition Provisional Authority. Thompson handled Shaways's schedule and itinerary and spent as much time in Irbil, Kurdistan, as he did in Baghdad. Det One Marines on Shaways's detail in Baghdad performed, in Thompson's words, "some very hairy missions."[2]

The Marines had not trained, as a unit, to do personal security work. Captain Thompson threw himself into educating and organizing his platoon, drawing from the SEALs' extensive knowledge and from the U.S. Department of State representatives who came out to assist them. A few of the Marines, including Gunnery Sergeant John A. Dailey, had some previous experience with personal security details. Dailey took it upon himself to read as much as he could on the tasks involved (because he thought it was something that Marines should know how to do), and he contacted one of his old platoon commanders, who had become a U.S. Secret Service agent, for advice. Dailey became the advance man for Vice President Shaways's detail, arriving first at all venues to check the physical security.[3] It was Dailey and the others from Task Unit Raider who did the "hairy missions," escorting Shaways in and out of Baghdad at a time when every terrorist and insurgent in the country wanted to kill him.

Just as quickly as the close protective mission came, it ended for Task Unit Raider. Within a week, Commander Wilson assessed the situation and decided he could cover his details and still reconstitute an offensive capability.* The resumption of the offensive supported the larger effort by giving Wilson the ability to hit first instead of simply standing by and waiting for an attack, trying to dodge it or worse yet, hoping just to withstand it. The SEAL task units stayed on the personal security detail, but the Marines were drawn out of it, and Task Unit Raider was again organized for direct action and other offensive missions. The Marines' role in the most important mission in Iraq would be to strike at the car-bomb makers and facilitators, since it was clear to Wilson that the vehicle-borne suicide bomb was the most dangerous weapon the insurgents possessed.[4]

Commander Wilson also had another force he could draw on: the Polish GROM was formed as a separate task unit, named Task Unit Thunder, and joined the Marines for direct action.** The GROM figured prominently in the Det One story, for in their members, the Marines saw kindred souls: big, aggressive, smart gunfighters, utterly reliable, and completely dedicated to the task at hand. To a man, the Marines were effusive in their praise of the Polish operators. Commander Wilson called them "the finest non-U.S. special operations force" of his experience. If the GROM had any limitation, it was only in certain command and control capabilities, specifically in fires, intelligence fusion, and liaison with conventional units. Wilson decided that he was going to set them up to succeed in independent operations, and in mid-June, he detailed Det One's Captain Stephen V. Fiscus and a small liaison cell of Marines and SEALs to embed with them.[5] In exchange for a handful of personnel, Wilson gained a completely new task unit, and the Raider/Thunder alliance proved to be a potent combination over subsequent weeks. Commander Wilson had girded his force for action.

---

* The terms of the 20 February 2003 memorandum of agreement with SOCom probably also played a significant part. The detachment was deployed to perform four missions, none of which was a personal security detail.
** *Grupa Reagowania Operacyjno Manewrowego*, which translates to Operational Mobile Reaction Group. The acronym GROM is the Polish word for thunder.

The SEAL task units formed the task group's shield around the Iraqi leaders, while Task Units Raider and Thunder formed the sword.

With the SEAL task units consolidating in Baghdad, individual personnel were also shifted. The intelligence Marines with what had been Task Unit West were brought back into the fold, while those with the former Task Unit North remained with the SEALs and moved into roles more directly related to protecting the Iraqi government officials. Most of the intelligence element remained in general support to the task group. Major Craig S. Kozeniesky shifted his duties to one job—command of Task Unit Raider.

One very important material result of the mission shift was that Task Unit Raider received several new, purpose-built M113 armored hunekers from the SEALs. This represented a substantial boost in their tactical capabilities, gave the Marines a deeper field of mobility assets, and covered the shortcomings of the assault vehicles they had built for themselves. That shift in assets caused some grumbling from the SEALs, but it made sense. If the Marines were to go out beyond the wire and hit targets, they needed the means to do so effectively.

After The Protective Detail

Task Unit Raider came off the brief period of protective duty by launching Objective Razor, the third in a series of raids targeting a notorious insurgent facilitator. Five days later, the Marines hit their next target, the leader of a large and active cell. Objective Radiate began a period of sustained direct action operations against cell leaders, bomb makers, and other major malefactors, leading up to the planned 30 June transfer of sovereignty to the new Iraqi government. The significance of these operations was clear: any threat to the emerging government needed to be dealt with quickly and decisively, not only to protect the principals, but to enforce their authority.

At 0230 on 13 June, the raid on Objective Radiate began. The operation netted several detainees, and while the Marine counterintelligence team sifted through them on site, one of them admitted he was the target; the others were released while he was taken back to task group headquarters. Several items were also taken that strongly suggested anti-Coalition activities, including "coffins draped with U.S. flags, Ansar Al Sunna videos, and a family photo with Saddam." The other curious aspect of the operation was substantial Iraqi police activity in the immediate vicinity. The Marines were wary of the police but did not interfere.[6]

On 18 June, the task unit executed a raid on Objective Raven. The target was a man suspected of being a car bomb maker. The information came once again from the always active source operations of 2d Battalion, 5th Special Forces Group. The target site was a farm not far outside Baghdad. The original plan for the mission was for Task Unit Raider, Task Unit Thunder, 1st Squadron, 5th U.S. Cavalry, and an Iraqi unit to strike several targets in sequence. Several individuals were targeted; Task Unit Raider's own target was a man who was suspected of regularly importing cars, which were then turned into suicide bombs at his farm and passed to cells around Baghdad. The intelligence on the targets came from a source who planned to attend a gathering of all the important figures targeted in the mission and provide the trigger for execution.[7] The detailed planning for Raven was upset when the source reported that the location for the meeting had been secured by a Coalition conventional unit conducting its own operations. The decision was made to execute the raid on the farm as planned, as the source expected that the targets would rendezvous there instead.

The Marines later reported that the approach to the target site was "uneventful." This was something of a misstatement, as a few things happened to enliven the proceedings. The convoy was navigating by global positioning system, but the source stated several times that the Marines had missed key turns. The convoy continued on its course, as the Marines had justifiable confidence in their equipment and their planning, and they assessed that "the source was obviously confused about exactly where he was." His confusion continued as, right after the convoy made its final turn into the target's street, he "belatedly indicated" that they had driven past the house. Having no more confidence in the man's sense of direction, the assault force headed for the target as they had planned.[8]

Moments before the assault began, a car left the target site and drove toward the convoy. When the car failed to obey warnings to stop, it was engaged first with a Marine's M4 and then with a .50-caliber machine gun, both bursts being directed across the front of the car rather than into it, in case it was rigged as a bomb. The driver of the car got out and "crawled down the street" until he was stopped by Marines as the assault was in progress.

From that moment, the raid proceeded without incident. Curiously, the door to the house was found open, so the assault force literally walked in instead of blowing the door in or breaking it down. While the house was being secured and searched, the assault teams moved a short way down the road to assault other buildings. The AC-130 and HH-60s reported several "squirters" escaping the house, who were promptly pursued and apprehended. Seventeen males were detained, so many that Major Kozeniesky decided that they would have to be airlifted out rather than taken back in the convoy. One of them was identified as the target of the raid. The operation yielded light weapons but no car bombs or bomb-making materials.* The raid force returned to Camp Myler without incident.⁹

Major Kozeniesky lauded the performance of the Marines on this operation, noting that the combination of a large target area, multiple structures, and vehicle threats prompted all hands to perform beyond even the normal high expectations. He logged the operation as another blow struck at the bomb makers and insurgent leaders threatening the Iraqi government. While accepting the reality of "less-than-perfect intelligence" on some of the targets, he noted: "The nature of the threat and the strategic significance of the turnover [transfer of sovereignty] dictate that we err on the side of action."¹⁰

Task Unit Raider continued to opt for action throughout June. At 0300 on 22 June, it executed its tenth direct-action raid, Objective Recoil. Second Battalion, 5th Special Forces Group, provided the high-quality intelligence sources that were becoming a regular feature of many of the task group's operations. What made Recoil exceptional was the timeline from notification to execution. Major Kozeniesky wrote that, while engaged in planning for Objective Relinquish, they were notified of the need to hit Recoil that night. "We began Recoil planning from a completely cold start around 2300, were on the objective a little over four hours later (0315), and were back inside friendly lines roughly a half hour after the first breach (0348)." This level of execution illustrated the high level of readiness maintained by the Marines and their ability to drop whatever they were doing and concentrate exclusively and effectively on a priority operation. The assault force hit the target's residence and place of business in rapid succession, detaining him and taking away items after a search of both places. In addition to praising the intelligence work by the special forces, Kozeniesky also singled out the naval pilots and crews of Helicopter Combat Support Squadron 4 (HCS-4), noting that they responded with admirable speed and efficiency to the short-notice call to arms.¹¹

Less than 24 hours after Recoil, the Marines executed a combined raid with the GROM on Objective Relinquish. This operation marked the first use of a source run completely by Det One counterintelligence Marines. The source was passed to them by other government agencies in Baghdad, where he had produced intelligence for task group targets in the past. Staff Sergeant Scott J. Beretz worked the source for two weeks to develop the intelligence on the target, which consisted of an individual or individuals strongly suspected to be producing car bombs for use against the Iraqi government. Descriptions and names were not known, but the source was reliable, and Major Kozeniesky's policy was to act on good intelligence rather than wait for perfect intelligence. The source indicated that the latest two vehicles, a van and a sport utility vehicle, had already been prepared as bombs and were almost ready for use. The two vehicles were at separate locations a few hundred meters apart. Task Unit Raider took one location, and the Task Unit Thunder, augmented for this mission by more counterintelligence and fires Marines, took the other.

The raid began with Task Unit Raider making a soft approach and a stealthy entrance to the target location. Inside the wall of the property, the Marines found three vehicles, one of them the van. The explosive ordnance disposal technicians swept the vehicles to make sure they were not loaded with explosives, and when they gave the signal that the vehicles were clear, the assault teams breached and entered the house. A short distance down the street, Task Unit Thunder did the same. Inside, the Marines found several people, including two military-age males who were detained. The Marines towed away the van and disabled the other two cars. After it was clear that the van was not a functional bomb at the moment, the only drama of the night occurred when Major Thomas P. Dolan, serving as forward air controller, saw a vehicle on a side street flash its lights three times. He asked the helicopters overhead to check it out. The pilots saw the car's lights flash three times again but reported no other visible activity. Dolan and the pilots thought that it could have been a prearranged signal by anti-Coalition forces, but it could just as well have been a remote entry device being used for its intended purpose. They took no further action.*

Based on the intelligence gathered from the site and from the two detainees, the raid on Objective Re-

---

* The intelligence debrief on the mission did note an unlikely combination of materials found on scene: "a picture of [Muqtada al] Sadr and *Maxim* magazines."

* In one of the bizarre side stories that always seemed to accompany these raids, the intelligence debrief noted that two men were seen outside a nearby building. "When the assaulters approached them the individuals asked in English, 'we go inside now?' The assaulter told them to go inside and they went."

Det One Sniper Rifles

.408-caliber Chey-Tac

.50-caliber M82 Barrett

7.62mm M40A3

7.62mm SR-25

Photos Courtesy of Det One

linquish was judged a success. The two men confessed to anti-Coalition involvement and provided actionable intelligence on local insurgent activities, which was quickly passed up the chain-of-command for other units to execute. Tests done by explosive experts on the van indicated traces of ammonium nitrate, a fertilizer compound used in improvised explosives, and it too was passed to higher headquarters for further exploitation.[12]

On 23 June, after resting and recovering from Relinquish, the Marines took a day off at the pool on the special forces' compound to mark the one-year anniversary of the unit's activation. As Major Kozeniesky wrote: "We have come a long way in a relatively short period of time—from moving into our new compound and putting names with new faces a year ago, to conducting direct action raids in Baghdad alongside Polish SOF, using Special Forces sources, with Navy and Air Force special operations aircraft in support."[13]

The birthday celebration called for a pause but not a vacation, and the task unit returned, refreshed, to Camp Myler, to address the business at hand. In the last few days before the transfer of sovereignty, Major Kozeniesky intended to keep the insurgent cells off balance by striking as many targets as he could since the general expectation in the task group was that the new government would take a somewhat less aggressive stance. They began to prepare for the next operation, Objective Recruit. The intelligence for Recruit was derived from the exploitation of detainees from Objective Radiate, executed on 13 June. The targets were individuals in the same cell who had eluded capture on that previous raid. Two in particular were targeted for capture or killing; the Marines took one, and the Poles of Task Unit Thunder took the other.

At 0208 on 29 June, Task Unit Raider's assault teams went over the wall of their assigned target house. During the approach, the AC-130 had reported figures fleeing from the roof of the house to an adjacent structure, so the assault force made ready to breach and enter that building too. At the first house, they attempted an explosive breach, which malfunctioned. Before the secondary breach could even be attempted, someone opened the front door from the inside. The assault teams entered and secured the residence, rounding up the occupants, including two males. The Marines also secured several items of interest, including a car, anti-Coalition propaganda, a washing-machine timer, and a remote-control car, the latter two both standard homemade bomb components. (There was also a page from a book showing the locations of U.S. military bases overseas.) The Marines also found, but did not touch, bloody bed linens, which the intelligence debrief later noted "would support some reporting on wounded foreign fighters" in transit through the area.[14]

Based on the in-stride surveillance of the target area by the AC-130, the Marines mounted a rapid assault on the adjacent building, where they detained six more males and more electronic components. On-site interrogations by Staff Sergeant Beretz turned into he-said/she-said finger pointing. One young man said that this was the target's house and that he was the target's nephew, but that he had not seen his uncle in a long time. One woman pointed to a man taken from the second house and said that he was the target. He, of course, remained silent. A third person said that the target lived across the street. Major Kozeniesky decided to take all the detainees back to task group headquarters and sort them out there, suspecting that they already had the man they wanted, and even if they did not, the others would be full of interesting information.[15]

Following the execution of Recruit, Gunnery Sergeant Joseph L. Morrison of Team 2 was injured in a training session. The injury was not life-threatening, but it aggravated a career's worth of hard use on his body, such that he needed to go home for surgery and recovery. The assistant team leader, Staff Sergeant Kevin J. Harris, took his place. The accident came during practice in hand-to-hand combat. Det One trained hard even while it was working hard.[16]

On 2 July, Task Unit Raider executed a raid on Objective Republican, the largest operation to date. The target of the raid was another car-bomb maker. Another target was assigned to Task Unit Thunder. The intelligence was supplied by 2d Battalion, 5th Special Forces Group, which also coordinated the participation of the 36th Battalion, Iraqi National Guard, a high-quality unit that the battalion trained and advised. The task group needed the Iraqis because the intelligence indicated that a mosque was being used for the construction and staging of car bombs.[17]

Task Units Raider and Thunder left Camp Myler and linked up with the Army and Iraqi units in the Green Zone, where they conducted rehearsals and final coordination. The individual units left in turn; Raider arrived at the set point just after 0200 and began a dismounted approach to the target house. While the Marines were scaling the wall, a male exited the front door and was immediately detained. The assault teams entered and cleared the structure, declaring it secure after five minutes. Outside, gunshots were heard down the block, but no one could pinpoint their origin, and no further action was taken.[18]

Three males, including the primary target himself, were detained and dropped off at the Green Zone, along with multiple bomb-making components, a computer, and several hundred blank Iraqi passports. The operation continued to strengthen the ties with the Polish unit and the special forces and gave the Marines an opportunity to work with Iraqi units. Major Kozeniesky concluded that Task Unit Raider had "dealt the cell a serious blow" that would "limit its ability to construct and employ car bombs for the foreseeable future. Mission was a success."[19]

Local Counter-Rocket Operations

Following the transfer of sovereignty from the Coalition Provisional Authority to the Iraqi interim government, Task Unit Raider stepped back from the spate of direct action missions against bomb makers that characterized much of the month of June and began a series of operations geared more toward protecting its own base. All Coalition bases were the targets of insurgent rocket and mortar attacks, but Camp Myler and Baghdad International Airport had recently received several attacks. The worst was a direct hit on the task group operations center that seriously wounded a SEAL and destroyed some equipment.* Major Kozeniesky turned the operational capabilities of his task unit to striking at these local threats.

On several days during the month of June, Marines had been compelled to man their assigned positions for base defense after incidents of small arms and indirect fire. On 30 June, the Marines established a sniper and observation position at Camp Myler, dedicated specifically to the base defense plan, to be occupied continuously until further notice. Even with only a pair of Marines on duty at any given time, this move represented a regular manpower drain. Once again, Colonel Coates's every-Marine-a-rifleman philosophy paid dividends, as support section and headquarters Marines ably addressed this requirement as well as serving on other missions, decreasing the burdens on the reconnaissance element.[20]

The intelligence element also turned its attention to the local threat. Master Sergeant Hays B. Harrington's signals intelligence section produced informa-

---
* HM1 Matthew S. Pranka treated the casualty, helped save his life, and was decorated. The citation read, in part: "Pranka leapt into action from his quarters several hundred meters away. Rather than seeking cover during the rocket barrage, he sprinted across open terrain to come to the aid of the wounded sailor."

tion that pointed to a certain residence in the vicinity. The high-tech SIGINT revelation was supported by an old but effective technique called crater analysis, in which a Marine measures and orients a shell crater to get a back azimuth to its point of origin and a rough indication of the size and type of round. Gunnery Sergeant Matthew A. Ulmer and Staff Sergeant Beretz began cultivating sources in the local area in order to root out information on the attackers.[21] While the intelligence was being gathered and analyzed, Major Kozeniesky and the staff coordinated with the Army unit that owned the local battlespace, 4th Battalion, 5th Air Defense Artillery. The soldiers had an immediate interest in the success of any raids directed at indirect fire threats and agreed to provide the quick reaction force. On this raid, the task unit would also employ a new technique, an eight-man "squirter control team" to deal with people fleeing the target house. This immediate reaction force, aloft in one of the HH-60s that always supported them, was provided by Task Unit Thunder.[22]

The series of raids aimed at the local indirect fire problem began with Objective Roundup. The attack launched at 0300 on 6 July. After a short approach to the target, which was less than five kilometers from Camp Myler, the assault force reached the set point and split up to assault the two target buildings simultaneously. It hit each building hard, then executed a rapid follow-on assault on another building, based on the questioning of the residents of the first two houses. The Marines detained three men, all of whom provided information on rocket attacks that led to subsequent operations.[23]

The detainee interrogations were fed back into the targeting cycle, along with more information from 4th Battalion, 5th Air Defense Artillery, and 2d Battalion, 5th Special Forces Group. Also thrown into the intelligence mix was a very useful item that was recovered by 1st Reconnaissance Battalion during a raid in al-Anbar Province: a global positioning system receiver. It contained hundreds of stored waypoints, many of which corresponded to locations associated with the Camp Myler rocket attacks, indicating possible points of origin or cache sites. Meanwhile, 2d Battalion, 5th Special Forces, was devising a plan, called Operation Serpent Strike, to bait the local insurgents into firing at the base by setting up a stage and leaking information that a large event was going to occur. They coordinated with an artillery unit to site a counterbattery radar set to track the incoming rounds, while aircraft circled overhead for surveillance. As part of the plan, Task Unit Raider was to stage its convoy and prepare to act on any rocket launch. If no rocket attacks occurred during Operation Serpent Strike, the plan called for Raider and Thunder to launch later on Objective Reform.[24]

The insurgents did not take the bait, so the two task units executed raids as planned. Task Unit Raider took one target set, Thunder the other. The Marine convoy left after nightfall on 9 June and arrived at the set point right after 2200. At the first of the three target sites, the Marines took no detainees and found no evidence of insurgent activity, so they proceeded directly to the next site. The watchful AC-130 passed information on activity there, and the Marines conducted a hard hit. They found scorch marks on the ground at this location that were indicative of possible rocket launches. The task unit mounted up and proceeded to the third objective, which also yielded nothing.[25] Major Kozeniesky, in his comments on the operation, admitted that they had "little to show" for the three hits of the night but pointed out that since every one of the individuals the Marines interrogated on site knew of rocket and mortar activity in the vicinity, it tended to validate the general intelligence picture and in no way deterred them from pursuing these targets.[26]

Following the local operations, Task Raider turned its attention again to high-value targets, striking at a former official in the Ba'athist regime chemical program, now dubbed Objective Reflector. This man was suspected of supplying explosives and chemicals to insurgent networks, and signals intelligence indicated that he was going to escape the country. Right before 0330 on 11 July, the assault force breached the man's house and entered it, finding it empty but very recently occupied. Experts from other government agencies brought along for the site exploitation found one ton of chemicals and chemical lab equipment, and they took several samples. "Technically and tactically, this was a superbly executed operation," wrote Major Kozeniesky. The disappointment at missing the target was balanced by a good haul of intelligence materials.[27]

Two days later, the task unit executed a raid on Objective Run Down, a leader of both insurgent and criminal activity. Second Battalion, 5th Special Forces, provided the intelligence and again organized the participation of the 36th Battalion, Iraqi National Guard. The raid proceeded on schedule and without incident. The force took the primary target as well as two other males.

By the third week of July, Task Unit Raider had conducted a total of 17 direct action raids. Most were successes, some were "dry holes." Some had been undertaken on short notice, while others were long planned. The Marines had hit former regime officials and common criminals, insurgents and bomb makers. Det One Marines were operating not only at Camp Myler but in the Green Zone and in Fallujah and served in key positions in the task group staff.* While the bulk of the task group was dedicated to the protective details, Task Units Raider and Thunder remained the forces of choice for direct action.[28]

Colonel Coates and the Fallujah Brigade

Colonel Robert J. Coates, who had the most accurate view of the Fallujah Brigade's operations and therefore no reason to have inflated expectations, also took a long view of the venture. Marines could crush the city in a matter of days—they nearly did in April, and would finally do so in November 2004—but he wanted to know if there was a better way to fight the battle. Iraqis needed to be pushed forward to solve Iraqi problems, and although their solutions might not be perfect by American standards, they would be Iraqi solutions.** But if the Iraqis could not come to a solution and the Marines needed to apply more forceful means, then every effort needed to be expended to use the Iraqi unit to shape the battlespace and contribute to victory.[29]

The one task the Fallujah Brigade needed to be able to do that it could not or would not do was take on the hard-core elements like the foreign fighters who made the insurgency immeasurably worse. The I Marine Expeditionary Force ceased support for its operations, namely in the form of payments delivered by Colonel Coates, and the Fallujah Brigade fell apart on 12 September. However, even as its parts melted away, then joined or rejoined the insurgency, Lieutenant General James T. Conway's staff was exploiting the discord it gradually had sown. And Colonel Coates was working with another Iraqi unit that had been formed, one that would prove to be a significantly more effective fighting force.

This second organization, which became known as the Shahwani Special Forces, grew out of the same general initiative that produced the Fallujah Brigade. It differed in that it was smaller and was made up of a much higher quality of Iraqi soldier than the *jundi* of the Fallujah Brigade. It took its name from its leader, Major General Mohammed Abdullah Mohammed al-Shahwani,* a figure with a long association with the Central Intelligence Agency (CIA) who had become head of Iraq's National Intelligence Service. He offered to form another unit of soldiers that were loyal to him and would do that which the Fallujah Brigade could or would not do.[31]

Colonel Coates was tasked with setting the Shahwanis up in a compound inside Camp Fallujah, supplying them with arms and equipment, and communicating Lieutenant General Conway's orders and guidance. He found General Shahwani and his men a refreshing change from the Fallujah Brigade and recognized that they would be able to accomplish a wide variety of tasks in shaping the Fallujah battlespace.

The Shahwani operational units formed under Colonel Khalis Ali Hussein, another professional and exceptionally capable officer.** Training progressed quickly, and the units began to operate first with the Marines, and then independently of them in many cases. They took over many duties from the Marines that they could do better, such as manning vehicle checkpoints and screening civilians. As the time drew near when it was clear that a more "kinetic" solution would be needed in Fallujah, the soldiers in the Shahwani Special Forces undertook several operations inside the city doing what Colonel Coates offhandedly described as "different things," meaning that they were involved in some very sensitive, high-risk shaping operations that contributed significantly to the success of the operation in November 2004.

The initiative that produced both the Fallujah Brigade and the Shahwani Special Forces was, in Colonel Coates's words, "an opportunity for those in there to choose what side they wanted to be on." The latter certainly chose more wisely than the former. Colonel Coates

---

* Shahwani, a Sunni, competed internationally as a decathlete in his youth and was sent for U.S. Army Ranger training in the late 1960s. He later headed the Iraqi Special Forces School and was a brigadier general in command of a Republican Guard unit during the first half of the Iran-Iraq War. His military success led Saddam Hussein to perceive him as a threat, and by 1990, Shahwani had fled to London. Shahwani was based in Jordan during the Gulf War, collecting intelligence from his abundant sources, and with CIA support, he tried to organize a military coup against Saddam in 1996. The plot failed, and while Shahwani escaped, 85 of the conspirators were executed, including his three sons. Shahwani continued to work with the CIA on various plots to turn the Iraq military against Hussein. After the invasion in 2003, he became director of the Iraqi National Intelligence Service.

** For their professionalism and steadfastness, the Shahwani officers suffered immensely. Col Khalis's family in Baghdad was kidnapped, but he remained loyal to the cause and stayed at his post, and Khalis and his protective detail were killed in early 2005 by terrorists in Baghdad. Col Coates called it "a statement to the effectiveness of his leadership and his Iraqi special forces." Many other Shahwani officers were also killed by the insurgents. Col Coates email to author, 7 August 2006.

---

* During the week of 10 July, Maj Wade Priddy assumed the job of task group operations officer after the SEAL officer in the post rotated home.

** Col Coates pointed out to the author that El Salvador's civil war brought to a close in much the same way as described.

Det One Weapons

5.56mm M4 SOPMOD Rifle

7.62mm M14 Rifle

5.56mm M249 Light Machine Gun

.45-caliber M1911 Pistol and Stryder Knife

Photos Courtesy of Det One

was involved with both units every day until he departed Iraq in October, was materially responsible for most of their successes, and consequently for much of the success in the decisive action of that part of the campaign.*

Intel Marines after the Protective Detail

With the onset of the protective detail mission, Det One's far-flung intelligence element became somewhat less far-flung as the task group contracted and consolidated. Master Sergeant Bret A. Hayes and Gunnery Sergeant Matthew Ulmer came back to Camp Myler, where they operated in general support of the task group and were able to work more directly with Task Unit Raider. Most of the radio reconnaissance section was sent to Baghdad for direct support of the SEALs. They occupied one floor of a hotel, and from that perch, they were able to provide timely and critical signals intelligence, employing new equipment and developing different techniques, tactics, and procedures. For example, Gunnery Sergeant James A. Crawford put together a significant target package based on his own collection that was passed up for execution by upper-tier units.[31]

The intelligence element performed other tasks in and around Baghdad as well, sometimes in support of conventional units. Gunnery Sergeant Crawford and Staff Sergeant William B. Parker were involved in a fierce day-long firefight on 12 August while attached to 1st Battalion, 9th U.S. Cavalry, seeking out insurgents responsible for indirect fire attacks on the Green Zone. They, along with two SEALs and a squad of cavalrymen, were posted on top of a building on Haifa Street. Throughout that day, they provided intelligence to the commander of the Army unit on the targets he was seeking. Later in the day, their mission was to scan the area for an insurgent mortar team, locate them, and take them out. The rest of the company had departed, and the small combined team was in a covert position. The mortarmen came, fired, and left, close to them but unfortunately out of sight, so they reported what they heard and remained in place. They saw a roadside bomb emplaced and subsequently detonated against an Army vehicle, but they did not engage those who planted it because they did not want to compromise their location.[32]

Their position was soon compromised for them, however, when the street filled with masked gunmen, massing for action and firing weapons in the air. They observed a dozen men get out of two vehicles at the base of their building and start to unload rocket propelled grenades and small arms. The SEALs, soldiers,

---
* Col Coates received the Bronze Star for his actions.

and Marines reasoned that this situation called for action, and they moved back to the roof, where they dropped grenades on the gunmen and engaged them with small-arms fire. They also called to alert the cavalry battalion's quick reaction force. The Haifa Street fight was on.[33]

Although his team had just engaged the gunmen below, Gunnery Sergeant Crawford was not sure that the enemy could pinpoint them, and so while he observed an enemy rocket team across the street, he did not shoot but instead alerted the rest of the team to its presence. Crawford quickly found out that the enemy did know his position, as they started to receive heavy small arms fire. The team returned it in kind. "Rounds were snapping over our heads at a very rapid rate, and they practically had us pinned," he later wrote. When the gunmen paused to reload, the Americans used the brief window of opportunity to descend to a more defensible part of the building.[34]

A young boy, perhaps 10 years old, appeared on the roof of the building next to them and threw a grenade. Shouts of "grenade!" went up, and most of the men were able to get out of the way, but one soldier was caught in the open and sustained severe injuries—one foot was severed and his legs had other wounds. "The rate of fire we were receiving was enormous," Crawford noting, adding that he later counted eight rocket-propelled grenade hits on just one side of the building. Parker counted 14 hits in all. Crawford called for an immediate extract.[35]

While the team treated its casualties and fortified its position, "all hell broke loose" on the street below. Smoke billowed up from the cars they had destroyed, and automatic weapons fire continued to sweep the position. The Marines, SEALs, and soldiers bounded down to an apartment below the roof under mutual covering fire and continued the fight. The incoming fire continued, as heavy as before. It shattered a window and sprayed Parker with glass. The Americans maintained a steady and accurate volume of fire going out. Crawford later wrote that they had 30 confirmed kills during the fight.[36]

The quick reaction force took an hour to arrive, but when it did, it was in force, with "Bradleys pouring out 25mm high explosive everywhere," as Crawford recalled. The Marines, SEALs, and soldiers took their wounded down to street level and loaded them into the vehicles, which drove straight to the 31st Corps Support Hospital. There they dropped off the wounded and then prepared to return and reengage the insurgents. Within an hour, Crawford and Parker found themselves back on Haifa Street, while 1st Battalion, 9th Cavalry, systematically retook the area and searched the buildings. The entire episode ran 20 hours. "By this time," Crawford wrote, "we were all smoked, no food, no rest, and hot as can be."[37]

The Haifa Street fight began with a radio reconnaissance mission and ended in a close-quarters fight, where gunfighting skills and sheer physical endurance won the day. The Det One Marines had again proved up to the task.

Staff Sergeant Daniel L. Williams of the counterintelligence section remained with the SEALs after Task Unit North moved to Baghdad, and he found himself working in the offices of the interim Iraqi president. Operating quietly, in civilian clothes, he was known simply as "Dan." It was his job to vet all of the Iraqi civilians working in the executive offices, questioning, screening, cataloging, indexing, and reporting. His inquisitive mind and exceptional memory took note of everything around him, and he patiently sifted through it all. He devised a system of credentials and enforced the wearing of badges. Through his efforts, he identified two immediate and potent threats to the president: one, "a foreign national with suspected ties to state-sponsored terrorism," and the other, "an individual with known anti-coalition ties."[38]

Another counterintelligence Marine, Gunnery Sergeant William G. Parsons, shifted after the protective detail from supporting Task Unit Central to more general human intelligence activities in the Green Zone. He screened meeting attendees, did physical threat assessments, and handled interpreters. In mid-July, he was recalled by Major Jerry Carter and assigned as the task force liaison to the intelligence agencies' combined surveillance and reconnaissance section, taking the place of an Army major. Parsons began coordinating requests from every special ops unit across Iraq, as well as from some conventional units. He stayed there, in a billet several levels above his pay grade, until Task Unit Raider stood down and Det One redeployed to Camp Pendleton.

An important part of intelligence support to the task group was the operation of the detention and interrogation facility. As the task group special activities officer, Captain Christopher B. Batts was responsible for handling detainees. Since he had few Marines to assist him, it meant that he pitched in as necessary to actually handle the detainees. Some were compliant, while some were not. One in particular went through substance abuse detoxification during his detention, flinging himself around his cell and defecating uncontrollably. Batts and others had to restrain him and then clean him up.[39]

The proper handling of detainees was crucial in

several respects. For one, humane and proper treatment of detainees is required by law and policy. For another, interrogations of detainees were some of the most productive feeds to the intelligence cycle. Maintaining the "shock of capture," as it was called, and getting a detainee to talk and give up information without overstepping boundaries is an art, and Batts and his Marines had the training to do it effectively. Once they were plugged into other government agencies and other task force units, they had the contacts to make sense of nearly everything detainees told them, and they were able to forward the results of their questioning to other interested parties. When detainees were brought in, Batts was there to meet them. They were checked for medical issues, given food or water as needed, and then photographed, fingerprinted, and questioned. Clever, effective, and timely interrogations more than once provided the primary actionable intelligence on key targets.[40]

The "One-Armed Bandit"

Two weeks of relative inactivity for Task Unit Raider ended with two more operations on targets close to home. These two raids, on Objectives Relapse and Roadster, struck at more local insurgents who had been firing rockets into Camp Myler. The sources were Iraqis who had been trained by Task Unit Raider's counterintelligence Marines.[41] The primary source for Objective Relapse was an Iraqi developed and handled by Staff Sergeant Scott Beretz. "He had excellent English, a very intelligent guy," said Beretz. The source began to bring in solid information on rocket launches, as well as promising informants of his own.

Beretz formed a plan, and he coordinated with higher headquarters for permission to proceed with it. He gave his source a vehicle and a global positioning system receiver. The source took one of the informants he had brought in, and together they went out and plotted three locations related to possible rocket launches. A few days later, Beretz sent them out again with a camera to photograph the locations. Through these efforts, the identity of the man who was behind the attacks finally surfaced. He would be easy to pick out, the source said, as he only had one arm; thus he became known as the "One-Armed Bandit."[42]

The assault on Objective Relapse occurred at 0220 on 27 July. Task Unit Raider was assigned to hit two targets: the "One-Armed Bandit" and his two-armed associate, described as a welder who made rocket launchers. Task Unit Thunder was assigned a third

Photos Courtesy of Det One

Det One Night Vision Devices

AN/PVS-17 Weapon Night Sight

AN/PVS-15 Binocular Night Sight

AN/PVS-14 Multipurpose Night Sight

PEQ-2A IR Laser Pointer

target. The unit that owned the battlespace was 2d Battalion, 2d Marines, commanded by Lieutenant Colonel J. Giles Kyser IV, the detachment's "godfather." The "Warlords" would provide the quick reaction force for the mission. The convoy, momentarily delayed by traffic coming in and out of Baghdad airport, proceeded to the targets with the AC-130 overhead, reporting on activity in the area. As the assault force reached the set point and dismounted, the gunship spotted two figures running from the one-armed man's residence. Marines from the containment teams gave chase across the adjacent field, grabbed both men, and dragged them back to the house. One was missing a forearm.[43]

By the time the containment teams returned, the assault teams had cleared the structure, and sensitive site exploitation was in full swing. Staff Sergeant Beretz was getting the customary evasions to his direct questions, but one of the young men under interrogation had a name that was related to that of the man for whom they were searching. At that moment, one of the assaulters uncovered a prosthetic arm, then the containment teams brought in the one-armed runner. The source positively identified him, and Beretz had his man.[44]

In addition to the "One-Armed Bandit," the raid turned up other damning evidence, including a detailed diagram of a main U.S. base and several military maps of Baghdad. On the search of the second objective, the GROM members also netted their target, along with 10 improvised rocket launch tubes complete with sights.[45] The raid was a dramatic success, and Major Kozeniesky was able to assess that "one of the active cells in the area has been decimated."[46i]

Based on the intelligence gleaned from Relapse, the task group then initiated a mission on Objective Roadster, targeting the man who was supplying the 57mm rockets that the "One-Armed Bandit" was shooting. Task Unit Thunder again took part, and there was excellent close target reconnaissance done by Army Special Forces and *jundi* from the 36th Iraqi National Guard. Task Unit Raider brought along a new source who had offered to identify the rocket supplier.[47]

The assault on Objective Roadster proceeded in the early hours of 5 August, with the assault teams making a dismounted approach to the target's house. After the Iraqi source confirmed that the building was the target's house, the force breached, entered, and cleared it, while other teams were assaulting another structure. At this point, it was found that the residence was a more complex building than it appeared, and Major Kozeniesky ordered his Marines to begin breaching and clearing the site until no room was left untouched. Several men were detained, and the source identified some as the target's relatives. The target himself was not there, and no items of significance were taken away.[48]

The general success of this series, despite the escape of Objective Roadster's primary target, highlighted the exceptional work of Staff Sergeant Beretz and validated Marine human intelligence abilities in the special operations arena. Beretz was able to pay his sources for their work and set them to further tasks. The chief Iraqi source became, in Beretz's words, "self-sufficient" and began to venture out to capture low-level targets on his own.[49]

Not only was Staff Sergeant Beretz having success in developing sources to counter the local indirect fire attacks, he was also becoming involved with sources for a much higher profile target, codenamed Rifle, a man who various organizations had been hunting for months. The assault on Objective Rifle grew into one of Task Unit Raider's hallmark operations, and one of its key features was the human intelligence operation run by Staff Sergeant Beretz.[50]

Al-Kut

In August 2004, the Shi'a militias began to rise up again in areas south of Baghdad, engaging in open combat with Iraqi and Coalition forces. In al-Kut, an important Shi'a center, gunmen were surging into the city and the Iraqi police were under siege. In a compound immediately west of the city were stationed a Ukrainian brigade and an Army Special Forces team, with a Marine ANGLICO team attached, and a small number of U.S. Army military police. The Ukrainians were unable or unwilling to intervene. The Special Forces, the ANGLICO Marines, and the military police were left to stand with the Iraqis in an increasingly difficult position, but they did not have the combat power to engage the militiamen and still serve as advisors to the Iraqis. The loss of Al-Kut would have been a severe blow to the interim Iraqi government and would have given the Shi'a militants an important victory.

Task Unit Raider's al-Kut operations begin on 11 August when the special operations task force sent down an order for Marines to reinforce the Special Forces team. The task unit staff did a quick mission analysis and advised that the best course of action would be to send a task-organized sub-detachment of 16 Marines, covering sniper, SIGINT, forward air control, and medical capabilities. Captain Eric Thompson was in command, and the senior enlisted Marine was Master Sergeant Charles Padilla. Within 12 hours of notification, that team, with two M113 hunekers and supplies for 96 hours, was en route to al-Kut on a pair of MC-130 aircraft.[51]

Upon arrival at the Special Forces team's house, the Marines received a brief on the situation. The battle was clearly still joined. On the roof of the house, the Air Force enlisted tactical air controller attached to the Special Forces team was working targets in the city with the AC-130 overhead. The Special Forces troopers extracted the governor of Al-Kut from the city the next day—by small boat across the Tigris River, as all other avenues were closed—to meet with senior U.S. Army commanders. Det One Marines accompanied them to and from the landing site and got a firsthand look at the aggressive tactics of the insurgents. The soldiers and Marines had to engage cars that would not stop when commanded and posed threats to the convoy. Master Sergeant Padilla and Staff Sergeant Chad Baker disabled several cars with the Barrett .50-caliber rifle and M240G machine gun.[52] Padilla noted with approval that the Special Forces were working with good, permissive rules of engagement and were not shy about using deadly force.[53] The situation in the city was assessed as very serious, and the governor needed American help to regain control.[54]

That evening, 12 August, the Marines established two positions by the river to gain observation on the city. Both had sniper teams; one post held Captain Daniel Sheehan, and Sergeants David Marnell and Miguel A. Cervantes to control the AC-130 when it came on station, and the other post held three radio reconnaissance Marines, Sergeants William S. Benedict, Jason Leighty, and Christopher E. Haug. Their mission was to support the beleaguered Iraqi police, still holding on in their fortified position in the city. During the night, the two posts observed several firefights across the river but found it difficult to discern if the shooters were Iraqi police or Shi'a gunmen. The Marines were cleared to fire if the figures they saw were attacking the police station. Staff Sergeant Baker took one shot from his M40A3 sniper rifle at a target of opportunity; the range was 750 meters. He saw the shot strike home, but no one could determine the effects, and so it was logged as a probable kill.[55] Fire was going in both directions, with a steady volume of rounds coming at them from across the river.

A friendly fire incident occurred that night when fires from the AC-130 hit the Iraqi police station. A member of the Special Forces team not located with the Marines was controlling the AC-130 while Staff Sergeant Baker observed another group of insurgents moving into position against the Iraqi police. In an effort to get a precise location on them and then engage them, Captain Sheehan designated the spot Baker identified with an infrared laser pointer and directed Sergeant Marnell to use the laser mark to produce the grid location. Unfortunately, the AC-130 saw the laser mark and mistook it for a target designation from the soldiers. The gunship fired, wounding several Iraqi police.[56] The same fire also stopped the insurgent attack for the night. The Marines shut down both posts and withdrew to the team house.

The heat at this time of the year was intense. The Marines preferred operating at night as much because it provided a small measure of relief from the heat. They also had the tactical edge because of their night vision equipment. They later noted, however, that thermal sights were degraded even at night because the ambient temperature was not much different from a human's temperature. Captain Sheehan remembered one day in al-Kut when the thermometer on his watch read 137 degrees.[57]

The next day, the Coalition forces once again retrieved the governor, and he began planning with the Special Forces leadership, the Marines, and the advance party of a U.S. Army Stryker battalion en route to provide the conventional force. The governor reported that the previous two nights of AC-130 strikes had turned the tide, and his forces were "90 percent" in charge of the city, but that a nearby town for which he was also responsible was still in the hands of the insurgents.[58] The group formed a plan to send the Stryker battalion across the river to retake the city, with the Special Forces team and the Marines occupying positions to support the assault. Operations in the other town, al-Hayy, were deferred pending action in al-Kut.

That night, the combined units moved into their positions. Four Marine snipers crossed the river with eight members of the Special Forces team and four of their ANGLICO Marines to occupy a clandestine position that gave them observation over much of the city.* In place to cover them and to support the

---

* The river crossing provided a brief moment of excitement when the engines on the Iraqi small boats cut out and the craft began to drift downstream. MSgt Padilla could see the event turning into a possible disaster; his first thought was that it was a set-up. He said to himself: "How am I going to explain this to Maj Kozeniesky? He's not going to like this." A special forces trooper broke the tension by quoting a line from a Snickers commercial: "Not going anywhere for a while?" Focused efforts restarted the engines and the boats made their way back upstream to an otherwise uneventful landing. SSgt Baker silently noted a lesson learned: "Marines need to plan and organize any water operation." Padilla intvw, 10Jan05 (MCHC); Baker intvw, 24Mar05 (MCHC).

Stryker assault later were eight Marines on the near side of the river, including the fires team and the radio reconnaissance team.

Once the Marines were in position across the river, Captain Sheehan began to prosecute targets. He directed the AC-130 onto one preplanned target, and for the rest of the night he coordinated the big gunship and a pair of Army OH-58D Kiowa helicopters as the Stryker units drove across the bridge into the city. It was later reported that he "described the situation on the ground to the battalion fire support coordination center and de-conflicted fires between the AC-130 and the friendly troop movements. The Stryker battalion rolled through al-Kut with no shots fired." In the wake of the battalion's movement, the Marines at the fires and radio reconnaissance position crossed the river in vehicles to link up with their fellow raiders and bring them out. The Marines then retired to the Special Forces detachment's compound.

When 15 August passed uneventfully, on the morning of the 16th it was determined that no clear requirement existed to keep the Det One Marines in al-Kut for further operations, and the sub-detachment returned to Camp Myler.[59] The al-Kut operation was a significant feather in the detachment's cap. Good mission analysis produced a balanced team to address an uncertain situation, and the resulting plan was rapidly executed. The careful application of precision fires, supported by tactical signals intelligence and effective command and control enabled the Marines to support both the Army Special Forces detachment and the Stryker battalion. The Stryker battalion, in turn, backed up the Iraqis in retaking the city. The al-Kut mission demonstrated that Det One could be a supporting effort as effectively as it could be a main effort, and that its conventional roots served it well in larger operations.

"Dry Holes"

As the al-Kut sub-detachment was returning, Task Unit Raider was executing a direct action raid on Objective Roulette, another combined operation with Task Unit Thunder. The target of the raid was the leader of a large cell in Mahmudiyah, a consistently restive city south of Baghdad. The intelligence on the target was drawn from a previous capture incarcerated in Abu Ghraib and from Marine counterintelligence teams operating in al-Anbar Province. Mahmudiyah was in the territory of 2d Battalion, 2d Marines, commanded by Lieutenant Colonel Giles Kyser. The "Warlords" again gladly stood up their quick reaction forces to support them and provided detailed information on the routes into and out of the target area.[60]

Intelligence sources had pegged two different buildings as the target's residence. When no clear determination could be made on which was the actual residence, the decision was made to hit each one simultaneously. The mission launched at 0200 on 16 August. Task Unit Raider's assault force numbered fewer than usual since Captain Thompson's al-Kut Marines were not part of the force. The ability of the support section Marines to step up and join the fight was crucial in this operation. All the drivers and gunners in the convoy except one were from the headquarters and intelligence elements, and that one was Hospital Corpsman First Class Matthew Pranka.

The approach to the target was difficult, due to a rough road network, billowing clouds of dust, and lack of natural illumination. The detailed route reconnaissance from Lieutenant Colonel Kyser's battalion, however, enabled the convoy to get through to the target. The Marine teams assaulted both structures in their target set, while Polish special forces took theirs down. Unfortunately, none of the individuals targeted in the raids was present. Sensitive site exploitation did reveal information that confirmed that the task force was correct to hit the sites, but the individual targets avoided capture. Major Kozeniesky concluded by noting that "egress back to Camp Myler was uneventful. Mission was a dry hole."*[61]

Three days later, Task Unit Raider executed a raid on Objective Resistor, the target being a former regime official running a large anti-Coaltion cell, which was allegedly tied to terrorist mastermind Abu Musab al-Zarqawi. This hit was synchronized with an Iraqi special operations unit and Task Force 626, a unit hunting the most important targets in Iraq. The plan called for those two units to hit a pair of financiers associated with Task Unit Raider's target; Raider was the supporting effort. The intelligence for this operation was derived from a 1st Cavalry Division report forwarded approximately one week before by

---

* One incident during the raid on Objective Roulette illustrated the strange things that the Marines sometimes found during the searches. The intelligence debrief from the raid noted matter-of-factly that, "One (1) woman was discovered sleeping outside." Actually, SSgt Zachary A. Reeves, one of the radio reconnaissance Arabic speakers, discovered her by stepping on her. He called MSgt Hays B. Harrington over, and asked him what they should do. There was a blanket lying on the ground, and Reeves said that there was an old woman underneath it. Harrington thought Reeves was playing a joke on him—"wrong place and time for a joke"—because he had searched that area and seen nothing. Harrington he lifted up the blanket and there indeed was an old woman: "This face is peering out at me, I mean, she is hideous-looking, has to be at least a hundred and fifty years old... That was the scariest thing I saw over there." Harrington decided just to leave her alone. Roulette operational summary; Harrington intvw, 13Jan05 (MCHC).

Major Carter to Gunnery Sergeant William Johnston in Baghdad. Johnston spotted the indicators that tied the Cavalry Division's target set to the higher-level target set and helped develop the combined, joint operation.

The target was a former Iraqi general and special forces operative. "Documents taken during the capture of Saddam Hussein identified the high value target as a key leader in Saddam's post-OIF I 'shadow government.'" Twenty-four hours before execution, the intelligence apparatus came to believe that their source in the target's group had been murdered, and they requested that Task Unit Raider hand off another operation then in progress to the GROM and prepare to execute Resistor on short notice. A new trigger for the target's presence was established by the officers from Baghdad intelligence cells, and all three forces planned to hit their targets simultaneously.[62]

In a convoy of six vehicles, with another slightly depleted force—the al-Kut team was back in the mix, but the first wave of Marines had gone to support operations in an-Najaf—Task Unit Raider moved out to the objective at 0200 on 19 August. Dismounting at the set point, the Marines assaulted the position on foot. One woman and five youths were found on site; the target of the raid was nowhere to be seen. Exploitation of the site yielded the target's identification card but little else. The major positive result of the raid was the opportunity to synchronize operations with the upper-tier Iraqi unit and Task Force 626. Major Kozeniesky stated that he thought the execution of the raid was based on a premature trigger, but he looked forward to getting another shot at the man later. As on Objective Roulette before it, he concluded, "Egress back to Camp Myler was uneventful. Mission was a dry hole."[63]

Chapter 7

An-Najaf, "Z," and Home

An-Najaf: "A Full-On Fight"

While Captain Eric N. Thompson's Det One sub-detachment was in al-Kut, another, much larger fight was breaking out in the city of an-Najaf, about 100 miles due south of Baghdad and home of the Imam Ali Mosque. This was holy ground for all Shi'a, and the stakes in this battle were even higher than at al-Kut. The malefactors were, again, the Shi'a militiamen following Muqtada al-Sadr. The al-Sadr militia had fought the Coalition here before; in April 2004, they had attacked Coalition forces but had been put down after hard fighting by U.S. Army units. The 11th Marine Expeditionary Unit (Special Operations Capable) was now responsible for the city and was being pressed hard by the large numbers of militiamen.[1] Multinational Force Iraq, the military high headquarters for the country, sent units to I Marine Expeditionary Force to reinforce 11th MEU (SOC); the Combined Joint Special Operations Task Force-Arabian Peninsula was ordered to provide a contingent under 1st Battalion, 5th Special forces Group, and Task Unit Raider was instructed to provide sniper support.

Nine Marines under Master Sergeant Terry M. Wyrick—seven snipers (under Gunnery Sergeant John A. Dailey), one fires Marine (Gunnery Sergeant Ryan P. Keeler), and one Corpsman (Hospital Corpsman First Class Robert T. Bryan)—were selected to go to Najaf. Wyrick initially reported to a SEAL officer, who was in overall command of the task group's personnel. Wyrick's team got sniper weapons from the returning al-Kut detachment and did a quick zeroing before departure. On 17 August, the Najaf sub-detachment mounted up in two hunekers, fell into an Army Special Forces convoy, and drove to Najaf.[2]

The 11th MEU (SOC) had been reinforced with 2d Battalion, 7th U.S. Cavalry, and it was to that unit that the task group's element was sent. Immediately upon arrival, the SEAL officer and Master Sergeant Wyrick reported to the battalion commander and received an update on the situation. The cavalrymen were inside the city, occupying positions south and east of the Imam Ali Mosque, which the enemy controlled and were using as a base, having assumed that the Americans would neither fire into it nor assault it. Once he was told that the special operations units were there just to support him, the battalion commander welcomed them with open arms. The SEAL officer and Wyrick did a quick planning session with the Army staff and came up with a workable plan to support their operations. By 0600 the next day (18 August), the Marines had a clear mission, an area of operations, and a base from which to work. The 10 Marines were sent directly to the battalion's Company C, named Task Force Cougar, positioned close to the Imam Ali Mosque—and in direct contact with the enemy.[3]

The trip into the city was an education in the conditions of Najaf. "It was the wild, wild west," remembered Master Sergeant Wyrick. "Rocket propelled grenades and gunfire were constant, and this was just on the outskirts of town." While Wyrick remained at the Task Force Cougar position to provide command and control, the rest of the force under Gunnery Sergeant Dailey pushed in toward the Imam Ali Mosque and occupied two observation posts (OP 1 and OP 2) near Task Force Cougar's forward platoons. While the Marines in these positions received "accurate but ineffective small arms fire," they did not engage any targets. They used the time to survey the area and gain a sense of the atmospherics, identifying key terrain and locating known and suspected enemy positions. They pulled out from these positions the next morning to prepare for the next phase of the operation.[4] Throughout the day of 19 August, Wyrick and Dailey worked with Task Force Cougar to devise a plan to support the unit's push north toward the Imam Ali shrine. When night fell, the soldiers' Bradley fighting vehicles took Dailey's Marines to another location, where they established their third observation post (OP 3).

At first light the next day, 20 August, the al-Sadr militiamen began to emerge from their positions. The Marines were already at work: Gunnery Sergeant Dailey and Sergeant Michael C. Mulvihill were on the roof of the structure, while the rest of the team was constructing covered and concealed sniper hides on the floors below. Dailey and Mulvihill began firing but were soon forced off the roof by enemy fire. During the day, they scored four confirmed and six probable kills. Gunnery Sergeant Keeler worked aviation support from every service, using his position's ex-

Photo courtesy of Capt Daniel B. Sheehan

SSgt Chadwick D. Baker mans a suppressed SR-25 7.62mm sniper rifle during the battle of an-Najaf in August 2004. Spotting for him is HM1 Matthew S. Pranka, and behind Pranka is SSgt Jack A. Kelly. Watching from the door are Sgts Miguel A. Cervantes and David D. Marnell. Although not apparent from this view, this sniper hide is covered and concealed, allowing the Marines to wear only soft body armor in the extreme heat. Det One snipers, firing from hides like this one and using the suppressed SR-25, slew dozens of Shi'a gunmen during the battle.

cellent fields of observation to find targets in and around the Imam Ali Mosque complex. At one point he had a laser spot on an enemy position inside the exclusion zone around the shrine and Lockheed F-16 Fighting Falcons overhead, but he was not granted permission to engage.

By the end of the day, the Marines' operations had already had an impact on the enemy. Reports began to come in that the gunmen's greatest fear was the "American snipers." Master Sergeant Wyrick said that from the excellent source operations the Army special forces units was running inside the mosque complex, the word was that the snipers "were just knocking the shit out of them, and morale was going down the tubes. . . . The sources were telling the Special Forces that there were piles of bodies inside the ring because of sniper shots." The Marines' own tally of confirmed kills bore this out.[5] As a result, a cease-fire was called, and the Marines withdrew from OP 3 back to the Task Force Cougar command post.

On 21 August, the snipers spent their time refitting and operating in the vicinity of the command post, waiting for further orders as the cease-fire played out. Apparently, not all the enemy was in compliance, as Marine snipers engaged several gunmen attempting to infiltrate the Army unit's position.

That night, more help arrived from Task Unit Raider: Gunnery Sergeant Fidencio Villalobos Jr. to handle the fires coordination, and Sergeant Jason V. Brackley, the detachment's radio technician, to help man the radios. Master Sergeant Wyrick had seen that he was not going to able to sustain operations as a one-man show at the command post. He also knew that he needed subject-matter expertise in fires. No Marine was more suited to that particular task than Villalobos, who, in addition to the special fires training he had by virtue of his service in ANGLICO and Det One, was fully capable of conventional fire support coordination at and above the regimental level. He began working with the company staff, Gunnery Sergeant Keeler, and Master Sergeant Wyrick to develop target lists and a comprehensive plan to shape the battlespace and support the company's scheme of maneuver.[6]

The shaky cease-fire soon collapsed, and during the afternoon of 22 August, the snipers left the command post and went forward again to occupy a new position, called OP 4. Gunnery Sergeant Keeler moved back to OP 1 and began sending target intelligence back to Villalobos, who submitted nine preplanned targets. That night, four of the nine targets were engaged by the AC-130 under Keeler's direction; one resulted in a secondary explosion, indicating that a quantity of munitions had been stored there. While these shaping operations were underway, Master Sergeant Wyrick attended a conference at the Army battalion command post to plan for the next phase of the assault into the city.[7]

Sergeant David D. Marnell from the fires element also arrived to reinforce Gunnery Sergeant Keeler, who, like Master Sergeant Wyrick, had been a one-man show in an indispensable job. While Keeler and Marnell were prosecuting the target list, they also looked for targets of opportunity. One such target presented itself at about 0120 on 23 August when Keeler observed enemy forces moving to attack Task Force Cougar positions. He directed the AC-130, with its superb surveillance capabilities, to relay information on the enemy, which he then passed to the Cougar commander. Once he had all stations fully appraised of the situation and the soldiers had broken contact, Keeler asked permission to engage. When he received word that the AC-130 was clear to hit the gunmen, he passed the approval to the plane's crew. His efforts were rewarded with a precisely delivered strike that killed five militiamen in the open and destroyed four buildings where the attacks had been massing. Four secondary explosions resulted.[8]

The work of Gunnery Sergeant Villalobos in the task force command post, particularly his skill at coordinating and deconflicting the fires, was as critical to success as Keeler and Marnell's presence and abilities on the frontlines. It became apparent that Villalobos could be even more effective in the battalion command post, and so he moved there. At the cavalry battalion headquarters, he virtually took over the fire support coordination duties for the unit, which did not have an air officer or terminal attack controllers other than Keeler and Marnell.

Villalobos, who knew fire support coordination measures and procedures intimately, began systematically planning to support the battalion commander's scheme of maneuver. When aircraft checked in on station, he wanted to be able to push them to Keeler and Marnell with preplanned and preapproved targets so no opportunities would be wasted while securing permission to engage. Sergeant Brackley made sure that Villalobos had uninterrupted communications, more than once exposing himself to enemy fire when setting up or adjusting antennas. When Master Sergeant Wyrick arrived at the battalion command post for meetings, he frequently found Villalobos both coordinating fire support and conducting ad-hoc classes, with the staff clustered around the radios listening to the AC-130 engage targets while "Big Daddy" provided the play-by-play commentary.[9]*

Dailey's snipers remained in OP 4 throughout most of 23 August, slipping out at 2130 when Task Force Cougar pushed north to get closer to the mosque complex. The enemy contested the move, and the soldiers took three casualties. Hospital Corpsman First Class Bryan assisted in their treatment and evacuation. As a result of the attack, Dailey's team occupied a fifth position, OP 5, and spent the rest of the night observing enemy activity, passing reports back to Master Sergeant Wyrick, and engaging targets with the AC-130. The Marines located one mortar position, which the gunship destroyed, resulting in four more confirmed kills.[10]

During this period, Gunnery Sergeant Dailey's snipers also located and eliminated an enemy sniper. Gunnery Sergeant Travis W. Clark was the first to spot an unseen hand slowly and carefully removing blocks from a wall to open up a firing port. Dailey directed Keeler to call an air strike on the position, but higher headquarters denied the request because of its proximity to the mosque. Instead, he called for Staff Sergeant D. T. Krueger to lay his .50-caliber Barrett rifle on the target, and then—operating under the unassailable logic that if one .50-caliber rifle was good, two would surely be better—he asked an Army sniper team to bring its Barrett over as well. When Dailey saw the hand remove the brick "one last time," the snipers hit the site with both weapons, each gun-

---

* For both Wyrick and Villalobos, the realities of being one deep in their positions meant long days and nights and very little sleep. Even after Villalobos and Brackley arrived to assist, Wyrick still found himself worn out. He would try to arrive for meetings 20 minutes early so he could crawl under the conference table and get a brief nap, which might be the only sleep he would get that day. Villalobos said that the mission in Najaf was "one big long Ranger episode—no sleep."

ner emptying several rounds into the wall. Where a loophole had been, there was now a hole "you could drive a truck through." It was impossible to assess the results of their fire with certainty, but the Marines felt confident that they had eliminated their adversary.[11]

Gunnery Sergeant Keeler also described the incident and its aftermath. "This," he explained, "did two things: A) anyone who was in that room was dead; and B) it pissed people off, because we took probably another 45 minutes of nothing but mortar rounds on top of the building. So we all dropped down to the center hall and weathered it out." Before they reached the inner core of the building, they had some close calls. Gunnery Sergeant Clark had left his uniform blouse in a room that faced onto an open shaft. A mortar round landed right in the shaft seconds after he left the room. The blouse was shredded, and Clark would have been had he not left when he did.[12]

Although most of the militia tactics were assessed as "basic and crude," there was evidence from incidents such as the sniper episode to indicate that at least some of al-Sadr's men had advanced training and good equipment, displaying "an elevated level of weapons proficiency." But most were just armed males of various ages, generally clad in black and wearing green headbands. They used women and children to screen their movements or to scout the Coalition positions when it suited them, and they even rigged rocket launchers on donkey carts. They preferred to operate during the daytime and seemed to yield the night to the soldiers and Marines.* Within the walls of the shrine complex, they carried weapons and munitions openly, at least until Det One snipers and forward air controllers worked their way into positions and began to put an end to the practice.[13]

The stars of the show, in terms of individual weapons, were the .50-caliber Barrett and the 7.62mm SR-25. The Barrett rifle had the range to hit any target the Marines could see and the strength to punch through masonry walls. The relatively close confines of Najaf meant that the Marines could not employ the rifle at its greatest ranges, so the bulk of the work on open targets was done with the SR-25. This rifle had everything that the Najaf Marines needed: semi-automatic action, range, accuracy, compatibility with a variety of optics, and most important of all, sound suppression. In a properly constructed urban sniper hide, a Marine with a suppressed SR-25 could engage multiple targets in quick succession without giving away the position. More than once, the Marines struck down gunmen and then watched as others frantically scanned the area for the origin of the fire.[14]

By 24 August, the initial sub-detachment had been in action in Najaf for a full week. Recognizing that fresh troops were needed if they were to maintain the high op-tempo, Master Sergeant Wyrick requested that Task Unit Raider dispatch a relief force. Accordingly, eight more snipers and two fires Marines were sent by air, arriving at OP 5 in the early afternoon. Captain Daniel B. Sheehan III came as forward air controller with Sergeant Miguel A. Cervantes to assist him. Master Sergeant Padilla was in charge of the snipers. Wyrick remained on station as the command and control element, and Gunnery Sergeant Villalobos continued to run the fire support coordination at the battalion command post.[15]

Gunnery Sergeant Dailey's original squad remained in place to allow Padilla's Marines to familiarize themselves with the situation. As 24 August proved to be one of the busiest days in Najaf, the new Marines got a taste of what the others had been living with for seven days. "Once we hit that building," said Staff Sergeant Chadwick D. Baker of their arrival at OP 5, "there was a full-on fight going on. . . . You ran in and threw your stuff off and crawled around avoiding all the windows." The relief force got to work. Baker was engaging targets within an hour noting that "once we got in, we set up our positions and started shooting people." The rules of engagement were clear, as Master Sergeant Wyrick had briefed the new arrivals. The Marines had identified several locations they suspected of being arms caches, and they were clear to shoot any armed military-aged males going in or out of those places. They were in their element. Padilla remarked that direct-action raids were one thing, "but I don't think there's anything like sniping."[16]

The Marines took fire throughout that day, from small arms, rocket propelled grenades, and enemy marksmen. Captain Sheehan and Sergeant Cervantes joined Sergeant Marnell and Gunnery Sergeant Keeler; together they brought fire on several targets, including one mission with the cavalry battalion's 120mm mortars. They conducted missions with whatever aircraft checked on station from Army, Air Force, or Marine aviation. In one incident, Keeler was controlling a section of Army Apaches when one of the aircraft experienced a weapons malfunction that put

---

* Marines also noted the probable presence of non-Iraqis in the enemy forces, including one "fair complexion male with blond hair," and others whose descriptions matched intelligence reports on Iranian agents and Hezbollah members. Najaf debrief, 27 Aug 2004.

a burst of 30mm cannon fire onto the Marines' position. Dust and concrete and metal fragments flew everywhere, and the Marines dove for cover. The pilots came up immediately on the radio to make sure there were no casualties. There were none, but the close call had knocked the wind out of a few of the Marines. The combined force of snipers and fires Marines that day scored another three confirmed and eight probable kills. Later that night, under the protective overwatch and firepower of Task Force Cougar's armored vehicles, they moved forward to another location, but they withdrew to OP 5 when they found the new position unsuitable.[17]

The Task Unit Raider Marines remained heavily engaged on 25 August. Master Sergeant Dailey and his Marines completed the turnover to the relief force and prepared to withdraw to the battalion command post for the trip back to Camp Myler. Before they departed, they took care of one last task, as Dailey's snipers had identified another enemy sniper nest.

This time it was Staff Sergeant Alex N. Conrad who spotted the signs of the enemy marksman. Something he saw looked out of place; as he looked closer, he recognized the loopholes. Then he observed a figure dressed in black with a green headband, and he saw that militiaman poke a gun barrel out of one hole and fire. Conrad withdrew farther into the building in case the enemy marksman had seen him. Setting up a new position slightly offset from where he had just been,

Three Marines (left to right: Sgt David D. Marnell, Capt Daniel B. Sheehan, and Sgt Miguel A. Cervantes) are shown in a Najaf schoolhouse, known as OP 5. With GySgt Ryan P. Keeler, they brought heavy but precise fires down on the Shi'a militiamen in and around the Imam Ali Mosque.

Photo courtesy of Capt Daniel B. Sheehan

he trained the .50-caliber rifle on the loophole and waited for movement. Master Sergeant Dailey took up the binoculars and spotted for him. After 40 minutes, their patience was rewarded. When Conrad saw the militiaman start to plug up the hole, he fired through it. Then he put three more rounds into the wall around it and several more rounds into another part of the structure in case the man had somehow escaped the four heavy rounds delivered in rapid succession. Confirmation of the kill proved impossible, but this enemy sniper was not heard from again.[18]

Master Sergeant Padilla's Marines kept the pressure on the enemy. Aside from the few and the proud among the enemy who had some training, Padilla thought they were "just a bunch of idiots" who virtually lined up to be shot. "We would take one guy out, and the next minute another guy was in the same spot trying to figure out what was happening." Even after the first wave departed, the Det One Marines still had sufficient manpower to keep a fresh sniper on a weapon at all times and man several positions 24 hours a day. Staring through optics, especially at night, is fatiguing, and the Marines needed to rotate regularly. The brutal heat also sapped strength and energy, and staying hydrated took constant effort. As Gunnery Sergeant Jack A. Kelly noted, "You sweated all day long, all night long. You slept and you sweated the whole time. You couldn't drink enough water." They got so filthy that Padilla could not remember having smelled that bad since Ranger school, years prior. Fortunately, they also had the soldiers of Task Force Cougar supporting them with logistics as well as security, so they did not have to be too concerned with their own maintenance and defense and could concentrate on the enemy. The ability to keep going and man their weapons was a critical element to their success. As Staff Sergeant Baker observed, "that's what killed the bad guys: they never got a break."[19]

The building where the Det One Marines had established their observation post 5 was a solidly built schoolhouse, which provided them plenty of room to operate and afforded protection against enemy fire, which was continuous and sometimes heavy. "It was a three-story building," said Gunnery Sergeant Kelly, "which allowed us multiple decks to observe from and shoot from. It got us about as close as we could possibly get to the shrine at the time without exposing ourselves completely, and we were able to observe and report on a lot of different activities." The snipers could use the lower decks while the fires Marines could get up high for better observation.

That the Marines were in the building was never a secret, and the enemy certainly wanted to eliminate them. But the Marines' urban sniper tactics kept the individual hides concealed and covered, and they were able to operate without interference. The snipers engaged targets and reported back constantly, sending information to Task Force Cougar and the battalion headquarters to flesh out the operational picture and feed the targeting cycle.[20]

Captain Sheehan, Sergeant Marnell, and Sergeant Cervantes continued to rain fire down on the enemy, manning Keeler's post at OP 5 that gave them excellent views of the battlespace. They settled into a battle rhythm based on the enemy's actions and the assets they had available. "The AC-130 would check on station at about 2220," Sheehan said. "We'd run the AC-130 all through the night on targets of opportunity as they would pop up. Then about three or four in the morning, the AC would check off station and we'd get our heads down for a little bit." He noted that "generally, the fighting was pretty quiet at night, at least in the dead hours, and then right around sunrise it would kick back off again. You'd hear the call to prayer—we were definitely within audio range of the mosque—so we got all the calls to prayer throughout the day. In that mosque they were using the loudspeakers to rally the troops, and as command and control for the fighters in there." Throughout the day, the Marines would control the sections of aircraft that were pushed to them by Gunnery Sergeant Villalobos, mostly Army Apaches and Marine Cobras. As night fell, the big Air Force gunship would reappear, and the cycle would begin again. During the night of 25 August, the Marines maintained observation of the area, engaged targets, and controlled preparatory fires for the long-planned ground assault on the Imam Ali shrine.[21]

The ground assault on the mosque never happened. Coalition operations in and around the city had had their intended effect on the noxious al-Sadr, and he was forced into negotiations with the interim Iraqi government by the reclusive but venerated chief Shi'a cleric in Iraq, Ayatollah Sayyid Ali Husseini al-Sistani. The Iraqi government announced at 0200 on 27 August that a truce had been reached and that hostilities would officially end at 1000.[22]

The stunned Det One Marines, only a few hundred meters from the shrine, reported large numbers of Shi'a gunmen "coming out of the woodwork," moving about openly with arms and ammunition, but the now-strict rules of engagement prevented the Marines from firing. For the aggressive Marines, holding their fire was hardest part of the operation; in fact,

Photo courtesy of Capt Daniel B. Sheehan

Capt Daniel B. Sheehan at his post in OP-5 in Najaf, August 2004. From this position he and the other fires Marines had excellent field of fire and observation on areas the Shi'a gunmen had previously enjoyed freedom of movement. The map and aerial photo taped to the railing was used for target identification.

they had just shot a man right before the cease-fire went into effect. They figured that the gunmen were just resting and refitting for the next action in Najaf or elsewhere. The discipline and maturity of the Marines ensured that the cease-fire would not be broken from within their ranks. If they were prohibited from firing, they could still observe, and they duly reported everything they saw in case the negotiations broke down and Coalition forces had to assault the militia's stronghold.[23]

Despite expectations to the contrary, the cease-fire did hold up, and the negotiations eventually resulted in al-Sadr and his forces withdrawing from the city. Although reports stated that the gunmen had sustained thousands of casualties in and around the city, the humiliating withdrawal was even more of a reverse for them than the battlefield defeat. More importantly, the authority of the interim Iraqi government had been enforced and upheld. Najaf was no Fallujah stalemate; the Coalition had won, and the insurgents had lost. On 27 August, Det One Marines pulled back to the cavalry battalion command post and waited for further instructions. The next day, they moved to another base in preparation for the trip home to Camp Myler, but they were told to hold there for 24 hours, just in case they were

Photo courtesy of Capt Daniel B. Sheehan

Det One Marines prepare to depart Najaf after the conclusion of operations there; SSgt Chadwick D. Baker mans an 50-caliber M2 machine gun while Capt Daniel B. Sheehan mans an 7.62mm M240G machine gun. This humvee is one of the purpose-built ground mobility vehicles transferred from the SEALs to the Marines when Task Unit Raider was reconstituted as a direct action force.

needed again. Finally, on 30 August they were released from further service in Najaf and traveled back to Baghdad by humvee and helicopter.

The actions of the Det One Marines during the battle of Najaf have no parallel in any other battle of Operation Iraqi Freedom. In a situation that called for a special operations force to completely integrate with a conventional unit as a supporting effort, Task Unit Raider's Marines shone brilliantly. The central theme was mutual support: Task Force Cougar soldiers provided security and support for the Marines, who in turn supported them, and more importantly, shaped the battlespace for their scheme of maneuver. Task Force Cougar led the 2d Battalion, 7th Cavalry, and that famous battalion led the fight inside the city. Together they were responsible for constraining the enemy's freedom of movement in the Imam Ali Mosque and contributing significantly to a major Coalition victory.

Det One Marines bridged the gap between "conventional" and "special" because they were regular Marines, grounded in conventional operations but organized and intensively trained for special operations.

It is important to note that except for Captain Sheehan, the teams were led by staff noncommissioned officers. The senior Marines did the liaison work with higher headquarters, led the snipers, and made all of the decisions on the ground. Major Craig S. Kozeniesky wrote that "one distinct advantage MCSOCom Det One personnel have over all SOF counterparts is their ability to coordinate and anticipate conventional force requirements and support." He stressed that more detachment capabilities could have been employed there if they had been requested.* Master Sergeant Wyrick agreed, noting that he wished they had had some counterintelligence and radio reconnaissance Marines to throw into the fight, and pointing out that the whole detachment could have been gainfully employed in the battle. Nothing in Najaf proved

---

* The after action report from the Naval Special Warfare element also alludes to Det One's capabilities in a conventional environment. The report, while not explicitly mentioning the Marines, stated, "The conventional forces are significantly more mindful of the military rank structure compared to SOF." No similar reference can be found in Det One after action reports. NSW AAR, 1 Sept 2004.

beyond the capabilities of the Marines of Det One.

Targeting "Z"

While a large number of Marines were involved in operations in Najaf, preparations back in Baghdad were well underway to execute the boldest and most daring operation Task Units Raider and Thunder had yet undertaken. Objective Rifle targeted "Z," a notorious insurgent commander, involved in scores of assassinations, bombings and indirect fire attacks. He was much like the insurgent "X," except that he was more violent, more cunning, and even harder to catch. As he did on the hunt for that first major target, Major M. Gerald Carter turned the entire resources of the intelligence element to catching "Z."[24]

Carter knew of "Z" as early as the first month of the deployment, when he was making contacts with every agency in Baghdad to get targeting intelligence. Over the course of the operation, the intelligence element kept alert for any sign on "Z," but nothing of significance turned up until early August, when solid information finally came to its attention.[25]

Captain Christopher B. Batts's counterintelligence Marines were given control of a source close to "Z." That source brought in new information that pointed to the man, and the hunt was back on. Through their own initiative, they developed another source they called "The Kid." Initially, only Captain Batts and Gunnery Sergeant William G. Parsons had met with the original source, but as the operation progressed, they brought in Staff Sergeant Scott J. Beretz. He began to feed "The Kid" information for their quarry, setting him up as an insurgent from another part of Iraq interested in buying weapons and bombs. "Z" took the bait.[26]

Due to the man's excellent operational security and tradecraft, he had never presented a clear enough picture to allow the task group to fix him and hit him. He moved constantly, had several houses, and never let anyone in on his plans. It became apparent that "Z" had not grown lax in his operational skills, and he did not present a target that was conducive to normal methods of operations. Through the work of the sources, however, it looked possible to lure him into a predetermined location in Baghdad where the assault force could descend upon him. But there was a catch: the location would be a crowded restaurant, at noon, deep inside the city, surrounded by traffic and crowds. There could be no fast convoy, no silent foot approach, and no AC-130 overhead. If shots were fired on this objective, it would not be a single burst but in all probability a major engagement with civilian casualties.[27]

The situation called for a far more ambitious plan than any the Marines had attempted before, and they were ready for the challenge. By the end of August, with a score of direct action hits under their belts, a stalwart force of Polish operators alongside them, and a relentless intelligence machine to pave the way, Task Unit Raider was on top of its game, and Major Kozeniesky argued persuasively for the chance to do the hit. Commander William W. Wilson approved the general concept and instructed them to proceed.

For the assault on Objective Rifle, almost none of the usual advantages were present, so the Marines and the men of Task Unit Thunder had to devise other means of stacking the deck in their favor. They needed to have some reasonable expectation that "The Kid" could deliver and could effectively trigger the assault. They needed to have a base of operations closer to the target area, since Camp Myler was too far away to launch a daytime convoy through congested streets. They needed air cover to replace the AC-130, which only operated at night, but which would also not seem out of place overhead at that time of day. And they needed an assault plan that was synchronized tightly enough to get the job done in a compressed time window but still allowed for flexibility as the situation dictated.

Staff Sergeant Beretz arranged through sources for "Z" to meet their source at a restaurant in one of Baghdad's better districts. The young man would pose as an up-and-coming anti-Coalition figure interested in buying weapons from "Z." He was given a cell phone to send text messages to the task force and a series of code phrases to transmit.[28] The trap was almost set.

The planners chose an American base close to the restaurant where units Raider and Thunder could wait for the trigger. The composition of the convoy needed to be addressed. Driving out of the gates at high speed in assault vehicles would alert the ever-watchful insurgency, and the planners had enough respect for the target's abilities to know that he would have surveillance out. They decided to use indigenous vehicles such as vans and panel trucks borrowed from the Special Forces, as well as some assault vehicles, trading the protection of the military vehicles for the anonymity of the Iraqi trucks. Up front would be dark-skinned Marines in native garb. Overhead would be Army OH-58D Kiowa helicopters, which had excellent surveillance equipment, carried weapons, and were usual sights in the skies over Baghdad. Task Unit Raider would handle the assault; Thunder would provide containment and backup force. Every man in each force who could possibly be spared was put on the raid force; with a dozen men still in Najaf, the support section Marines again stepped up to fill gunfighting roles.[29]

On 30 August, the pieces for the operation were complete and the assault forces staged, with Task Unit Raider mounted in four hunekers and three indigenous vehicles. In the cab of the lead Iraqi truck wearing a robe, a dish-dash, was Staff Sergeant Glen S. Cederholm, who had grown as much of a beard as he could after the return from Najaf. (Ironically, he and others had long advocated that some Marines should maintain facial hair for just such a contingency. He had a fairly good beard after a week in Najaf but had shaved it off before his return to Camp Myler.) The meeting was set for any time between 1100 and 1600. At 1132, the OH-58Ds checked on station and began to watch the target area. A quick reaction force from 3d Battalion, 82d Field Artillery, quietly prepared to go. "The Kid" sent a message to say that he was en route to the meeting.[30]

Shortly afterward, the message came from the source that "Z" was on site. Task Units Raider and Thunder left the gates and moved toward the objective. The approach was far more difficult than any they had previously undertaken. Traffic was heavy, the vehicles experienced communications blackouts, and at one point, an Iraqi male was seen watching the convoy and talking on a cell phone. The Marines were certain he was tipping off someone.

In the lead vehicle, the bearded Staff Sergeant Cederholm in his dish-dash navigated the force on its route. His disguise worked, and he never got a second look from any bystander. At one point, his computerized navigation system seized up because of the excessive heat, and it was only his excellent memory of the route that kept the force on schedule while the system reset. All during the approach, Master Sergeant Keith E. Oakes kept thinking that they would get compromised, but he knew that with his Marines ready for action and Task Unit Thunder alongside, "it would have been a wicked fight," but a fight they definitely would have won.[31]

The units did manage to avoid detection, though, and they soon were on the target site. The indigenous vehicles pulled up to the site, and the assault teams dismounted and ran toward the site while other teams from Raider and Thunder took up blocking positions. Staff Sergeant Cederholm jumped out, ripped off his "man dress," and took up a position in the cordon. With complete surprise, Teams 2 and 5 burst into the building just seconds after they exited the vehicles, with Captain Eric N. Thompson and Staff Sergeant Beretz carrying photographs of the targets. "These guys were just sitting at a table, drinking tea,"

Thompson recalled. None of the targets put up a fight; they never had a chance. The Marines seized several men, flexicuffed and blindfolded them, and took them outside individually to load them into different vehicles. The source was able to covertly identify "Z." No shots were fired, and no one attempted to interfere. The entire force remounted and returned to Camp Myler.[32]

Major Kozeniesky trumpeted this operation, with good reason, as a hallmark for the detachment as a whole.* He praised all involved, especially Task Unit Thunder, which selflessly joined the high-risk mission as a supporting element. The capture of "Z" was a real triumph, as he was an important insurgent figure in central Iraq, not just Baghdad. The operation illustrated the depth of the unit's capabilities and its willingness to alter its tactics, techniques, and procedures and accept a higher level of risk to take down a higher-level target. The preparation for it highlighted the ability of the counterintelligence section to operate at the special operations level with or without a designation, and it was Det One's own human intelligence Marines who placed and ran the source that gave them the trigger. Staff Sergeant Alex N. Conrad called it "the most exhilarating hit of them all."[33]

After Objective Rifle, the Task Unit executed a raid on Objective Ruby on 15 September. The target was a significant figure—a former Iraqi general, a cousin of Saddam Hussein, and a numbered figure on the famous Coalition blacklist. He was wanted for suppressing the post-Gulf War Shi'a uprising and for running major insurgent operations. Several incidents occurred during the execution of Ruby. A vehicle trailing the convoy had to be stopped by warning shots. The breach proved difficult, as a heavy metal grate prevented easy placement of the charge, but the lead breacher, Hospital Corpsman First Class Michael Tyrell, fully recovered from his gunshot wound in Objective Ricochet, quickly worked the charge onto the door. During the search of the house, Gunnery Sergeant Andre K. Bosier of Team 2 discovered what appeared to be a circuit board taped to a frying pan, which he immediately recognized as a bomb. He called the explosive ordnance disposal teams, which immediately cleared the building. When the device began emitting sounds, they destroyed it.[34]

The main house was a "dry hole," and Major Koze-

---

* Ironically, this operation, as risky as it was, was something that all of the reconnaissance Marines had practiced during work-ups for MEU (SOC) deployments, but never thought they would have a chance to execute. Part of the standard MEU (SOC) training package was the execution of a direct action raid in indigenous vehicles. Capt Thompson called the raid on Objective Rifle "MSPF 101."

niesky directed that the assault teams breach an adjacent structure. Team 5 accessed the roof of the building, breached, and entered it. It too yielded nothing. Interrogation of detainees found there indicated that the target lived there once but had not been seen for some time. Meanwhile, outside the house a commotion arose. There was an explosion some distance to the east, the nature of which was never discovered. The containment teams fired warning shots at two vehicles approaching the site, and as the force was re-embarking, an unknown person fired a burst from some weapon. None of the rounds hit the Marines, and no fire was returned. The raid force returned, intact but empty-handed, to Camp Myler. Objective Ruby was the last direct action raid mounted by Task Unit Raider.[35]

Departing Iraq

Immediately following the execution of Objective Ruby, Task Unit Raider stood down as a direct action force, and the Marines of Det One began to reassemble in Baghdad. Squadron One was turning over with its relief, and those Marines who were either in direct or general support to the task group briefed their replacements. Task Unit Raider had no replacement, there being no "Det Two" following in trace, and the main task they had was to return the assault vehicles they had received in June. The Marines concerned themselves with packing up for the trip home, documenting the lessons learned from this landmark deployment, and planning for an uncertain future.

Capt Stephen V. Fiscus talks with one of the members of the Polish special operations unit, the GROM, which formed Task Unit Thunder in the Naval Special Warfare Task Group. Every member of the task group, and especially the Marines, had the highest respect and admiration for the Poles.

Photo courtesy of Capt Stephen V. Fiscus

Much nonessential gear had been shipped home over the course of the summer, and the only substantial additions to the movement plan were an abandoned humvee that Gunnery Sergeants Jaime Maldonado and Jaime J. Sierra had recovered, rebuilt, and added to the detachment's table of equipment, and a small dog that Gunnery Sergeant Villalobos had adopted. The advance party flew home in mid-September. The first planeload of the main body departed on 27 September, and the last on 1 October. All Marines, save one, were back at Camp Pendleton, California, by 2 October.[36]

The one remaining Marine, Captain Stephen V. Fiscus, stayed behind in Baghdad to finish a job in progress. He had been asked to remain at his post with Task Unit Thunder in order to take part in a final operation west of Baghdad.[37] The target for this operation was a cell of major insurgent figures. Originally, the operation belonged to an Iraqi unit, but subsequent planning revealed that the target set was too large for this one unit to hit, and through the task group's liaison in the Green Zone, Task Unit Thunder was asked to join the effort. Captain Fiscus, in his role as liaison officer and planner for Thunder, saw that the operation would also require coordination with an Army brigade, in whose area it would occur. Fiscus arranged to meet with the brigade commander and his staff and was pleased to find that they were fully on board and offered full support. Fiscus noted that the brigade commander "was a former Special Forces guy, and he understood the deal completely." In fact, Fiscus remembered that when the general saw the target packages, "he stopped what he was doing, looked at me, and said, 'I've been looking for these guys for a while. You're damn right I'll support you!'" The Iraqi unit was the main effort; Task Unit Thunder and the Army brigade were supporting efforts. All parties agreed on a concept of operations and a timeline, and Fiscus went back to task group headquarters to prepare for execution.[38]

When the operation kicked off, the various elements of the force converged on their targets. The brigade commander had turned out his entire unit for a supporting sweep of the area, recognizing the opportunity that the operation presented. Communications problems began to crop up, due probably to the extensive electronic jamming employed to thwart command-detonated bombs (a problem Task Unit Raider had also experienced), and Thunder was blacked out for approximately 15 minutes, during which time they did not hear calls from the Iraqi unit that they were delayed. Adding to the confusion, at one point the AC-130 mistook Thunder for the Iraqi unit and began passing incorrect information.

Task Unit Thunder proceeded straight to its target location, stopped, and waited. After eight minutes—a near-eternity on an operation like this—the Poles still could get no communications. They assaulted the target as briefed and captured the individuals they were seeking. On the egress off the target, they picked up Commander Wilson from his post, where he had tracked the operation with the Army commander. Both of them were ecstatic at the overall results of the operation.[39]

Following that operation, Captain Fiscus detached from the GROM amid much heartfelt praise from those warriors with whom he had lived and operated for months, and for whom all of the Marines had developed strong respect and admiration. The Polish operators made Fiscus an honorary member of the GROM, and he carried back to California several tokens of their esteem for him, and for all the Marines of Det One.[40]

Major M. Wade Priddy, the fires element leader and operations officer, summarized the deployment best with one understatement: "We acquitted ourselves pretty well."[41]

Chapter 8

A Proven Concept

Making the Case for the Future

The majority of the Marine Corps U.S. Special Operations Command Detachment returned to the United States by 2 October 2004.[1] The Det One Marines wore their newly won laurels with pride, but they faced an uncertain future. Even while still deployed to Iraq, Colonel Robert J. Coates and the staff had been holding internal discussions on future courses of action, building their lessons learned, and planning to incorporate them into what they expected would be a new training cycle. They now had to submit those courses and recommendations to Headquarters Marine Corps and lay out their case. The formation and training phases had been challenging and difficult, the deployment even more so. But the post-deployment phase would prove to be the greatest challenge of them all.

Administrative and logistics matters occupied the detachment's time after its arrival at Camp Pendleton. The mountains of gear needed to be inventoried, checked, cleaned, serviced, stored, turned in, or sent up for maintenance or disposal. New equipment was coming in and had to be absorbed. Classified data and phone lines were being installed. A new training schedule had to be drawn up and implemented. In the absence of a clear decision from Headquarters Marine Corps on the future of the detachment, Colonel Coates chose to begin anew with the fundamental skills and improve the unit's capabilities by absorbing the lessons of the deployment. He also began an aggressive campaign of leveraging the solid relationships that the Det One Marines had built with units in Iraq, such as the Army's 2d Battalion, 5th Special Forces Group, to continue to improve their ability to operate with Special Forces units.

In October, Colonel Coates, Lieutenant Colonel Craig S. Kozeniesky, Major M. Wade Priddy, and Major M. Gerald Carter attended a "Way Ahead" conference at Joint Special Operations University, Hurlburt Field, Florida. The purpose of the conference was to develop courses of action for the upcoming USMC-SOCom Warfighter Conference scheduled for December. On 17 November, Colonel Coates and his primary staff, along with Commander William W. Wilson and his staff, presented their after action reviews to the commander of Naval Special Warfare Command, Rear Admiral Joseph Maguire, USN, at the SEALs' headquarters at Coronado, California. Lieutenant Colonel Kozeniesky, Major Priddy and Captain Stephen V. Fiscus began with a brief on the deployment and the lessons learned from it. The responses from the Navy side varied. Rear Admiral Maguire was openly "laudatory;" others chose to question the value of the Marine air-ground task force model and "expressed their opinions that the intelligence and fires sections were the only parts of the Detachment that should continue into the next phase."*

Colonel Coates answered the points by stressing the value of the detachment's task organization. He emphasized that Det One brought capabilities that SOCom did not otherwise possess in a standing, stand-alone unit: the detachment could perform all six warfighting functions (command and control, fires, maneuver, logistics, intelligence, and force protection); had the depth to field effective liaison officers to varied commands and agencies; and could operate either as a supporting effort or a main effort with equal facility. Coates closed by alluding to higher-level discussions taking place on the same subject and declined to speculate on the future. The Commandant of the Marine Corps and the commander of SOCom are "locked in a room," he said, referring to the service-level discussions then underway. "We'll wait for the puff of white smoke or black smoke."[2]

Colonel Coates and Lieutenant Colonel Kozeniesky next presented the detachment's after-action brief to General Michael W. Hagee and General Bryan D. Brown during the USMC-SOCom Warfighter Conference in December. What emerged from the meeting was that the Marine and SOCom leadership did not see a future for the detachment beyond the terms of the current memorandum of agreement.[3] Indeed, as Colonel Coates remembered it, General Brown stated definitively at the end of the brief that he did not see a requirement for Det One or any

---

*RAdm Joseph Maguire, USN, was the head of Special Operations Command's Directorate of Force Structure, Resources, and Strategic Assessments when Col Paul Hand served there and was strongly in favor of greater Marine participation in special operations.

Col Robert J. Coates and MGySgt Thomas P. Muratori furl and case Det One's colors at the detachment's de-activation ceremony, 10 March 2006, Camp Pendleton, California.

other Marine force contribution to SOCom.[4] The two generals owed a final recommendation to Secretary of Defense Donald H. Rumsfeld in January 2005, and his decision would follow.

Back at Camp Pendleton, training resumed for Det One. In December, the Marines of the reconnaissance element validated a four-day selection test designed for the anticipated accession of new members. The by-name selection of the original detachment could not be repeated, and a tough but fair process was required to screen and evaluate applicants. Instead of an epic ordeal designed to cull a handful from a field of hundreds, they opted for a series of straightforward tests aimed at an already qualified and screened pool of senior Marines and Navy Corpsmen. Day one consisted of a standard Marine Corps physical fitness test, followed by a swim test, and then an eight-part test that measured more of an applicant's strength and agility as well as shooting skills. Day two included a five-mile run and then a 12-mile road march. It ended with a double obstacle course run and a pistol qualification course. Day three saw a day and night land navigation test that consumed more than half the day and rolled into the fourth and final day, with more land navigation. The whole event finished with a run with full pack.[5]

One of the most significant training events oc-curred early in 2005. Beginning on 18 January, Det One reconnaissance and counterintelligence Marines participated in a month-long exercise with Company B, 2d Battalion, 5th Special Forces Group, with whom they had worked so closely and successfully in Iraq. Some Marines were embedded in the operational detachments, giving them the opportunity to observe and absorb the soldiers' techniques and procedures for human intelligence collection. Others were embedded at the company headquarters and assisted in the coordination of the unit's overall intelligence collection plan. Reconnaissance Marines shared their expertise in close-quarters battle with the soldiers of the operational detachments.[6]

The Secretary of Defense Responds

On 20 February 2005, Det One was scheduled to reach the end of its two-year existence as a proof-of-concept unit. At the USMC-SOCom Warfighter conference in December 2004, the detachment's leadership had been left with the impression that their unit's days were numbered. All hands anticipated a definitive answer on or about 20 February and prepared themselves for the order to deactivate. As January turned into February, the detachment's Marines waited to hear their fate, but the 20th passed without a decision. When no word came down, all began to have hopes that their unit would live to fight another day.

Behind the delayed announcement were Pentagon policy discussions. General Hagee and General Brown did not see a clear requirement for Det One to continue. General Hagee favored the enhancement of the traditional role of the Marine Corps with respect to special operations: interoperability with the theater special operations commands, cooperation on research, development and acquisitions, as well as the addition of Marines to perform such duties as foreign military training in order to free SOCom assets to pursue more specialized tasks. He considered that the Det One experiment had proven the point, but the long-term value of the experiment lay in the ties that the unit had made with Special Operations Command operating forces, the lessons learned in equipment and tactics, and the enhanced interoperability that would result from all of the above. He and General Brown recommended to the secretary of defense that the Marine force contribution to Special Operations Command not be continued, but that the Marine Corps could and should provide certain other capabilities to the special operations community.

Secretary of Defense Rumsfeld's reply to them, dated 4 February 2005, began, "Subject: Marines Special Operations Command." In it, he told them to reassess the problem and "think through the idea of a MarSOC," giving them 30 days to report back on "what it might look like, how many Marines might be involved, where it might be located, and so forth."[7] Staff officers at Headquarters Marine Corps and Special Operations Command accordingly began to examine the problem and work up courses of action to be submitted to the secretary. The progressive versions of the briefs they prepared show a large and ambitious force contribution, numbering more than 2,000 Marines.*

The detailed story of the rise of Marine Special Operations Command (MarSOC) is beyond the scope of this monograph. It is, however, necessary to mention certain facets of the discussion on the future of the Marine Corps and Special Operations Command following the experience of Det One. Two studies were written on the performance of the detachment and its future utility to Special Operations Command and the Marine Corps. One was written for SOCom by a team from Joint Special Operations University, the members of which traveled to Iraq and interviewed Marines and SEALs on a variety of topics, including the effectiveness of the command relationships and the value of their training. The study, titled *MCSOCOM Proof of Concept Deployment Evaluation Report,* undertook a realistic assessment of the detachment's performance and its value to Special Operations Command.

While citing several questions concerning the basic requirement for such a unit, the nature of its command relationships, and the frictions associated with integration—notably what the authors saw as the large amount of time Commander Wilson needed to devote to handling Det One issues[8]—it concluded, "Research and analysis strongly indicate that the initial force contribution was an overall success and should be continued. The Marine Corps successfully demonstrated the ability to interoperate with SOF during combat operations."[9] Significantly, the study recommended that the Marine Corps maintain the Det One model, increase its size to 130 members to address shortfalls identified during the deployment, and increase the number of detachments in order to provide "continuous availability."[10] The study also cited comments by U.S. Army Colonel Michael S. Repass, commander of Combined Joint Special Operations Task Force-Arabian Peninsula, that Det One should have been an "independent unit."

At the same time, researchers from the Center for Naval Analyses in Alexandria, Virginia, compiled a study for the Marine Corps on the costs and benefits of the detachment. Titled *MCSOCOM Det: Analysis of Service Costs and Considerations,* it sought to answer the following questions: was the value of the detachment worth its price, and what courses of action should be pursued with respect to the Marine Corps and special operations? This study presented mixed views. While recognizing that the detachment brought significant capabilities to the task group in Iraq, it also questioned the validity of the deployment as a comprehensive test of the unit since it performed only one of the four missions given to it.* The study cited the high price in resources and personnel involved in the detachment's creation and projected expansion and concerns about the Marine Corps' insistence on maintaining its hallmark air-ground task force model. The study observed that "the Marine Corps can make a valuable contribution in the SOF

---

* Although the idea of a Marine Special Operations Command was moving above and beyond Det One, one of the early draft MarSOC briefs did use the Det One logo as the prospective MarSOC logo on the cover slide. MarSOC document binder, Marine Corps Historical Center, Quantico, VA.

* That "one mission" was direct action, according to the Center for Naval Analyses study. Det One members, however, were adamant that their liaison work with the GROM as well as the missions to al-Kut and an-Najaf constituted Coalition support. The Joint Special Operations University study credited them with performing special reconnaissance as well.

realm, both at the unit level and by individual Marines supporting SOF units," but it noted that the other lesson from the proof of concept was that "the Marine Corps cannot expect to operate completely on its own terms when supporting SOCom forces."[11] It discussed several courses of action, echoing the Joint Special Operations University study's recommendation of maintaining and expanding the Det One model, as well as others, such as providing a component-like command to SOCom without a large contribution and a formal structure, or simply leveraging existing Marine Corps units and capabilities to support SOCom missions.*

While the Center for Naval Analyses study's final version was published on 18 February 2005 and made available to Det One, the Joint Special Operations University study was not released; it was finished in December 2004 but held at Special Operations Command. Det One knew of its existence, having worked with its authors during and after the deployment, but the Marines could not obtain a copy of the report during the first half of 2005 when Colonel Coates and the staff were trying to make the case for their unit's continued existence. They finally received a copy on 12 December 2005."[12]

Colonel Coates and his staff saw the formation of Marine Special Operations Command itself as a significant and necessary step forward for the Marine Corps, but they saw in the organizational details some points with which they did not agree. In their opinion, the proposed MarSOC structure was not the task-organized model that they had formed and validated. As they saw it, they had the experience to recommend the right courses of action, having demonstrated that their unit produced a solution that minimized impact on the Marine Corps while providing a uniquely Marine capability to address Special Operations Command shortfalls.

Their proposed alternative course was a component commanded by a major general, with two organizations under it: a Marine Special Operations Group, and a Foreign Military Training Unit. As the Det One officers outlined it, under the Marine Special Operations Group initially would be two standing detachments, called Marine Special Operations Units, task organized to perform all warfighting functions and having the missions of special reconnaissance, direct action, coalition support, advanced special operations, and combating terrorism. Det One, with personnel augments, would form the basis for the first of the two units and would deploy again in January 2006. The Marine Special Operations Group would also be a deployable warfighting headquarters, and could form the core of a joint special operations task force. In this plan, the component would be ready for initial action in the second quarter of fiscal year 2006, a matter of months from the time they proposed it. An aviation detachment would come on line starting in fiscal year 2008, followed by third and fourth special operations units in 2009 and 2010, respectively. This plan, as the Det One staff designed it, carried with it the philosophy and integrity that the unit's founders had built into it, namely a uniquely Marine contribution to an identifiable need, which also leveraged existing Marine Corps structure and returned value to the operating forces.[13]

As 2005 progressed, however, Colonel Coates and his Marines had less and less effective voices in the new command's structure. The Det One plan did not find favor with the Marines working on the Marine Special Operations Command structure, and the detachment's command chronology asserted that the proposal being worked by the action officers at Headquarters Marine Corps "was constructed with virtually no input from the detachment." It would not be incorrect to say that from the Det One perspective, the debate inside the Marine Corps on the size and shape of MarSOC was acrimonious.

The Detachment Presses On

For most 2005, the status of Det One took on a peculiar aspect, separate from but related to the frictions at the service level. Although it was no secret that the unit's days were numbered, there was a lingering question on the extent to which it would provide, in part or in whole, the foundation for the new Marine component command.[14] Det One was not slated for further deployments. It could not take on more recruits. Its men were, for the most part, held on station. The only Marines allowed to transfer were those retiring, those who were slated for command, and a selected few others who were assigned to high-demand billets. Lieutenant Colonel Kozeniesky, pro-

---

* The Center for Naval Analyses study explicitly used the Det One model as the basis for examining options for a continued and expanded force contribution to Special Operations Command, from one detachment augmented to a strength of 130 (just as the Joint Special Operations University study did) and with the current command relationships, to four detachments, eight detachments, and finally a 2,500-Marine component command with eight "independently deployable detachments with an aviation combat element."

** In an email to the author on 12 December 2005, Maj Priddy wrote, "Amazing that it takes the subject of the study a year to get a copy of it. Haven't had a chance to digest the whole thing, but overall seems to be a very favorable review, which probably explains why it's taken a year to get a copy. Interesting conclusions and recommendations, but since they were completely ignored they're probably also irrelevant at this point."

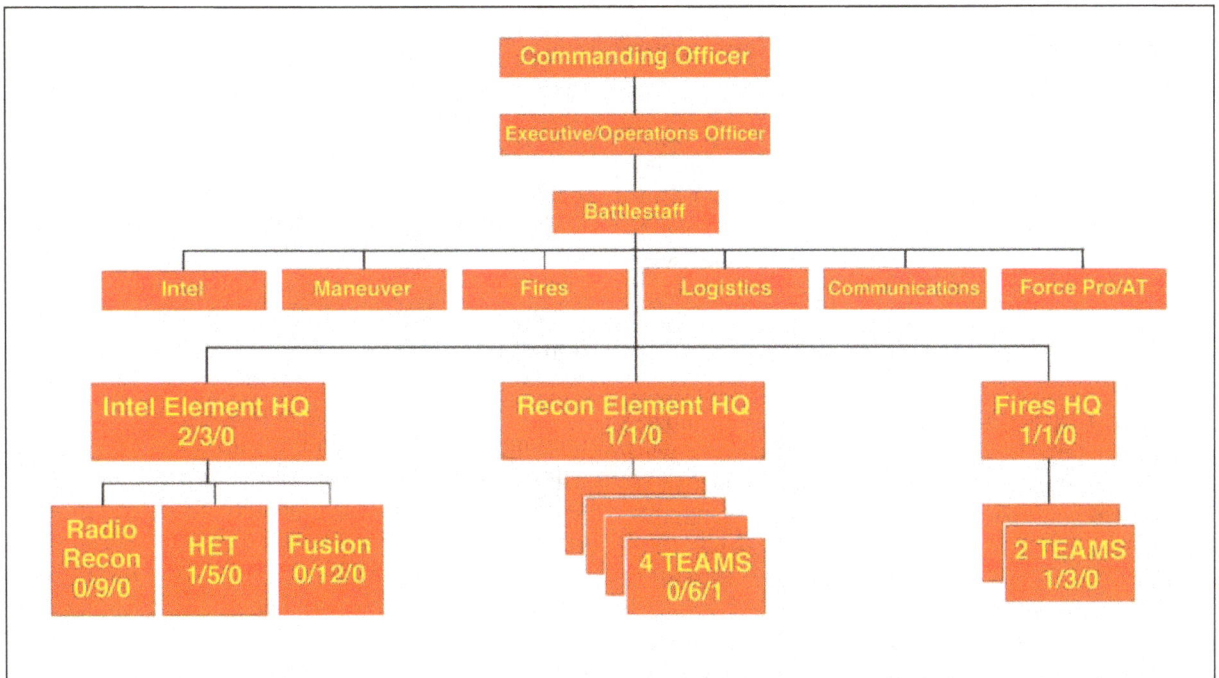

This diagram shows the original structure and manning levels for Det One. The unit was allotted 86 personnel, but due to shortfalls discovered during the formation and training phase, it was augmented to approximately 100; the reconnaissance element was also reorganized from four teams to six.

moted after return from Iraq, left to assume command of an infantry battalion. His place was taken by Lieutenant Colonel Francis L. Donovan, another veteran of 1st Force Reconnaissance Company under Colonel Coates. Donovan had played multiple roles in the formation of the detachment. While on recruiting duty, he helped reenlist some of the reconnaissance Marines who were out of the Corps, then as a staff officer in Special Operations Training Group, he had helped evaluate part of the Capstone Exercise in Nevada. Additionally, he had done some time with Special Operations Command and knew the SOCom realm well.[15]

This state of suspended animation put the detachment in a difficult position. It could train with what it had, but to what end? Colonel Coates chose to press on, regardless of the policy-level discussions, over which he had little influence and no control. He wanted to keep his Marines sharp, and even if the unit was to be disbanded, his intent was to hand over Marines who were fully trained and had skills no others had. If they happened to be called upon to deploy again, he was determined to be ready when the call came.

During 2005, training continued at a brisk pace.[16] Det One Marines attended several schools, including breaching, parachute, communications, and medical courses. The fires element Marines maintained their joint terminal attack controller qualifications with live close air support training. The reconnaissance element and radio reconnaissance section worked on ever-greater integration, embodying the lessons they had learned in Iraq. In July, the reconnaissance Marines went to the wilds of southwestern Utah for a four-week sniper package. In September, the unit shifted to element training and returned to Bridgeport, California, for mountain operations, followed in October by more close-quarters battle training at Camp Pendleton and a week-long raid force exercise at a former U.S. Air Force base in southern California.[17]

By the fall of 2005, the detachment had again achieved a high state of readiness despite personnel shortfalls and an uncertain future. One proposal they brought up was deployment with I Marine Expeditionary Force as a "counter-intimidation task force," reprising their role in Baghdad by providing a stand-alone unit solely dedicated to striking at the insurgent cells that were interfering with the nascent Iraqi security forces. The commander of Marine Forces Pacific, Lieutenant General Wallace C. Gregson, pressed for that and other options for the continued employment of the detachment and was one of its most vocal advocates among Marine general officers.[18] On 30 November, however, Colonel Coates was informed that the detachment would be deactivated.

Although he was not given a final date, Coates informed the staff, and they began to prepare a program of actions and milestones.

Deactivation

On 7 February 2006, nearly one year to the day after Secretary Rumsfeld's memorandum, Det One got the official word on its fate. Captain Daniel B. Sheehan III forwarded a message to the author with the comment, "There you have it. The fat lady sang." Attached to his e-mail was the full text of Marine Corps Bulletin 5400, dated 6 February 2006. It directed the deactivation of MCSOCom Detachment no later than 1 April 2006 and laid out the subordinate tasks in detail. The manpower structure that was shuffled to create the billets for the detachment would be reshuffled to return each of the slots to the 42 commands from which they had come. The equipment would be transferred, after inventory and limited technical inspection, to Marine Corps Logistics Command. From there, service-common equipment would enter the pool for reissue to other units in the operating forces; the special operations-specific gear would remain in the hands of Logistics Command for use by Marine Special Operations Command.* Personnel orders would follow; most Marines would be sent to units in the operating forces, and many of them would deploy to Iraq. Approximately two dozen Det One Marines received orders to Marine Special Operations Command units on the East and West coasts.[19]

On 10 March 2006, in between rain showers on a brisk afternoon, Det One held its deactivation ceremony. On the same spot where the detachment was activated nearly three years before, a much-reduced unit stood in a final formation. Among the guests present were the Commanding General, Marine Forces Pacific, Lieutenant General John F. Goodman, the Commanding General, 1st Marine Division, Major General Richard F. Natonski, and Mr. Charles Meacham from the Marine Raider Association. Family, friends, and retired members of the detachment looked on from the stands. As the band played, Colonel Coates and Master Gunnery Sergeant Thomas P. Muratori cased the unit's colors. Then, Lieutenant Colonel Frank Donovan called out the command, "Dismissed," and the Marine Corps U.S. Special Operations Command Detachment ceased to exist.

---

* Col Coates and LtCol Kozeniesky's .45-caliber pistols, serial numbers DET 1-001 and DET 1-002, went to the National Museum of the Marine Corps, Quantico, VA, along with an M4 carbine and its accessories.

The Legacy of Det One

After Det One passed into history, Colonel Coates was assigned to the staff of I Marine Expeditionary Force (Forward) as the officer responsible for overseeing the training, equipping, and directing of the Iraqi security forces. Lieutenant Colonel Kozeniesky took command of 2d Battalion, 5th Marines, and deployed with the 31st MEU (SOC) from Okinawa. Lieutenant Colonel Donovan took command of 2d Battalion, 1st Marines, within weeks of the deactivation of Det One.

Major Carter elected to do another joint intelligence tour. Major Priddy was assigned to a border training team in Iraq and left for a one-year tour at a fort on the Jordanian border. Major Thomas P. Dolan returned to a light attack helicopter squadron and deployed to Iraq, while Captain Daniel B. Sheehan III was assigned as an instructor in the helicopter training squadron at Camp Pendleton. Captain Christopher B. Batts, who had left active duty soon after the detachment's return from Iraq, went to work at an organization in Special Operations Command. Captain Mathew H. Kress returned to the Marine Corps Reserve, while Captain Olufemi A. Harrison stayed until the end and oversaw the transfer of the unit's facilities and equipment. Both Captain Eric N. Thompson and Captain Stephen V. Fiscus took command of infantry companies, and Captain Thompson deployed to Afghanistan in 2005.

Several Det One Marines retired, including Master Sergeants James R. Rutan, Joseph L. Morrison, and Terry M. Wyrick and Gunnery Sergeants Monty K. Genegabus and James E. Wagner. Staff Sergeant Victor M. Guerra left active duty and took a civilian information technology position with a Special Operations Command organization.

The Marines who stayed on active duty secured various assignments, some in the nascent Marine Special Operations Command units, others in conventional units. Master Sergeant Fidencio Villalobos Jr. was assigned to the fires section of I Marine Expeditionary Force and deployed immediately after the deactivation for a one-year tour in Iraq. Master Sergeant Charles H. Padilla remained on the West Coast as a special operations training group instructor; Master Sergeant John A. Dailey took a similar billet on the East Coast. Gunnery Sergeant Jack A. Kelly was assigned to Expeditionary Warfare Training Group Pacific as an instructor. Master Gunnery Sergeant Thomas P. Muratori became the operations chief at 1st Marine Special Operations Battalion, the West Coast operating unit of Marine Special Operations Command. Master Sergeant Mark S. Kitashima received orders to Okinawa. Gunnery Sergeants Jaime J. Sierra and Jaime Maldonado both transferred to 1st Force Reconnaissance Company, which was destined to be part of Marine Special Operations Command. (The humvee they recovered and rebuilt is now in the outdoor museum at Camp Pendleton.) Gunnery Sergeant Chadwick D. Baker reported to the Ranger Training Brigade at Fort Benning, Georgia, to be an instructor.

Master Sergeant Bret A. Hayes became the intelligence operations chief at Marine Special Operations Command headquarters, Camp Lejeune, North Carolina. Gunnery Sergeant Kenneth C. Pinckard was assigned to the Marine Corps Intelligence Activity at Quantico, Virginia, where he was of great help to the author in the preparation of this monograph. Master Sergeant Hays B. Harrington was sent to 1st Radio Battalion and deployed to Iraq. Gunnery Sergeant James A. Crawford became the signals intelligence chief at Marine Special Operations Command, while Staff Sergeant William B. Parker went to the Defense Language Institute to learn Farsi. The counterintelligence Marines remained in their community as well, in various capacities and different locations.

The founders of Det One had sought to ensure that the special operations experiences of the Marines in the unit would be fed back into the Corps at different levels by returning them to the operating forces. Ironically, the members of Det One, which were conceived as the modern descendants of the Marine Raiders of World War II, shared the fate of those Marines: their unit was disbanded, but they seeded other units with their experience and training. Although perhaps in a manner not originally intended, that is what Det One's Marines are doing: as commanding officers, instructors, staff officers, and team leaders, they are continuing the work they began in June 2003. This project is a testament to what they did, and what the Marine Corps can and will do when called upon to excel. They were, in the words of Major Priddy, "one of the most talented groups of Marines ever assembled."[20]

Epilogue

Where No Group of Marines Had Gone Before

By the findings of various reports and assessments, the Marine Corps U.S. Special Operations Command Detachment proved the concept it was designed to test, despite, as both the Joint Special Operations University and Center for Naval Analyses studies pointed out, the lack of a clearly stated requirement. Det One conducted two of the four missions it was assigned: direct action and Coalition support, and, by one account, a third mission as well, special reconnaissance. The true value of its performance lies not in the statistics—this many raids conducted, that many sub-detachments deployed, or this many task group staff positions filled—but in the task-organized capabilities it brought to bear over the course of the deployment. It demonstrated the applicability of the Marine Corps warfighting approach to the special operations realm, and it proved that the Marines could field a special operations unit that had value to Special Operations Command but still remained uniquely Marine.

The combat actions of the deployment clearly validated the pre-deployment training plan. This is a significant point, as it demonstrated that Marines could develop and execute a plan to train themselves to special operations standards. In a similar manner, the deployment validated the selection of the Marines, although not necessarily the selection process itself, which was a singular event. Det One secured the right mix of individual Marines, some with special operations backgrounds, most without those experiences, but all with a solid Marine Corps background.

No less significant for the Marine Corps, then, is that Det One also validated the special operations-capable program. The discussions and debates of the 1984 Fleet Marine Force Atlantic working group ordered by General Paul X. Kelley had produced two results. One was a rigorous examination of what the Marine Corps could, should, could not, and should not do in the area of special operations. The second was the subsequent transformation of a standing organization—the Marine amphibious unit—into something that was neither a solely conventional force nor an explicitly special force. With the success and value of the forward-deployed Marine expeditionary units taken as such an article of faith by Marines today, it is difficult to appreciate objectively how singular the emergence of that capability was within the Department of Defense, and the potential it revealed. Det One was a product of the maturation of the overall development of the training, equipment acquisition, operational philosophy, and practical experience that was the special operations capable program, and especially the maritime special purpose forces.* If a Marine expeditionary unit is a conventionally organized force with certain special operations capabilities, Det One was a logical progression from it: a standing special operations task force that was fully grounded in conventional operations.

Since there was no "Det Two" and no follow-on deployment for Det One, questions will linger on what the outcome might have been had the circumstances of the deployment been different. What if, for example, Det One had been deployed as a whole, and its task-organized capabilities preserved to the greatest extent possible? What then would have been the result of its operations in Iraq? Unfortunately, what-if ruminations, even if cast into known parameters, do little for concrete evaluation. The fact is that the 20 February 2003 memorandum of agreement empowered the commander of Squadron One to task-organize his forces, and much of the detachment's capabilities were accordingly placed in general support of the task group rather than in direct support of Task Unit Raider. In light of this fact, it is more useful to evaluate what effect those capabilities brought to the task group as a whole, and on the campaign in Iraq.

Clearly, the intelligence element dominated its field, having no peer in any other organization in Iraq, excepting only perhaps the high-tier Special Operations Command units, which are in a class by themselves.[1] In fact, Colonel Robert J. Coates regarded his intelligence capability as comparable to that of the highest tier SOCom units.[2] The radio re-

---

* It should be noted that Det One's training in close-quarter battle tactics illustrated that one segment of the Marine Corps effort had not kept pace with the times.

connaissance and counterintelligence Marines proved themselves able to work in the SOCom realm, if anything lacking only a label. The Joint Special Operations University study mapped both of those specialties to special operations designations but did not note the key point: radio reconnaissance and counterintelligence are standard Marine capabilities, not "special" capabilities.[3] The individual intelligence Marines serving with the outlying task units certainly distinguished themselves and contributed skills and abilities that would not have been present without them. Likewise, the Marines of the fires element occupied a niche all their own in a SOCom unit, proving that basic combined arms thinking is as applicable in special operations as in conventional fighting.

What effect did Det One have on Operation Iraqi Freedom? Here again, the statistics, although impressive, do not tell the full story. The Marine participation in the close-in duties of the personal security detail lasted only a few days, and thus that episode does not provide much substance for evaluation. Their direct action missions, however, had a substantial effect in preventing the insurgents from being able to deal a death blow to the fledgling Iraqi government. Task Unit Raider, even when depleted by requirements in al-Kut and an-Najaf, formed a powerful striking force that hit insurgent networks relentlessly, alone and in conjunction with the men of the GROM whom they supported with a liaison cell, while the SEAL task units did the dangerous and unheralded work of the personal security details. It was neither the SEALs nor the Marines nor the Poles alone who protected the Iraqi government; it was the task group that won the day, and Marines clearly added significant value to Commander William W. Wilson's warfighting capabilities and his ability to accomplish that "most important mission in Iraq."

At al-Kut and an-Najaf, the Marines provided timely capabilities to special and conventional units and in both cases materially contributed to the ability of the Coalition to hold the line against insurgent forces. Their actions enabled the emerging Iraqi government to enforce its authority, demonstrate resolve in the face of mortal challenges, and assert basic legitimate governance over glowering brute force.

Finally, what effect did Det One have on the organization and training of the Marine Corps? It is too early to answer that question fully; the exact ways in which the Marine Corps will operate in its traditional expeditionary role while achieving greater interoperability with Special Operations Command will emerge in due course as the Global War on Terrorism continues and Marine Special Operations Command reaches full operational capability. The acrimony attending the discussions on the demise of the detachment and the concurrent rise of MarSOC make it contentious to say that Det One was MarSOC's direct lineal predecessor. Yet it is also difficult to say that Det One had no effect at all on the formation of that command, as Det One was certainly the first Marine unit ever to serve with U.S. Special Operations Command. This much is true: "They went where no group of Marines had really gone before, and they proved their worth," said Lieutenant General Jan C. Huly, Deputy Commandant for Plans, Policies, and Operations. "It was a great proof-of-concept under some trying and actual combat conditions, and they did very, very well. And I think that the Marine Corps and the nation owe them a debt of thanks for what they did in blazing the trail for the Marine Corps component to the Special Operations Command."[4]

Notes

Chapter 1

1 Department of Defense, Secretary of Defense Memorandum on Special Operations Forces, 3 October 1983 (hereafter SecDef SOF Memo).
2 U.S. Special Operations Command History and Research Office, *United States Special Operations Command History: 15th Anniversary* (MacDill AFB, 2002), 10.
3 USMC, PP&O Information Paper, LtCol J. Giles Kyser IV, "History (Supported By 'Hard Data') As To Why The Marine Corps Did Not Participate In The Standup Of SOCom," 5 March 2003. This view is also asserted in similar language in Maj Robert E. Mattingly, USMC, *Herringbone Cloak—GI Dagger* (Washington, D.C.: USMC History and Museums Division, 1989)
4 SecDef SOF Memo
5 Headquarters II Marine Amphibious Force, Special Operations Study Group, "Examination of Marine Corps Special Operations Enhancements," 19 November–17 December 1984, pp. 3–5 (hereafter II MAF Examination).
6 Ibid., 6.
7 Ibid., 7–8.
8 Ibid., 9.
9 Ibid., 24–25.
10 Ibid., 25.
11 Headquarters Fleet Marine Force Atlantic, "Report of Examination of Marine Corps Special Operations Enhancements," 26 March 1985, para. 3.c (hereafter FMFLant report).
12 II MAF Examination, 16.
13 FMFLant report, para. 10.a.
14 Ibid., para. 11.
15 Ibid., cover letter, para. 3.
16 CG, Fleet Marine Force Atlantic, "Marine Corps Special Operations Capabilities, Discussion with the Commandant of the Marine Corps," 27 April 1985 (briefing slides; hereafter CMC/FMFLant SOC brief).
17 Ibid.
18 Ibid.
19 CMC, "Memorandum for the Record: The Marine Corps and Special Operations," 7 June 1985.
20 CMC, "Memorandum for the Joint Chiefs of Staff on the Marine Corps and Special Operations," 22 July 1985; and USMC, CMC P4 to USCinCEur, CinCPac, CinCMAC, CinCLant, USCentCom, USCinCSO, USCinCRed; Subject: The Marine Corps and Special Operations, 220915ZJul85.
21 Col Melvin G. Spiese intvw, 16 May 2005 (Marine Corps Historical Center [MCHC], Quantico, VA).
22 U.S. Marine Corps, ALMAR 023/88, para. 2.
23 24th MEU (SOC) ComdC, 1 January–30 June 1995 (Gray Research Center [GRC], Quantico, VA).
24 24th MEU (SOC) ComdC, 1 January–30 June 1993 (GRC).
25 4th MEB ComdC, 1–31 January 1991 (GRC).
26 LtCol J. Giles Kyser IV intvw, 25 May 2004 (MCHC).
27 Col Paul A. Hand intvw, 26 August 2005 (MCHC).
28 Kyser intvw.
29 Hand intvw.
30 Kyser intvw.
31 Ibid.
32 Hand intvw
33 Ibid.
34 MGySgt Joseph G. Settelen III 1st intvw, 3 August 2004 (MCHC).
35 MSgt Troy G. Mitchell intvw, 12 August 2004 (MCHC).
36 Kyser intvw.
37 Joint Publication 1-02, *Department of Defense Dictionary of Military and Associated Terms, 12 April 2001* (as amended through 31 August 2005).
38 The special operations section of Plan, Policies, and Operations had been pushed out of its Pentagon office and back into the Navy Annex after the damage to the Pentagon on 11 September 2001.
39 Settelen-1 intvw.
40 Ibid.
41 Kyser intvw.
42 Hand intvw.
43 Kyser intvw.
44 Ibid.
45 Ibid.
46 Ibid.
47 Settelen-1 intvw.
48 Ibid.
49 Mitchell intvw.
50 Kyser intvw.
51 USMC, PP&O Information Paper, LtCol J. Giles

Kyser IV, "Marine Support To Special Operations Forces (SOF) And Contributions To Address USMC Expanding Relationship And Interoperability Concerns," 2 July 2002.

[52] Hand intvw.
[53] Kyser intvw.
[54] Ibid.
[55] Ibid.
[56] CMC P4 Message, First Marine Corps Force Contribution to the United States Special Operations Command (USSOCom), 281330ZOct02.
[57] 5400 MCBUL 040900ZDec02 para. 2B.

Chapter 2

[1] LtCol J. Giles Kyser IV intvw, 25 May 2004 (Marine Corps Historical Center [MCHC], Quantico, VA).
[2] Sgt Victor M. Guerra intvw, 16 November 2004 (MCHC).
[3] GySgt James A. Wagner intvw, 12 January 2005 (MCHC).
[4] Guerra intvw.
[5] Ibid.
[6] MSgt James R. Rutan intvw, 10 January 2005 (MCHC).
[7] Wagner intvw. The problems of creating and forming the new unit were occasionally relieved by minor gaffes. A unit is assigned various codes that serve as shorthand for the automated data systems, so that large numbers of orders can be efficiently cut for Marines to report in, check out of, or otherwise be detached from that unit. Det One was assigned a monitor command code of "1F9," naming its home station as Camp Del Mar, on Camp Pendleton. In the course of the stand-up phase, a large number of orders were efficiently cut for Marines to report to Pensacola, Florida. "1F9" was an old code, belonging to some unit that had not been in existence in years, but the data systems had never been updated to say, "Camp Del Mar, Camp Pendleton, California," instead of "Pensacola, Florida." MGySgt Joseph G. Settelen III intvw, 3 August 2004 (MCHC).
[8] Capt Eric N. Thompson intvw, 14 October 2004 (MCHC).
[9] MSgt Terry M. Wyrick intvw, 23 March 2005 (MCHC).
[10] MSgt Joseph L. Morrison intvw, 14 April 2006 (MCHC).
[11] MSgt Charles H. Padilla intvw, 10 January 2005 (MCHC).
[12] MSgt John A. Dailey intvw, 10 March 2006 (MCHC).
[13] MSgt Keith E. Oakes intvw, 11 January 2005 (MCHC).
[14] HM1 Matthew S. Pranka intvw, 10 January 2005 (MCHC).
[15] SSgt Chadwick D. Baker intvw, 24 March 2005 (MCHC).
[16] Maj M. Wade Priddy intvw, 13 October 2004 (MCHC).
[17] Maj Thomas P. Dolan intvw, 13 October 2004 (MCHC).
[18] GySgt Fidencio Villalobos Jr. intvw, 13 January 2005 (MCHC).
[19] GySgt Ryan P. Keeler intvw, 12 January 2005 (MCHC).
[20] LtCol Francis L. Donovan intvw, 24 March 2006 (MCHC).
[21] Maj M. Gerald Carter intvw, 13 October 2004 (MCHC).
[22] GySgt Kenneth C. Pinckard intvw, 14 October 2004 (MCHC).
[23] MSgt Hays B. Harrington intvw, 13 January 2005 (MCHC).
[24] Capt Christopher B. Batts intvw, 6 January 2005 (MCHC).
[25] Ibid.
[26] CWO2 Kevin E. Vicinus intvw, 23 June 2006 ((MCHC).
[27] 5400 MCBUL 040900ZDEC02, para. 4A.
[28] Capt Matthew H. Kress intvw, 18 November 2004 (MCHC).
[29] Ibid.
[30] Carter intvw.
[31] GySgt Mark S. Kitashima intvw, 18 November 2004 (MCHC).
[32] Ibid.
[33] Ibid.
[34] Ibid.
[35] 20 February 2003 MOA, para. 5.
[36] MCSOCom Det One Mission Training Plan, 1 March 2003, para. 3.a.(3).(a).

Chapter 3

[1] MCSOCom Det One Mission Training Plan, 1 March 2003, para. 3.a. (1), emphasis in the original (hereafter 2003 MTP).
[2] MSgt Charles H. Padilla intvw, 10 January 2005 (Marine Corps Historical Center [MCHC], Quantico, VA).
[3] Capt Stephen V. Fiscus intvw, 17 November 2004 (MCHC).
[4] Maj Thomas P. Dolan intvw, 13 October 2004 (MCHC).
[5] MCSOCom Det One ComdC, 1 January–30 June 2003, Sect 2 (Gray Research Center [GRC], Quantico VA).

6 2003 MTP, para 3.a (1).
7 2003 MTP, Encl. 3: Detachment Training Packages.
8 Maj M. Gerald Carter intvw, 13 October 2004 (MCHC).
9 Capt Eric N. Thompson intvw, 14 October 2004 (MCHC); MCSOCom Det One ComdC 1 July–30 December 2003 (GRC).
10 Thompson intvw.
11 MSgt Keith E. Oakes intvw, 11 January 2005 (MCHC).
12 Ibid.
13 SSgt Andrew T. Kingdon intvw, 24 March 2005 (MCHC).
14 GySgt Jaime Maldonado and GySgt Jaime Sierra intvw, 22 March 2005 (MCHC).
15 GySgt Monty K. Genegabus intvw, 1 November 2004 (MCHC).
16 MCSOCOM Det One ComdC, 1 July–31 December 2003, Section 2 (GRC).
17 Thompson intvw.
18 Col Robert J. Coates intvw, 6 May 2004 (MCHC).
19 Dolan intvw.
20 Padilla intvw.
21 Dolan intvw.
22 LtCol Kozeniesky email to author, 5 April 2006.
23 Dolan intvw.
24 Thompson intvw.
25 Padilla intvw.
26 SSgt Alex N. Conrad intvw, 1 August 2005 (MCHC).
27 Padilla intvw.
28 Dolan intvw; Thompson intvw.
29 Department of Energy, Nevada Test Site Web page (www.nv.doe.gov/nts/default.htm.).
30 Thompson intvw.
31 MGySgt Joseph G. Settelen III, USMC, 2d intvw, 24 Febuary 2006 (MCHC) (hereafter Settelen-2 intvw).
32 Sgt Victor M. Guerra intvw, 16 November 2004 (MCHC).
33 GySgt Kenneth C. Pinckard intvw, 14 October 2004 (MCHC).
34 Padilla intvw.
35 HM1 Matthew S. Pranka intvw, 10 January 2005 (MCHC).
36 Thompson intvw.
37 Ibid.
38 Settelen-2 intvw.
39 Ibid.
40 Ibid.
41 Cmdr William W. Wilson, USN, intvw, 24 March 2005 (MCHC).
42 Settelen-2 intvw.
43 Pinckard intvw.
44 MSgt John A. Dailey intvw, 10 March 2006 (MCHC).
45 Settelen-2 intvw.
46 Pinckard-2 intvw.
47 Fiscus intvw.
48 Oakes intvw.
49 LtCol Kozeniesky email to author, 5 April 2006.
50 MCSOCOM Det One ComdC, 1 January–30 June 2004, 3–4 (GRC).
51 Ibid.
52 Oakes intvw.
53 LtCol Craig S. Kozeniesky intvw, 15 October 2004 (MCHC).
54 I Marine Expeditionary Force, "I MEF SOTG Tactical Evaluation of MCSOCOM Det One capstone Exercise," 21 January 2004, para. 3.(2).c.
55 LtCol Kozeniesky email to author, 5 April 2006.
56 Dailey intvw.
57 MSgt Terry M. Wyrick intvw, 23 March 2005 (MCHC).
58 Pinckard intvw.
59 Carter intvw.
60 Dolan intvw.
61 Kozeniesky intvw.

Chapter 4

1 Cmdr William W. Wilson, USN, intvw, 24 March 2005 (Marine Corps Historical Center [MCHC], Quantico, VA).
2 MCSOCOM Detachment One, Daily Sitrep, 20 April 2004, para. 4.c (U) (hereafter Daily sitrep]).
3 Daily sitrep 28 April 2004, para. 4.c.
4 Capt Matthew H. Kress intvw, 18 November 2004 (MCHC).
5 Daily sitrep, 28 April 2004, para. 4.c.
6 Wilson intvw.
7 Ibid.
8 LtCol Craig S. Kozeniesky intvw, 15 October 2004 (MCHC).
9 MCSOCOM Detachment One, Deployed Weekly Sitrep 020 (hereafter Weekly sitrep 020).
10 Daily sitrep, 25 April 2004.
11 Deployed weekly sitrep, 021, para. 3.A.1.
12 Deployed weekly sitrep, 021.
13 MSgt Terry M. Wyrick intvw, 23 March 2005 (MCHC).
14 MSgt Keith E. Oakes intvw, 11 January 2005 (MCHC).
15 Daily sitrep, 4 May 2004; MSgt Charles H. Padilla intvw, 10 January 2005 (MCHC).
16 Padilla intvw.
17 Padilla intvw.
18 MCSOCOM Detachment One, Operational Summary, Objective Racket.

[19] Ibid.
[20] Daily sitrep, 2 May 2004, comdrs comments.
[21] Daily sitrep, 6 May 2004, comdrs comments.
[22] Daily sitrep, 6 May 2004, comdrs comments.

Chapter 5

[1] MCSOCOM Detachment One, Operational Summary, Operation Raccoon (hereafter Raccoon opsum).
[2] MCSOCOM Detachment One, Daily Sitrep, 17 May 2004.
[3] LtCol Craig S. Kozeniesky intvw, 15 October 2004 (MCHC).
[4] Rambler opsum.
[5] Revenge opsum.
[6] MSgt Terry M. Wyrick intvw, 23 March 2005 (MCHC).
[7] MCSOCOM Detachment One, Deployed Weekly Sitrep 024.
[8] Wyrick intvw.
[9] Wyrick intvw; Cederholm award citation
[10] SSgt Andrew T. Kingdon intvw, 24 March 2005 (MCHC).
[11] Tyrell award citation.
[12] GySgt James A. Crawford intvw, 13 January 2006 (MCHC).
[13] SSgt Daniel L. Williams intvw, 23 March 2005 (MCHC).
[14] Williams intvw and award citation.
[15] Sgt William B. Parker intvw, 3 August 2005 (MCHC).
[16] Williams intvw.
[17] MSgt Bret A. Hayes intvw, (MCHC).
[18] Ibid.
[19] Ibid.
[20] Author's conversation with Capt Shannon Johnson, 23 April 2004.
[21] LtGen James T. Conway, press conference, 1 May 2004.
[22] LtCol John C. Coleman invtw, 3 August 2005 (MCHC).
[23] Author's conversation with Col Coates, 23 June 2004, as detailed in the author's official journal.

Chapter 6

[1] Cmdr William W. Wilson, USN, intvw, 24 March 2005 (Marine Corps Historical Center [MCHC], Quantico, VA).
[2] Capt Eric N. Thompson intvw, 14 October 2004 (MCHC).
[3] MSgt John A. Dailey intvw, 10 March 2006 (MCHC).
[4] Wilson intvw.
[5] MCSOCOM Detachment One, Deployed Weekly Sitrep 028 (hereafter Weekly sitrep 028).
[6] MCSOCOM Detachment One, Operational Summary, Operation Radiate (hereafter Radiate opsum).
[7] Raven opsum and conops.
[8] Raven opsum and debrief.
[9] Ibid.
[10] Ibid.
[11] Recoil opsum.
[12] Relinquish opsum and debrief.
[13] Deployed weekly sitrep 029, commander's comments.
[14] Recruit opsum.
[15] Recruit opsum and debrief.
[16] MSgt Joseph L. Morrison intvw, 14 April 2006 (MCHC); MCSOCOM Detachment One, Daily Sitrep, 30 June 2004 (hereafter daily sitrep, 30 June 2004).
[17] Republican opsum.
[18] Ibid.
[19] Ibid.
[20] Weekly sitrep 030; Daily sitrep, 30 June 2004.
[21] Roundup opsum; Capt Christopher B. Batts intvw, 6 January 2005 (MCHC); SSgt Scott J. Beretz intvw, 23 March 2005 (MCHC).
[22] Roundup opsum.
[23] Ibid.
[24] Reform opsum.
[25] Ibid.
[26] Ibid.
[27] Reflector opsum.
[28] Weekly sitrep 032.
[29] Coates-2 intvw.
[30] Coates intvw and award citation
[31] GySgt James A. Crawford intvw, 13 January 2006 (MCHC); Sgt William B. Parker intvw, 3 August 2005 (MCHC).
[32] Crawford/Parker AAR and intvws.
[33] Ibid.
[34] Ibid.
[35] Ibid.
[36] Ibid.
[37] Ibid.
[38] SSgt Daniel L. Williams intvw, 23 March 2005 (MCHC); Williams award citation.
[39] Batts intvw.
[40] Ibid.
[41] Relapse opsum.
[42] Ibid.; Beretz intvw.
[43] Ibid.
[44] Ibid.
[45] Relapse opsum.

46 Ibid.
47 Roadster opsum
48 Ibid.
49 Ibid.; Beretz intvw
50 Deployed weekly sitrep 035.
51 Daily sitrep, 12 August 2004.
52 SSgt Chadwick D. Baker intvw, 24 March 2005 (MCHC).
53 MSgt Charles H. Padilla intvw, 10 January 2005 (MCHC).
54 al-Kut opsum.
55 Baker and Thompson intvws; al-Kut opsum.
56 Capt Daniel B. Sheehan intvw, 21 April 2005 (MCHC).
57 Ibid.
58 al-Kut opsum.
59 Ibid.
60 Roulette conops.
61 Roulette opsum.
62 Resistor opsum and conops.
63 Ibid.

Chapter 7

1 For an overview of the Marines' role in the fight for an-Najaf, see Francis X. Kozlowski, *U.S. Marines in Battle: An-Najaf, August 2004* (Washington, D.C.: U.S. Marine Corps History Division, 2009).
2 MCSOCOM Detachment One, Operational Summary, Najaf (hereafter [Name] opsum).
3 Ibid.; MSgt Terry M. Wyrick intvw, 23 March 2005 (MCHC).
4 Ibid.
5 Wyrick intvw; Najaf debrief.
6 Wyrick intervw; GySgt Fidencio Villalobos Jr. intvw, 13 January 2005 (MCHC).
7 Najaf opsum; Wyrick intvw.
8 Najaf opsum; GySgt Ryan P. Keeler intvw, 12 January 2005 (MCHC).
9 Najaf opsum; Wyrick and Villalobos intvws.
10 Najaf opsum.
11 Keeler intvw; MSgt John A. Dailey intvw, 10 March 2006 (MCHC); SSgt Alex N. Conrad intvw, 1 August 2005 (MCHC).
12 Ibid.
13 Najaf debrief and opsum.
14 SSgt Chadwick D. Baker intvw, 24 March 2005 (MCHC); MSgt Charles H. Padilla intvw, 10 January 2005 (MCHC); SSgt Glen S. Cederholm intvw, 12 January 2005 (MCHC); GySgt Jack A. Kelly intvw, 22 March 2005 (MCHC).
15 Najaf opsum; Wyrick intvw.
16 Najaf opsum; Baker intvw.
17 Najaf opsum; Capt Daniel B. Sheehan intvw, 21 April 2005 (MCHC); Keeler, Baker intvws.
18 Najaf opsum; Conrad intvw.
19 Kelly, Padilla, and Baker intvws.
20 Kelly intvw.
21 Najaf opsum; Sheehan interview
22 Kozlowski, *An-Najaf*, 42.
23 Najaf opsum; Kelly and Baker intvws.
24 Rifle opsum.
25 MCSOCOM Detachment One, Deployed Weekly Sitrep 036 (hereafter Weekly sitrep [number]).
26 Capt Christopher B. Batts intvw, 6 January 2005 (MCHC); SSgt Scott J. Beretz intvw, 23 March 2005 (MCHC).
27 Beretz intvw; Rifle opsum.
28 Beretz intvw.
29 Rifle opsum; LtCol Craig S. Kozeniesky intvw, 15 October 2004 (MCHC).
30 Rifle opsum.
31 Rifle opsum; MSgt Keith E. Oakes intvw, 11 January 2005 (MCHC); Cederholm intvw; Cederholm award citation.
32 Rifle opsum; Capt Eric N. Thompson intvw, 14 October 2004 (MCHC).
33 Rifle opsum; Conrad intvw.
34 Ruby opsum; GySgt Andre K. Bosier intvw, 24 March 2005; Tyrell award citation.
35 Ruby opsum.
36 MCSOCom Det One ComdC, 1 July–31 December 2004 (Gray Research Center, Quantico VA). ComdC, 1 July–31 December 2004; Weekly sitrep 041.
37 ComdC, 1 July–31 December 2004.
38 Capt Stephen V. Fiscus intvw, 17 November 2004 (MCHC).
39 Ibid.
40 Ibid.
41 Maj M. Wade Priddy intvw, 13 October 2004 (MCHC).

Chapter 8

1 MCSOCom Det One ComdC, 1 July–31 December 2004 (Gray Research Center [GRC], Quantico VA). Although the command chronology states the final flight returned on 2 October, Col Coates remembers it as 6 October.
2 Author's notes on Naval Special Warfare Command AAR, 17 November 2004.
3 Det One ComdC, 1 July–31 December 2004.
4 Col Coates' emails to author, 22 August 2006, about manuscript draft 4. Det One's future might have been determined before the Warfighter conference. LtGen Jan C. Huly stated that "there was never a plan for

this unit to continue that I know of. It was a one-time proof of concept. . . . We put it up, we formed this thing, let's see how it will work. And it was never planned on it becoming a permanent entity in the Marine Corps that I know of." LtGen Jan C. Huly intvw, 31 July0 2006 (Marine Corps Historical Center [MCHC]).

[5] Det One ComdC, 1 July–31 December 2004.

[6] Det One ComdC, 1 January–30 June 2005 (GRC).

[7] Department of Defense, Secretary of Defense Memorandum, 4 February 2005.

[8] *MCSOCOM Proof of Concept Deployment Evaluation Report* (Hurlburt Field, FL: Joint Special Operations University, 2005), App. C (hereafter JSOU study).

[9] JSOU study, conclusion, p. II.

[10] JSOU study, conclusion, p. III.

[11] *MCSOCOM Det: Analysis of Service Costs and Considerations* (Arlington, VA: Center for Naval Analyses, 2005), conclusions, p. 55.

[12] Maj Priddy's email to author et al., 12 December 2005, with JSOU study attached.

[13] Det One ComdC, 1 January–30 June 2005.

[14] Huly intvw.

[15] LtCol Francis L. Donovan intvw, 24 March 2006 (MCHC).

[16] Det One ComdC, 1 January–30 June 2005.

[17] Det One ComdC 1 July–31 December 2005 (GRC).

[18] Col Coates' emails to author, 22 August 2006.

[19] 5400 deactivation bulletin, 060043Z FEB 06; Capt Sheehan email to author, 7 February 2006.

[20] Det One Final ComdC (GRC).

Epilogue

[1] LtCol Francis L. Donovan intvw, 24Mar06 (MCHC).

[2] Col Coates e-mails to author, 22 August 2006.

[3] Joint Special Operations University study, "Findings," 4-5.

[4] LtGen Jan C. Huly intvw, 31Jul06 (Marine Corps Historical Center [MCHC]).

Appendix A
Command and Staff List

Commanding Officer
Col Robert J. Coates   01 March 2003–10 March 2006

Executive Officer
LtCol Craig S. Kozeniesky   17 March 2003–15 April 2005
LtCol Francis L. Donovan   16 April 2005–10 March 2006

Senior Enlisted
MSgt James R. Rutan   17 June 2003–31 March 2005
MGySgt Thomas P. Muratori   01 April 2005–10 March 2006

Adjutant
GySgt Jeffrey King   20 June 2003–16 January 2004
SSgt Barrett M. Rhodes   17 January 04–06 July 05
SSgt Jesus Garcia   07 July 2005–10 March 2006

Intelligence Officer and Intelligence Element Leader
Maj M. Gerald Carter   24 March 2003–10 March 2006

Intelligence Chief
MSgt Bret A. Hayes   03 March 2003–10 March 2006

Counterintelligence Officer
Capt Christopher B. Batts   19 February 2003–31 December 2004

Operations Officer
LtCol Craig S. Kozeniesky   17 Mar 2003–30 June 2004
Maj M. Wade Priddy   01 July 2004–10 March 2006

Assistant Operations Officer
Capt Stephen V. Fiscus   01 July 2004–29 November 2004
Captain Eric N. Thompson   29 November 2004–31 December 2004

Operations Chief
MSgt James R. Rutan   17 June 2003–30 June 2004
MSgt Thomas P. Muratori   01 July 2004–10 March 2006

Fires Officer
Maj M. Wade Priddy   21 March 2003–30 June 2004
Maj Thomas P. Dolan   01 July 2004–31 December 2005
Capt Daniel B. Sheehan III   01 January 2005–10 March 2006

Air Officer

Maj Thomas P. Dolan	01 March 2003–31 December 2004
Capt Daniel B. Sheehan III	01 January 2005–10 March 2006

Logistics Officer

Capt Matthew H. Kress	01 March 2003–31 December 2005

Logistics Chief

GySgt Monty K. Genegabus	07 May 2003–12 August 2005
GySgt Jaime Maldonado	13 August 2005–10 March 2006

Supply Officer

Maj Ronald J. Rux	02 June–30 August 2003
Capt Olufemi A. Harrison	19 September 2003–10 March 2006

Communications Officer

GySgt James A. Wagner	09 June 2003–5 May 2005
GySgt Ryan P. Keeler	06 May 2005–10 March 2006

Reconnaissance Element Leader

Capt Eric N. Thompson	28 February 2003–29 November 2004
Capt Stephen V. Fiscus	29 November 2004–31 January 2006

Appendix B

Chronology of Significant Events

2001

9 November 2001 — Commandant of the Marine Corps signs a memorandum of agreement with the commander of SOCom to reestablish the SOCom/USMC Board to examine enhanced interoperability between the two forces in the wake of the 11 September attacks.

2002

22–24 January 2002 — Lieutenant Colonel Giles Kyser proposes a Marine force contribution to SOCom during the meeting of the SOCom/USMC Board.

5–7 March 2002 — Naval Special Warfare Command, as executive agent for SOCom, hosts a conference to discuss the nature of the Marine force contribution to SOCom.

4 December 2002 — Commandant of the Marine Corps directs the activation of Marine Corps Special Operations Command Detachment for a two-year proof-of-concept operation with SOCom.

2003

20 February 2003 — Deputy Commandant of the Marine Corps for Plans, Policies and Operations signs a memorandum of agreement with the deputy commander of SOCom to delineate the scope and nature of the initial Marine force contribution to SOCom.

1 March 2003 — Personnel for the command element begin to report for duty to Camp Pendleton, California; Detachment One headquarters are temporarily housed in the offices of I MEF Special Operations Training Group.

20 June 2003 — Marine Corps Special Operations Command Detachment One is activated in a ceremony at the unit's new compound at Camp Del Mar, Camp Pendleton, California.

1 July 2003 — Detachment One begins unit training phase.

14–26 September 03 — Detachment One conducts its first full unit training exercise at Marine Corps Mountain Warfare Training Center, Bridgeport, California.

6–24 October 2003 — Reconnaissance Element conducts close quarters battle training at Range 130, Camp Pendleton, California.

1 December 2003 — Detachment One transfers from Marine Forces Pacific to the operational control of Naval Special Warfare Command in accordance with the 20 February memorandum of agreement and in preparation for deployment.

1–19 December 2003 — Detachment One conducts its Capstone Exercise, evaluating the unit's full spectrum of operational capabilities at the Department of Energy's Nevada Test Site.

2004

13–16 January 2004	Detachment One senior leadership travels to Qatar, Bahrain and Iraq for pre-deployment site survey.
22–29 February 2004	Detachment One, as part of Naval Special Warfare Squadron, conducts a pre-deployment certification exercise at Edwards Air Force Base, California; personnel from the detachment staff and intelligence element augment the squadron's capabilities; the reconnaissance element remains intact as a separate task unit.
6 April 2004	Detachment One deploys to Iraq, establishing a base of operations near Baghdad International Airport; selected personnel from the intelligence element are detached to serve with outlying task units and with other government agencies; the remainder of the detachment forms Task Unit Raider under Naval Special Warfare Task Group-Arabian Peninsula, and commences direct action raids and other operations.
28 May 2004	Commanding Officer Naval Special Warfare Task Group-Arabian Peninsula receives orders to shift operations and provide personal security details to the four principal figures of the interim Iraqi government; Task Unit Raider Marines are assigned to protect one of the two Iraqi vice-presidents.
3 June 2004	Commanding Officer Naval Special Warfare Task Group-Arabian Peninsula reconstitutes Task Unit Raider for offensive operations; a small liaison cell is sent to the GROM, the Polish special forces unit, which is then constituted as Task Unit Thunder.
8 June 2004	Task Unit Raider executes "Objective Razor," the third in a series of three raids on a high-value target, in which the complete spectrum of the task-organized capabilities of the detachment were fully employed.
11–17 August 2004	Marines from Task Unit Raider reinforce U.S. Army Special Forces units in al-Kut, providing sniper, intelligence and fires support in operations against Shi'a militias; their support enabled coalition forces to help the governor of al-Kut rid the city of enemy forces and reestablish his authority.
17–30 August 2004	Marines from Task Unit Raider reinforce U.S. Army cavalry units in an-Najaf, providing sniper, intelligence and fires support in operations against Shi'a militias; their support enabled coalition forces to compel the Mahdi Militia to cease operations and withdraw from the key city.
30 August 2004	Task Unit Raider, in conjunction with Task Unit Thunder, executes a daylight raid into Baghdad to capture or kill a high-value target, "Objective Rifle," who had been tracked for five months; the raid is successful and all forces withdraw without casualties.
2 October 2004	Naval Special Warfare Task Group-Arabian Peninsula stands down from operations; Detachment One reconstitutes and redeploys to Camp Pendleton, California; the unit commences sustainment training and examination of future employment options.
17 November 2004	Detachment One leadership briefs after action report and lessons learned to ComNavSpecWar at Coronado, California.

1 December 2004	Detachment One leadership briefs lessons learned and recommended courses of action for the future at the USMC/SOCom Warfighter Conference.
4 February 2004	Two-year proof-of-concept phase expires; Detachment One continues sustainment training and examination of employment options.

2006

6 February 2006	Commandant of the Marine Corps directs the deactivation of Marine Corps Special Operations Command Detachment no later than 1 April 2006.
10 March 2006	Marine Corps Special Operations Command Detachment deactivates in a ceremony at the unit's compound at Camp Del Mar, Camp Pendleton, California.

Appendix C
Lineage and Honors

Lineage

2003–2006

Activated 1 March 2003 at Camp Pendleton, California, as Marine Corps U.S. Special Operations Detachment

Participated in Operation Iraqi Freedom, Iraq, April–October 2004

Deactivated 10 March 2006

Honors

Navy Unit Commendation Streamer

Arabian Peninsula
2004–2006

Meritorious Unit Commendation Streamer
2003–2004

National Defense Service Streamer

Global War on Terrorism Expeditionary Streamer

Global War on Terrorism Service Streamer

Appendix D

Individual Awards

Bronze Star:

SSgt Scott J. Beretz (w/V)
HM1 Robert T. Bryan (w/V)
Maj M. Gerald Carter
Col Robert J. Coates
GySgt James A. Crawford (w/V)
GySgt John A. Dailey (w/V)
Maj Thomas P. Dolan
Capt Stephen V. Fiscus
GySgt Ryan P. Keeler
LtCol Craig S. Kozeniesky (w/V)
MSgt Keith E. Oakes (w/V)
MSgt Charles H. Padilla
Capt Daniel B. Sheehan III (w/V)
Capt Eric N. Thompson (w/V)
GySgt Matthew A. Ulmer
SSgt Daniel L. Williams
MSgt Terry M. Wyrick (w/V)

Meritorious Service Medal:

Capt Christopher B. Batts
Maj M. Gerald Carter
MSgt Victor M. Church
Maj Thomas P. Dolan
GySgt Monty K. Genegabus
MSgt Hays B. Harrington
MSgt Bret A. Hayes
LtCol Craig S. Kozeniesky
MSgt Joseph L. Morrison
MGySgt Thomas P. Muratori
GySgt Kenneth C. Pinckard
Maj M. Wade Priddy
MSgt James R. Rutan
GySgt James E. Wagner

Navy and Marine Corps Commendation Medal:

SSgt Jason M. Bagstad
SSgt Terry L. Beckwith Jr.
SSgt Chad E. Berry
Sgt Stephen J. Bolden
SSgt Glen S. Cederholm (w/ V)
SSgt Benjamin J. Cushing (w/ V)
GySgt Stephen C. Davis (w/ V)
Sgt Benjamin J. Dreher
SSgt Stuart C. Earl
GySgt Monty K. Genebagus (w/ V)
Sgt Victor M. Guerra
GySgt Tyler M. Hammel
Capt Olufemi A. Harrison
GySgt Christopher E. Haug
SSgt Patrick M. Hegeman
GySgt William M. Johnston
GySgt Jack A. Kelly (w/ V)
GySgt Jason T. Kennedy
SSgt David T. Kirby (w/ V)
GySgt Mark S. Kitashima
WO Michael L. Kuker
Sgt Joseph B. Mooring
Sgt Michael C. Mulvihill
SSgt William B. Parker (w/ V)
HM1 Matthew S. Pranka (w/ V)
SSgt Barrett M. Rhodes
SSgt Frederick L. Riano. III
HM1 Michael D. Tyrell (w/ V)
CWO2 Kevin E. Vicinus
GySgt Fidencio Villalobos Jr. (w/ V)
GySgt Sidney J. Voss (w/ V)

Navy and Marine Corps Achievement Medal

Sgt Russell T. Cook
Sgt Christopher J. Houston
SSgt David T. Kirby
Sgt Frankie Lebron
GySgt Jaime Maldonado
Sgt Michael C. Mulvihill
SSgt Jaime J. Sierra
Cpl Oscar Vazquez
SSgt Adam C. Wallman

Appendix E

Navy Unit Commendation Citation

THE SECRETARY OF THE NAVY
WASHINGTON, D.C. 20350-1000

The Secretary of the Navy takes pleasure in presenting the
NAVY UNIT COMMENDATION to

MARINE CORPS SPECIAL OPERATIONS COMMAND DETACHMENT ONE

for service as set forth in the following

CITATION:

For exceptionally meritorious service in support of Combined and Joint Special Operations Task Force-Arabian Peninsula from 19 April 2004 to 3 March 2006. The personnel of Marine Corps Special Operations Command Detachment ONE consistently displayed a high level of professionalism, while forward deployed to the Iraqi theater of operations, and during post deployment tactical experimentation for the design of a permanent U.S. Marine Corps component to Special Operations Command. Demonstrating tenacity and esprit de corps, unit personnel conducted a sustained and unprecedented demonstration of Marine Air Ground Task Force principles during a successful execution of a full range of special operations missions. Taking full advantage of their advanced skills, unique training, and specialized equipment, the Marines and Sailors of Marine Corps Special Operations Command Detachment ONE aggressively sought opportunities to locate and destroy an elusive enemy, inflicting significant damage on the Iraqi insurgent movement, resulting in the safe and expeditious transfer of authority to the Interim Iraqi government and safety of principal government officials. Detachment ONE's accomplishments proved conclusively that the Marine Corps could operate at the level of other special operations units and contributed directly to the Secretary of Defense's decision to add a U.S. Marine Corps component to Special Operations Command. By their truly distinctive achievements, personal initiative, and unfailing devotion to duty, the officers, enlisted personnel, and civilian employees of Marine Corps Special Operations Command Detachment ONE reflected great credit upon themselves and upheld the highest traditions of the Marine Corps and the United States Naval Service.

Secretary of the Navy

Appendix F

Meritorious Unit Commendation

COMMANDANT OF THE MARINE CORPS

The Secretary of the Navy takes pleasure in presenting the
MERITORIOUS UNIT COMMENDATION to

MARINE CORPS SPECIAL OPERATIONS COMMAND
DETACHMENT ONE

for service as set forth in the following

CITATION:

For meritorious service from 20 June 2003 to 18 April 2004. The personnel of Marine Corps Special Operations Detachment One conducted operations of major significance to the national defense of the United States. During this period, Marine Corps Special Operations Detachment One activated and prepared for deployment in support of Operation IRAQI FREEDOM II as the Marine Corps' first purpose-built force contribution to U.S. Special Operations Command (USSOCOM). Detachment personnel overcame a lack of precedent and established doctrine, challenges in the arrival of personnel and equipment as well as their deployment schedule and method of employment and executed a very demanding Mission Training Plan, transitioning from concept to full operational capability in nine months. The Marines and Sailors of the Detachment demonstrated exceptional professionalism, innovativeness and a mission-oriented mindset as they developed and validated standing operating procedures and evaluated and fielded emerging technologies. Throughout the nine month pre-deployment training phase, they executed some of the most dynamic and difficult training ever undertaken by a Marine Corps unit. By their unrelenting determination, perseverance, and steadfast devotion to duty, the officers, enlisted personnel, and civilian employees of Marine Corps Special Operations Command Detachment One reflected credit upon themselves and upheld the highest traditions of the Marine Corps and the United States Naval Service.

For the Secretary of the Navy,

M. W. Hagee
Commandant of the Marine Corps

Index

Abu Ghraib prison (Iraq), 50, 57, 61
Afghanistan, 13, 17, 20, 21, 28, 34, 43, 60
American Rifleman, 17, 27
Al-Anbar Province, Iraq, 47, 70, 77
Anderson, Sergeant Daryl J., 60, 61
Arnold, Hospital Corpsman First Class Michael I. (USN), 21

Baghdad, Iraq, 43, 47, 49, 50, 52, 53, 56, 57, 58, 60, 61, 62, 65, 67, 68, 71, 72, 75, 77, 78, 79, 87, 88
Bagstad, Staff Sergeant Jason M., 26
Baker, Staff Sergeant Chadwick D., 21, 53, 76, 80, 82, 83, 85, 97
Balkans, 5, 60
Bargewell, Major General Eldon A. (USA), 7, 11
Batts, Captain Christopher B., 24, 48, 52, 55, 56, 57, 73, 86, 96
Bedard, Lieutenant General Emil R., 7, 8, 10, 14
Benedict, Sergeant William S., 60, 61, 76
Beretz, Staff Sergeant Scott J., 56, 57, 67, 69, 70, 74, 75, 86, 87
Berg, Nicholas E., 58
Berry, Staff Sergeant Chad E., 49
Bosier, Gunnery Sergeant Andre K., 87
Bosnia, 5
Brackley, Sergeant Jason V., 80
Brown, General Bryan D., 43, 91, 93
Brown, Colonel Larry K., 63
Bryan, Hospital Corpsman First Class Robert T. (USN), 21, 59, 79, 81
Burma, 20

Calland, Vice Admiral Albert M. III (USN), 29
Carter, Major M. Gerald "Jerry," 23, 24, 25, 26, 32, 33, 41, 43, 44, 45, 48, 50, 51, 55, 56, 57, 73, 78, 86, 96
Cederholm, Staff Sergeant Glen S., 59, 87

Cervantes, Sergeant Miguel A., 76, 80, 82, 83, 84
Church, Gunnery Sergeant Victor M., 26
Clark, Gunnery Sergeant Travis W., 81, 82
Clausewitz, Carl P.G. von, 31
Coates, Colonel Robert J., v, 14, 17, 18, 20, 21, 23, 24, 25, 26, 27, 29, 31, 32, 33, 34, 39, 41, 48, 49, 62, 63, 64, 69, 71, 91, 94, 95, 96, 99
Coleman, Colonel John C., 64
Conrad, Staff Sergeant Alex N., 37, 58, 83, 87
Conway, Lieutenant General James T., 63
Cooney, Mary, 13
Crawford, Gunnery Sergeant James A., 60, 61, 72, 73, 97
Cushing, Staff Sergeant Benjamin J., 41

Dailey, Master Sergeant John A., 20, 21, 25, 34, 36, 37, 44, 51, 53, 55, 65, 79, 81, 82, 83, 96
Desert One (Iran), 1
Djibouti, 35
Dolan, Major Thomas P., 22, 31, 35, 36, 38, 44, 45, 48, 67, 96
Donovan, Lieutenant Colonel Francis L., 23, 95, 96

Earl, Staff Sergeant Stuart C., 25
El Salvador, 14, 63, 71

Al-Fallujah, Iraq, 47, 50, 62, 63, 71
Fallujah Brigade, 18, 63
Fiscus, Captain Stephen V., 19, 31, 42, 48, 65, 88, 89, 91, 96

Genegabus, Gunnery Sergeant Monty K., 19, 33, 34, 35, 96
Goodman, Lieutenant General John F., 96
Gray, General Alfred M., 2, 3, 4, 5
Gregson, Lieutenant General Wallace C., 95

Grupa Reagowania Operacyjno Manewrowego (GROM), 47, 51, 52, 65, 67, 75, 78, 88, 89, 93, 100, 110,
Guerra, Sergeant Victor M., 18, 20, 28, 39, 41, 49, 96

Hagee, General Michael W., 14, 17, 91, 93
Hailston, Lieutenant General Earl B., 29
Hand, Colonel Paul A., 7, 8, 11, 12, 13, 14, 29
Harrington, Master Sergeant Hays B., 23, 53, 59, 61, 69, 77, 97
Harris, Staff Sergeant Kevin J., 69
Harrison, Captain Olufemi A., 24, 96
Haug, Sergeant Christopher E., 76
Hayes, Master Sergeant Bret A., 23, 62, 72, 97
Al-Hayy, Iraq, 76
Hejlik, Brigadier General Dennis J., 13, 29
Holland, General Charles R. (USAF), 8
Horn of Africa, 28, 43
Huly, Lieutenant General Jan C., 100
Husaybah, Iraq, 62
Hussein, Colonel Khalis Ali, 71
Hussein, Saddam, 71, 78, 87

Irbil, Iraq, 65

Johnston, Gary Paul, 27
Johnston, Gunnery Sergeant William M., 51, 52, 55, 78
Jones, General James L., Jr., 8, 9, 11, 31

Keeler, Gunnery Sergeant Ryan P., 22, 23, 79, 81, 82, 83
Kelley, General Paul X., 2, 3, 4, 5, 29, 99
Kelly, Staff Sergeant Jack A., 36, 37, 80, 83, 96
Kennedy, Gunnery Sergeant Jason T., 49
Kingdon, Staff Sergeant Andrew T., 58, 59
Kirkuk, Iraq, 57
Kitashima, Gunnery Sergeant Mark S., 26, 27, 33, 37, 96
Korea, 2
Kozeniesky, Major Craig S., 19, 20, 31, 34, 35, 38, 42, 43, 44, 45, 48, 50, 51, 54, 55, 56, 57, 58, 60, 66, 67, 68, 69, 70, 75, 77, 78, 85, 86, 87, 91, 94, 96

Kress, Captain Matthew H., 19, 24, 25, 31, 43, 49, 96
Krueger, Staff Sergeant D. T., 81
Kurdistan, 57, 65
Al-Kut, Iraq, 75, 76, 77, 78, 93, 100
Kyser, Lieutenant Colonel J. Giles, IV, v, 6, 7, 8, 9, 10, 11, 12, 13, 14, 23, 75, 77

Laplume, Jonathan, 25, 39
Leighty, Jason, 76

Maguire, Rear Admiral Joseph (USN), 91
Mahmudiyah, Iraq, 77
Maldonado, Gunnery Sergeant Jaime, 26, 34, 35, 38, 88, 97
Marine Corps Gazette, 7
Marine Corps Times, 17
Marnell, Sergeant David D., 53, 76, 81, 82, 83, 84
McHaty, Captain Rodrick H., 63
Meacham, Charles, 29, 96
Merle, Robert, 13
Mitchell, Master Sergeant Troy G., 9, 10, 11, 12, 13, 18, 23
Mogadishu, Somalia, 6
Morrison, Master Sergeant Joseph L., 20, 37, 53, 54, 57, 69
Mulvihill, Sergeant Michael C., 79
Muratori, Master Sergeant Thomas P., 19, 34, 96
Myler, Christian W., 34, 48

An-Najaf, Iraq, 79, 82, 84, 93, 100
National Defense Magazine, 17
Natonski, Major General Richard F., 96
Netherlands, 20

Oakes, Master Sergeant Keith E., 21, 33, 34, 37, 42, 43, 53, 59, 87
O'Grady, Captain Scott (USAF), 5

Padilla, Master Sergeant Charles H., 20, 31, 34, 35, 37, 40, 53, 55, 56, 76, 82, 83, 96
Parker, Staff Sergeant William B., 60, 61, 72, 97
Parsons, Gunnery Sergeant William G., 73, 86

Philippine Islands, 28
Pinckard, Gunnery Sergeant Kenneth C., 23, 41, 45, 97
Pranka, Hospital Corpsman First Class Matthew S. (USN), 21, 40, 69, 77, 80
Priddy, Major M. Wade, 22, 44, 45, 48, 55, 71, 89, 91, 96, 97

Al-Qaim, Iraq, 62

Ar-Ramadi, Iraq, 62
Reeves, Staff Sergeant Zachary A., 77
Repass, Colonel Michael S. (USA), 93
Riano, Staff Sergeant Frederick L., III, 24
Rogers, Patrick J., 23, 27
Rumsfeld, Secretary of Defense Donald H., 92, 93, 96
Rutan, Master Sergeant James R., 19, 25, 31, 42, 96

al-Sadr, Muqtada, 79, 82, 84
San Diego Union-Tribune, 17
Settelen, Master Gunnery Sergeant Joseph G., III, 9, 10, 11, 12, 13, 18, 23, 25, 39, 40, 42
al-Shahwani, Major General Mohammed Abdullah Mohammed, 71
Shahwani Special Forces, 18, 71
Shaways, Rowsch, 65
Sheehan, Captain Daniel B., III, 35, 53, 76, 77, 82, 83, 84, 85, 96
Sierra, Staff Sergeant Jaime J., 26, 34, 35, 38, 88, 97
Sierra Leone, 8
Sine, Chief Hospital Corpsman Eric D. (USN), 21, 55

al-Sistani, Ayatollah Sayyid Ali Husseini, 84
Somalia, 5
Stars and Stripes, 17
SWAT Magazine, 17, 27

Thompson, Captain Eric N., 20, 21, 33, 35, 38, 39, 65, 75, 77, 79, 87, 96
Toolan, Colonel John A., 18
Toothaker, Gunnery Sergeant Adam C., 23
Tyrell, Hospital Corpsman First Class Michael D. (USN), 21, 59, 87

Ulmer, Gunnery Sergeant Matthew A., 24, 62, 70, 72

Vicinus, Warrant Officer Kevin E., 24, 53
Vietnam, 2
Villalobos, Gunnery Sergeant Fidencio, Jr., 22, 80, 81, 82, 84, 88, 96
Voss, Gunnery Sergeant Sidney J., 21, 37

Wagner, Gunnery Sergeant James E., 19, 20, 96
Weinberger, Secretary of Defense Caspar W., 1, 4
Westphal, Michael A., 13, 29
Williams, Staff Sergeant Daniel L., 60, 61, 73
Wilson, Commander William W. (USN), vi, 41, 44, 45, 47, 48, 50, 51, 52, 54, 55, 64, 65, 86, 89, 91, 93, 100
Wyrick, Master Sergeant Terry M., 20, 37, 45, 53, 58, 59, 79, 80, 81, 85, 96

al-Zarqawi, Abu Musab, 77

Back Cover: The device reproduced on the back cover is the oldest military insignia in continuous use in the United States. It first appeared, as shown here, on Marine Corps buttons adopted in 1804. With the stars changed to five points, the device has continued on Marine Corps buttons to the present day.

www.ingramcontent.com/pod-product-compliance
Lightning Source LLC
Chambersburg PA
CBHW080516110426
42742CB00017B/3131